Clerical Errors

Clerical Errors

How Clericalism Betrays the Gospel
and How to Heal the Church

Peter Murnane

RESOURCE *Publications* • Eugene, Oregon

CLERICAL ERRORS
How Clericalism Betrays the Gospel and How to Heal the Church

Copyright © 2022 Peter Murnane. All rights reserved. Except for brief quotations in critical publications or reviews, no part of this book may be reproduced in any manner without prior written permission from the publisher. Write: Permissions, Wipf and Stock Publishers, 199 W. 8th Ave., Suite 3, Eugene, OR 97401.

Resource Publications
An Imprint of Wipf and Stock Publishers
199 W. 8th Ave., Suite 3
Eugene, OR 97401

www.wipfandstock.com

PAPERBACK ISBN: 978-1-6667-4000-4
HARDCOVER ISBN: 978-1-6667-4001-1
EBOOK ISBN: 978-1-6667-4002-8

08/01/22

Scripture quotations are from *New Revised Standard Version, with the Apocryphal/ Deuterocanonical Books.* Copyright ©1989, Division of Christian Education of the National Council of the Churches of Christ in the United States of America. Used by permission. All rights reserved.

Contents

Acknowledgements | vii
Abbreviations | ix
Introduction | xi

1   The Trials of George Pell | 1
2   "... To All Nations" | 18
3   A Lifetime Sentence | 46
4   How Could It Come to This? | 57
5   Clericalism | 69
6   The Failure of Canon Law | 86
7   The Amoral Institution | 103
8   Temple and Priesthood Restored | 120
9   How Clerics Have Changed the Eucharist | 140
10 Reshaping the Pyramid | 156

Bibliography | 169
Index | 175

Acknowledgements

I THANK ALL THOSE who have helped me in bringing this book to completion by their encouragement and criticism. To name just a few: Gideon Boas, Margaret-Mary Brown, Raymond Canning , Michael Elligate, Helen Ferrara, Sheila Flynn, Eric Hodgens, Vincent Long, Frank O'Loughlin, John Murphy, Lara Pollard, and John Warhurst. The chapter on Canon Law draws particularly on Kieran Tapsell's book *Potiphar's Wife*; the writings of Tom O'Loughlin shaped the chapter on the Eucharist.

I'm particularly grateful to the team at Wipf & Stock, who have patiently helped to shape the book.

Not least I thank the many people whose friendship has formed me over the years, but I stress that none of the persons mentioned above, nor my Dominican community, is responsible for the book's conclusions. Indeed, some will have quite different views. The opinions I have expressed, and any errors, are mine entirely.

Camberwell, March 27, 2022

Abbreviations

ACR   *Australasian Catholic Record.*

AAS   *Acta Apostolicae Sedis.*

CCC   *Catechism of the Catholic Church.*

Code   *Code of Canon Law* (1983).

Codex   *Codex Iuris Canonici* (1917).

CR   *Clergy Review*

Dz   Denzinger, Heinrich, *Enchiridion Symbolorum.*

Fontes   *Codex Iuris Canonici Fontes.*

GS   *Gaudium et Spes: Pastoral Constitution on the Church in the Modern World.*

LG   *Lumen Gentium: Dogmatic Constitution on the Church.*

NCR   *National Catholic Reporter.*

NRSV   *New Revised Standard Version.*

NYT   *New York Times.*

PO   *Presbyterorum Ordinis: Decree on the Ministry and Life of Priests.*

RCFR   *Royal Commission into Institutional Responses to Child Sexual Abuse: Final Report.*

Abbreviations

SC Sacrosanctum Concilium: Constitution on the Sacred Liturgy.

S Th Summa Theologiae.

VPI Victorian Parliamentary Inquiry. *Betrayal of Trust: Inquiry into the Handling of Child Abuse by Religious and other Non-government Organizations.* 2013.

Introduction

THE CATHOLIC CHURCH IS a remarkable phenomenon: the world's oldest and largest trans-national corporation. But the Catholic church is in serious decline. One obvious sign of its deterioration is that most of its members—in Australia about 90 percent—choose not to attend Sunday Mass. The situation is similar in North America and Europe. In Germany in 2019, some 272,000 Catholics formally left the church, the largest number in any year so far. As a partial counterbalance to these figures, church attendance continues to be high where there is political or religious repression and in poorer countries where people still take the Scriptures and their faith in a more "literalist" way.

The declining influence of the Catholic church—and of other churches—does not necessarily indicate a decline in people's *belief* in a Transcendent Reality. But the downward trend in religious *practice* presents the churches with an enormous challenge. It is urgent for them to understand the reasons for the decline. This book seeks reasons within the Catholic church itself, and suggests that these often stem from erroneous choices made by the clerics who lead the church-institution.

When we listen to church members themselves, they give all kinds of reasons why they no longer attend church: that it is irrelevant to life today; that it fails to provide them with a community, or give them intellectual stimulation; that the non-attender is too busy, or is confused about what to believe. Prominent among the reasons given is that a minority of clerics have misused their authority and power to sexually abuse children.

Introduction

This tragic clerical error will be examined here in some detail: first in the case of the high-ranking cleric Cardinal Pell, who was accused, imprisoned and then acquitted (Chapter 1). Then the world-wide picture is looked at, with particular attention to Australia, to show that the abuse crisis applies "... to all nations." (Chapter 2).

Most sexual abuse of children is committed by persons within the child's own family. However the Australian Royal Commission heard several thousand first-hand stories of sexual abuse committed by approximately 7 percent of all Catholic priests who ministered in Australia between 1950 and 2010. It is important to acknowledge that these are only the crimes we have heard about, for it is known that most sexually-abused children never publicly reveal the abuse.

It was found by the Royal Commission, and by many other investigations, that clerics' status and prestige gives them unique access to children and therefore more opportunities to abuse them. The Commission's extensive research also revealed how children suffer particular harm when abused by a "man of God"; and that they and their families endure further trauma when their church's leaders conceal or deny the abuse, so as to protect the offenders (Chapter 3).

Clerical Errors explores the reasons why clerics commit those crimes, and why so often bishops conceal the abuse (Chapter 4). In this way the book may help victims/survivors[1] of clerical abusers and those close to them who share their pain and grief. These chapters also offer access to the basic findings contained in the multi-volume *Final Report* of the Australian Royal Commission; to the excellent work by Cahill and Wilkinson, and to other sources.

One reason for the abundance of clerical child-abuse has been deficiencies in the church's own Canon Law. It is not uncommon for people with authority in institutions to write laws that unjustly benefit themselves, but it is shocking to find this happening in the church. When bishops in our own time concealed the crimes of child-abusing clerics so as to protect the "image" or "good name" of the organization, they were often obeying the church's own Canon Law (Chapter 6).

The Christian church began as a collection of small communities, but when it began to evolve into a large institution, it suffered from the weaknesses which occur in all institutions (Chapter 7). It was a basic error that clerics formed themselves into a "caste". The members of this caste began to

---

1. Each abused person is at first a victim, but to varying degrees is healed and survives.

Introduction

describe themselves as "priests", like those who served in Jewish and Pagan temples. By restoring a priesthood with elements from the Jewish temple, the clerical elite attained status and power, contrary to the teaching of Jesus (Chapter 8). Clerics also made gradual but significant changes to the Eucharist, the central act of Christian worship (Chapter 9). It is argued here that all these were serious "clerical errors", even if sometimes unintended.

When I point out fundamental errors that clerics have made, I am not attacking the church. My aim is to analyze and understand, so that we, the church, may change and grow. I say *we*, for my "declaration of interest" is that I was ordained as a Catholic priest in 1965 and am still serving as one. Many disillusioned people have walked away from the church. At times I too have felt like walking away, as those two sad disciples walked away from Jerusalem towards their home in Emmaus after Jesus was murdered.[2] However like them I have found at the heart of the church community the One who has passed through death and whose Spirit guarantees that the church continues to point us towards the Transcendent Mystery which brought us into being and is our ultimate future. It is this conviction that compels people to continue working to reform the church's human structures (Chapter 10).

At every stage of its history, many people *have* attacked the church, particularly today when the crimes of some of its clerics are widely publicized. But to attack produces anger and resistance. It is more fruitful to ask questions, even radical ones. When a person's beliefs and actions are seriously harming others, Jesus advised us to point this out,[3] and he himself questioned and radically challenged the religion in which he had been raised. So my aim here is to question grave errors that clerics have made since the early centuries; errors that have become systematic and are still distorting Jesus' teaching.

The book proposes that many of the church's substantial errors stem from the phenomenon of clericalism (Chapter 5). This can be defined as the *attitudes and culture that excessively idealize the role of clerics, and give them preference as persons*, as if clerics are superior to other church members. Clericalism can be found in different forms in most institutions, and it is always unjust. I propose that it is a principal cause of the church's deterioration, even corruption

---

2. Luke 24:13–15.
3. Matt 18:15.

Introduction

Some clerics and some Catholics will find my conclusions unsettling. The book invites them to examine objectively the claims made here and try to respond to them. There is value in every discussion that might lead us towards understanding the church's current plight. In this crisis, more than ever, we need to acknowledge that "the truth will set you free."[4]

Clericalism is a central error which allows clergy to expect privileges. It descends into favoritism and cronyism. Clericalism has also persuaded lay people to accept clerics as superior, and to obey them without sufficient discernment. Clericalism tries to justify itself by claiming that ordination as a priest brings about an "ontological change", which transforms the *being* of the cleric. Clericalism has seriously distorted our understanding and practice of the Eucharist and how that ceremony is led. Clericalism's assumptions have produced a church made up of two classes: ordained clerics and the rest. This book contends that all such errors betray the gospel, which— by strong contrast—shows Jesus establishing a community of persons who have various gifts and tasks, but are radically equal.

There have been other clerical errors. For example:

1. The clerical church allowed exceptions to Jesus' radical teaching to love our enemies and shun violence and war.[5]

2. In their teaching, clerics have focused on personal sin but overlooked structural sins by which whole populations have been oppressed and classes of poor folk exploited, while clergy often collaborated with the wealthy perpetrators of those crimes.

3. The clerical church—mainly its Western branch—promoted the belief that God will punish in eternal fire persons who die unrepentant.[6]

4. Church leaders' concern for control and uniformity led to inquisitions and crusades that at their worst used torture, the death penalty and war to enforce "right belief".

It is a further serious error to claim that the church's sacraments and its authority structure of pope, bishops and priests were received ready-made from Jesus, when in fact they evolved through time. It is also obviously false to suppose that the church is or ever was a "perfect society", although this has often been claimed. The surviving records of the earliest Christian

---

4. John 8:32.
5. Matt 5:43–45, 26:52; Luke 6:27, 35; John 18:11; Luke 22:35, 51.
6. The belief is convincingly challenged by Hart: *Saved*.

Introduction

communities show ordinary, imperfect people; communities who sometimes quarreled and split and whose leaders tried to restore peace. But it is beyond the scope of this book to study these clerical errors. Our focus is on the error of clericalism itself.

The Catholic church is not the *institution* made up of some 3000 dioceses around the World; nor is it ordained officials; nor the vast array of cathedrals, churches, schools, hospitals and other works. It is not the elaborate *culture* of art, music and scholarship that Christians have developed through twenty centuries. The Church is essentially *people*; about 1.3 billion baptized persons now living, and a greater number of the dead who have gone before us. The church identifies all these people as making up the mysterious "Body of Christ".

As the church has struggled to survive and grow, its members inevitably made mistakes. We still do. Throughout its history the church has undergone enormous changes, even paradigm shifts. Jesus left us a seed, not a mature forest, and his commission to bring about the Reign of God is always a work in progress. So it is false to think—as so-called "traditionalist" Catholics do—that the church will be repaired by restoring the liturgy and institutions of some earlier stage of its growth.

Despite some severe disappointments, I am enormously grateful to the church. From my earliest years it showed me the transcendent dimension of reality. Through the mythical stories of Genesis, I heard that the universe has its origins in a Creator, the Source of Being, whom we call God. From the gospels I learned about the life and teachings of Jesus of Nazareth, in whom God was uniquely present. Jesus, like many others who have spent their lives defending the victims of injustice, was tortured and murdered, but—I was taught—he passed through death and offers us the amazing Good News of eternal life.

In my childhood, the church's rituals inspired me with awe. Later I absorbed from its tradition the astonishing truth that God dwells within us. Only slowly, during the half-century since my ordination, have I become more aware that Jesus did *not* come to establish the church-institution as we know it, but to give us the Good News that every person, within and outside the church, is loved by God. We all have free access to "eternal life", and everyone can grow without limit in loving other people and God. When we begin to see this, we can be deeply joyful. It can be difficult, however, to shake off the teaching that the church-institution is the essential or the only path by which people can learn about and reach God. I now see that

Introduction

this exclusiveness is another fabric of errors spun by clerics. While I respect those many Catholics who have not yet "seen through" clericalism, I have been greatly helped by others who, like Pope Francis, solidly condemn it.[7]

In criticizing the church, there is need for deep compassion. This is true when we expose the crimes of those unfortunate clerics who commit the worst errors of abusing children. It is no less true when we point out other errors in the institution. All of us who err need to be told of our mistakes, and the mistakes corrected. But we all also need to be given every help, and to have our dignity respected, as our healing is sought. All this is integral to our Christian belief.

So it is not helpful merely to condemn the institution. In pointing out its huge mistakes, we need to understand that just as every object casts a shadow, so every person and institution has a "shadow side" and ambiguously produces both gain *and* loss. It would be short-sighted and illogical, for instance, merely to condemn the ruthless violence of past empires like those of Rome or Britain. They became empires by conquering and enslaving Indigenous peoples; by ravaging communities and destroying environments. But we must also admit that those empires brought stability—not a true peace—which enabled greater material prosperity, better health and education for a fortunate minority, and enabled arts and culture to flourish. We need to recognize such good as those empires achieved, even while exposing the truth that it was accomplished by cruel exploitation. The same analysis needs to be made of the Industrial Revolution, which also brought vast benefits of prosperity and comfort, but at the cost of bringing our planet to the brink of ruin.

The evolution of the church has been similarly ambiguous. Through the centuries countless Christian communities have enabled their members to draw close to God; they have produced art and scientific discoveries, even while some church leaders accumulated wealth and abused power. Those leader's errors have gravely distorted the church, but while we recognize and deplore their errors, we need also to recognize the institution's achievements and its goodness.

Although clericalism contributes to the church's sickness, the church carries its unique share of truth, incomparably greater than the institution's structural weaknesses or the shameful crimes and deceits of some members. So after chapters that seek to explain the church's systemic errors, the final

---

7. E.g., https://cruxnow.com/vatican/2018/08/clericalism-the-culture-that-enables-abuse-and-insists-on-hiding-it/.

Introduction

chapter suggests how the church might be healed. This re-forming needs to be radical, at the roots, through local communities. As the two disciples who hurried back from Emmaus to re-join their grieving companions found Christ there among them, we can hope that we will rediscover the Transcendent Mystery, the Risen Christ in our wounded communities. The church does not have to remain the flawed institution that it has become. It can be transformed and freed to bring about the Reign of God, in which love prevails over power.

This book is not an academic thesis, but an attempt to contribute to the continuous work-in-progress of healing and re-forming the Christian church. It can be read without bothering with the footnotes, which are intended only to show that the arguments are based on sound scholarship in Scripture, theology, history, psychology and sociology.

In the interests of openness and truth, I have used the names of persons and organizations, but only where these have already been published.

1

The Trials of George Pell

OUR SUBJECT IS CLERICAL errors. These are not abstract matters, but human choices that can have enormous consequences. This first chapter looks at the various trials of the Australian Cardinal George Pell, which have had a world-wide impact on the Catholic church. In June 2017, the cardinal was charged with a series of historic sexual assaults against a number of victims. In the first County Court trial of alleged "cathedral" crimes, the jury could not reach a decision, but in a re-trial Pell was found guilty and jailed in November 2018. His first appeal failed, but on April 7 2020, the High Court overturned the guilty verdict and acquitted him. Some people take this to mean that the senior cleric is innocent of all the alleged crimes,[1] but many still have serious doubts.

The question continues to be hotly debated because in sexual crimes where the victim/survivor is the only witness, it is notoriously difficult to determine the truth. As professors of law have pointed out, the High Court did not declare the cardinal innocent, but merely that the Prosecution did not prove its case beyond reasonable doubt.[2] We can be certain that an

---

1. Notably Frank Brennan, SJ, in many articles and lectures, summed up in Brennan, *Observations*.

2. 1. Professor Gideon Boas, Barrister and Adjunct Professor of Law at La Trobe University: ".what's to say the High Court had it right?" Quoted in Davey: *The Case* 338.
2. Professor Jeremy Gans, Melbourne Law School: "The High Court's key ruling—that there is a 'significant possibility' that Pell is innocent of the charges against him—isn't a conclusion that he is innocent; it is a conclusion that the prosecution failed to prove that he isn't." https://insidestory.org.au/pell-in-purgatory/

Clerical Errors

enormous error lies concealed in this matter. If Pell is innocent, the mistake was made by the jury at the second County Court trial and repeated by the majority of two judges in the Victorian Court of Appeal. If he is guilty, the wider justice system has compounded a clerical error of the worst kind, in failing to prevent clerical power and wealth from once again hiding the truth and so preventing sordid crimes against children from being brought to justice.

On a late-spring morning in November 2018, I stood in the lobby of Melbourne's County Court, checking the electronic board that listed trials to be heard that day. Among them I saw the simple line: Pell, George: Courtroom 3–4. I could scarcely believe what those words implied. In Melbourne during the 1950s and 1960s, as schoolboy and then seminarian, I saw Catholic priests as holy men in black suits, a world-wide army who ran parishes "saying Mass" and hearing confessions. Bishops were higher up, more remote. In those days I could never have imagined that any priest, much less an archbishop or cardinal, would be tried in a criminal court.

Cardinal Pell is a big man and a forceful personality. On the football field at St Patrick's College in Ballarat he had played strongly and skillfully. At Corpus Christi seminary they remembered him as an assertive student. After being ordained priest in 1966 then studying in Rome and Oxford he climbed the clerical ladder with unusual speed. Within twenty-one years he was appointed as an auxiliary bishop in Melbourne, Australia's largest diocese, having already served as a consultor to Ballarat's bishop and become rector of his former seminary.

Consecrated as Melbourne's archbishop in August 1996, Pell's Vatican connections made it inevitable that he would climb further. Five years later he was appointed to the older see of Sydney and soon afterwards received the cardinal's red hat. This brought additional power, for cardinals elect the pope and lead the Vatican departments that control the church's network of more than 3,000 dioceses. Pell had already worked on several Roman committees, and in 2013 the new pope Francis called him to Rome to be part of a select group of advisers. Soon afterwards, Cardinal Pell was given the complex task of sorting out the Vatican's tangled financial affairs.

Inside Courtroom 3.4 there was seating for about fifty members of the public, but only half the chairs were occupied. Very few people knew about this trial—I had heard about it only "on the grape-vine"—for it was under a strict media ban to prevent intense publicity from influencing the jury when Pell came to trial again on other charges.

The Trials of George Pell

The cardinal sat alone in the dock, a low gallery at the rear of the court, railed off from the public. A handful of journalists typed furiously from time to time on their little computers, although they were strictly forbidden to publish anything until after the later trial. During breaks in the proceedings, I learned that they represented Reuters; the *New York Times;* the *Washington Post;* Melbourne's local dailies and sundry other news-media.

Judge Peter Kidd presided, and Senior Counsel Mark Gibson addressed the jury, reading out five charges. These alleged that Cardinal George Pell, when Archbishop of Melbourne, after high Mass in St Patrick's Cathedral one Sunday in 1996 had found two thirteen-year-old choir boys trespassing in the sacristy. The boys' names were read out in court, but later reduced to the single initials 'J' and 'R'. The charges alleged that Pell found the boys helping themselves to altar-wine; told them that they were in trouble and began to assault them, exposing himself and forcing his penis into the mouth of 'R'. Despite the boys' tears, and their pleas for him to stop, it was alleged that he proceeded forcibly to assault the second boy, commanding him to remove his trousers, and handling the boy's genitals while masturbating himself.

There was a fifth charge: 'J' had also claimed that sometime later, when passing 'J' in the cathedral corridor, Pell had suddenly pushed him against a wall and groped his genitals. 'J' was the sole complainant, giving evidence also on behalf of his companion, who had died in 2014. The jury was told that 'R's death was accidental, but not told that it was caused by a drug overdose. Following the alleged assaults, both boys' lives had deteriorated, and 'R' had begun to use heroin while still in his teens.

When the Prosecutor had finished reading the charges, Robert Richter QC rose to speak in Pell's defense. He spoke calmly, chatting to the jury members as if they were his equals. He first told them how Pell had been hounded by the media and reviled in a popular song, and yet had returned from Rome to answer these charges. Because 'J' claimed the offenses had occurred before Christmas, Richter said, they must have taken place on either December 15 or 22, the only Sundays in 1996 on which Pell had celebrated the 11am Mass after being installed as archbishop in the previous August.

At one point Richter told the jury that they did not have to think about the complainant's past history, or his psychological state. But by that simple statement he immediately put doubts in their minds about 'J's personal life and mental stability. Later, when the jury was out of the courtroom, the

Clerical Errors

prosecutor rather timidly objected to this and the judge rebuked Richter, but the proverbial horse had long since galloped from the stable.

The court was closed to the public for two and a half days while the jury watched the video recording of 'J's evidence at the earlier trial on these same matters, which had ended in a hung jury. It would have been inhuman to submit 'J' once again to several days of Richter's grueling questions. When the court re-opened, the jury heard a series of witnesses called by the prosecution: former choir boys, the former choir master and his assistant, the former choir-marshal, organist, sacristan and master of ceremonies. Even the wine dealer was called to give evidence about the kind of wine used in 1996.

Pell's supporters would later claim that all these witnesses were "exculpatory" and that they "exonerated" Pell, but in fact none of their evidence proved anything conclusively. From them we learned that Pell was well-known to the choir boys. Sometimes vested in regalia, sometimes in clerical street clothes, he would visit and chat with them at morning tea in the Diocesan Center, or in the corridor, before Mass.

Richter's "proof" that Pell could not have committed the crimes depended on such points as the following, which are not presented here in the order he made them:

1. That the crimes must have taken place very soon after the procession from the altar had dispersed. This, like the entire case, was based entirely on 'J's evidence. Whatever he told the jury has never been made public, but his memory seems to have been quite unclear, for at different times he gave different accounts of how the two boys got to the sacristy. Was his uncertainty caused by the trauma he claimed to have suffered, and magnified by the lapse of twenty-two years? Was he further confused by Richter's severe grilling over more than two days? His lack of precision did not cause the jury, or any of the three judges at the subsequent appeal, to doubt his truthfulness or reliability. At that appeal, the dissenting Justice Weinberg reasonably claimed that the jury must have had grounds for reasonable doubt, but he based this conclusion not on 'J's lack of credibility, but on the sequence of events as the Prosecution had presented them. Weinberg correctly concluded, and the High Court later unanimously agreed, that as the evidence was presented, it failed to prove "beyond a reasonable doubt" that the offenses had been committed. Would the Prosecution case

have ultimately succeeded if the police had gathered evidence more thoroughly, and the Prosecution argued more carefully?

2. That if the truant boys had left the choir procession as it emerged from the cathedral, they would have been seen departing by their fellow choristers, by the choir marshal, by Br Finnegan, and possibly the organist. When questioned, however, those persons denied that they would *necessarily* have noticed if two boys had absented themselves.

3. That after Mass the sacristy and the corridor beside it would have been busy with people coming and going: the master of ceremonies; sacristan; altar servers; choristers and possibly concelebrating priests. But against this, witnesses attested that the choristers would have hurried from their changing room within about five minutes, and the others would normally have dispersed within about ten.

4. That the two boys would have been missed from their noon choir practice, which normally followed immediately after Mass. However, the former choir master Mallenson recalled that rehearsals were held at different times and places, especially at that time when the cathedral was being renovated. Sometimes rehearsals were *before* the 11am Mass; sometimes in the cathedral itself, rather than the locked rehearsal room to which it would be difficult for truant boys to return unnoticed. Mallenson could not recall that two boys ever came late for an after-Mass rehearsal. Nor was the former choir marshal Peter Finnegan certain on this point. But when asked whether he would notice if any boys were missing from Sunday rehearsals, he replied: 'It never occurred, that I know of, *but I might not know*.' Richter's claims were not so certain after all.

5. That "canon law" demanded that the MC must always accompany the robed archbishop. This naïve error went uncorrected. The obvious truth emerged later that the MC's role was not so much to "look after the archbishop," but to manage the liturgy. One former choir boy, Carl Muller, recalled that although the MC and the archbishop were *often* together, this was *not always* the case. He recalled how the boys joked about the contrast between the tall, clean-shaven archbishop and the shorter, bearded MC, and found it amusing that the two were often together, but sometimes not. The sacristan Potter's evidence too, reinforced the fact that they were *not* always together.

6. One of Richter's main "proofs" was lack of opportunity. His case hung on his claim that the crimes must have been committed within ten minutes after the procession ended, which made them impossible if the archbishop stayed at the front of the cathedral talking with people for perhaps fifteen or twenty minutes. Later in the trial, the 84-year-old former sacristan Max Potter—who quaintly kept addressing the judge as "Your Majesty"—stated that Pell might remain on the front steps for up to half an hour. But when this claim is more closely examined, a long delay on the steps works *against* Richter's argument, for it would have considerably broadened Pell's opportunity to assault the boys. By the time he had finished chatting—which as new archbishop he certainly would have done for some time—the people who had been busy around the sacristy area would all have dispersed. If the boys on that day did *not* have a choir practice, or had skipped it unnoticed, there would be ample time for the crimes to occur.

7. That the two boys never told their parents, nor discussed the crimes with each other, even though they were friends. When asked by his mother, 'R' had explicitly denied that he had been abused. 'R's father too had suspected that his son had suffered abuse.[3] The boys' failure to disclose proves nothing, for it is well established that many victims/survivors *never* admit or report the abuse that traumatized them.

8. That sacristan Potter would *always* lock the sacristy during Mass and after he had finished tidying up. But people are fallible, and their habits are not inflexible. The defense depended heavily on people always following the same routines: that Potter for instance *always* locked the sacristy during Mass and whenever it was empty. It is interesting that Pell later wrote in his *Prison Journal*[4] that "Potter did *different* things after Sunday Mass, [my emphasis] sometimes travelling with the procession of servers and choir, sometimes breaking off as they left the sanctuary and then opening the sacristy door, either immediately or when his server helpers arrived." Might Potter on that one occasion have left the sacristy unlocked, either through forgetfulness or for the archbishop's convenience when he returned from the front steps? Minor acts of forgetfulness can sometimes have momentous consequences.

---

3. Louise Milligan, *Cardinal*, Kindle Location 5648.
4. Pell, *Journal*, Vol 2, 131.

In view of all these loose ends, it remains possible that after the procession had dispersed, the two boys had "nicked off" in search of some minor adventure and continued to loiter among the many potential hiding places at the east end of the cathedral. It is also possible that, after the flurry of servers, choristers and possibly priests had left the area, the boys had trespassed into the empty sacristy. Meanwhile the archbishop, having chatted on the front steps of the cathedral for fifteen or twenty minutes or more, might—alone for once—have returned to the sacristy to disrobe.

At one point prosecutor Gibson questioned Potter about the vestments that Pell would have been wearing: a long alb, with possibly a cassock beneath it. Did the alb have slits for access to trouser pockets beneath? Richter had tried to prove that the continuous cloth of the vestments would make impossible the crimes of exposure and rape, but Gibson's questions were quite inept. The present writer has been wearing albs and religious habits, similar to cassocks, for 56 years, and like any priest, well knows that to answer a call of nature it is a simple matter to lift the hem of the garments to the required height.

Apparently 'J' had also mentioned in his evidence that Pell had "parted" or "moved aside" the vestments. If the boy's memory had retained that vivid detail during the terrible moments of the attack, he might well have been recalling the outer *chasuble* being moved aside. This vestment has no sides but merely hangs like a sandwich board in back and front. It can easily be moved *aside* and then the hem of the alb lifted without difficulty. A strong elbow could simply hold all the bunched cloth against the attacker's ribs, leaving both hands free for the awful assault. Such an attack was entirely possible; a fact reinforced by the evidence which a Mr Gray gave to the Royal Commission some time before Pell's trial. When Gray was a boy, the Anglican priest Father Rushton often abused him, and on one occasion compelled him to perform oral sex in the vestry of the church *while Father Rushton was wearing his church robes.*[5]

On December 11, I was in the courtroom for what proved to be the final day of the trial. After three and a half days of deliberation the jury returned a verdict of "guilty on all five counts." I felt stunned at the news. So did most people, whether or not they could believe the verdict to be true. Many Catholics found it simply unthinkable that a cardinal could be guilty of such crimes, despite being convicted in a criminal court. Their response seemed to confirm the psychological principle that when we are confronted

---

5. *RCFR*, 16, 1, 416. [My emphasis.]

Clerical Errors

with a fact that goes against everything we believe, we look everywhere for evidence to prove it can't be true and continue to see everything through the lens of our previous assumptions.

Was it still possible that Pell was innocent? The issue at stake was enormous. I could hardly bear to think of the terrible wrong of falsely accusing *any* innocent person of gross offending against children, and then wrongfully jailing them. But the opposite wrong was equally frightening: if we failed yet again to hear a victim's cries, how many other victims would we be keeping forever silent and helpless because powerful churchmen can afford expensive lawyers? Either way, any sensitive person must have shuddered at the thought of the elderly cardinal now suffering the indignity of being strip-searched by guards; verbally abused by fellow-prisoners; confined to a narrow cell and, for only one hour each day, allowed to limp around a dingy prison-yard.

It is folly to think that any justice system always "gets it right." The courts wrongly convict many innocent persons. Between 1922 and 2015, among the thousands of persons convicted in Australian courts, seventy-one were later *found* to be innocent. Among them, fifteen had been given "life": up to twenty years. Three were told that they were to be hanged, but two of those were later freed. The other unfortunate, Colin Campbell Ross, was killed by the state in 1922, but "pardoned" somewhat tardily eighty-six years later. These figures tell only of persons who were later *found* to be innocent. How many other innocent people have been jailed, or are still in jail? But it goes the other way too: many guilty persons are acquitted by the courts because there is not enough evidence to convict them; or because their highly-paid lawyers can skillfully sway a jury.

The "gag" that prevented all media from reporting Pell's verdict was not lifted until three months later, on February 26, 2019. The suppression had been intended to prevent possible "contamination" of the jury at another proposed trial, concerning allegations that Pell had abused boys at a Ballarat swimming pool in the 1970s. That trial was cancelled, but the accusations will be mentioned later. Soon after the news of Pell's conviction was released, the Jesuit priest and lawyer Frank Brennan published an article opposing the jury's verdict. It appeared first in the national newspaper *The Australian* and then in the London *Tablet*.[6] I had often admired Brennan's writings on social justice issues and recalled that he had sometimes challenged Archbishop Pell, notably contesting Pell's erroneous teaching

---

6. *Tablet,* March 2, 2019.

that the conscience of the individual is not superior to law and authority. I had met Brennan at the County Court, and later learned that the Australian bishops had commissioned him to report on the trials.[7] Now he was challenging Pell's accuser: "... the complainant got all sorts of facts wrong"; and "... many of the details he gave were improbable if not impossible." Brennan himself got a few of the details wrong, for instance describing the sacristy door as being "*wide* open," when the evidence was merely that Pell had not *locked* it. Even if 'J' had accurately remembered this detail, an unlocked door is irrelevant if, long after Mass, the cathedral beyond it is virtually empty of people. Brennan also claimed that the witnesses "gave compelling evidence that it was impossible to produce an erect penis through a seamless alb." As shown above, this was not at all true. Like other commentators, Brennan seemed to assume that the accumulated circumstantial evidence of many witnesses "proved" that the crimes could not have happened. Against this opinion, another experienced journalist noted that the circumstantial evidence did *not* show that the crimes were impossible, but was at best ambiguous and at times contradictory.[8]

Neither Brennan nor Pell's many other defenders had heard 'J' give his evidence. The court had been closed for the several days in the first trial during which Richter had grilled him, and also in the second trial when the evidence was replayed. After doubting 'J's evidence, Brennan went on to pity him, hoping and praying that he "can find some peace; able to get on with his life, whichever way the appeal goes." This seemed to suggest that the accuser's lack of peace and his courageous challenge of the cardinal arose not from being raped at the age of thirteen but because he was troubled or disturbed for some other reason.

As shown above, there *were* ways in which the crimes might have been possible. For the sake of 'J' and countless others who had in vain made complaints against clerics, I believed Brennan's presumption needed to be challenged. In addition to my thoughts about opportunity to commit the crimes, there were other reasons why I could believe that Pell *might* be guilty. I had read Louise Milligan's book *Cardinal: The Rise and Fall of George Pell* and discussed it with its author. From her and from several legal people who had close dealings with 'J', I heard that he was a reliable and credible person. The jury had reached the same conclusion. In addition to

---

7. Interview, Sky News, April 7, 2021.
8. Terry Laidler: https://www.abc.net.au/radionational/programs/lawreport/2019-12-26/10850390.

this, I sadly recalled that 'J' was not the only person who had made serious accusations against Pell.

In 2002 a Melbourne man's memory was jogged when he saw Archbishop Pell on television. He came forward to accuse the new archbishop of Sydney of having sexually abused him at a Catholic youth camp in 1961. At that time Pell was a seminarian and the accuser twelve years old. Pell denied the accusations and stood down from his position during an inquiry by the National Committee for Professional Standards. Retired Justice Southwell found the complainant to be speaking "honestly and from actual recollection," but could not reach a conclusion because of lack of evidence after such long delay.[9]

A number of other accusers have claimed that as a young priest Pell had often indecently groped them when playing with them in a Ballarat swimming pool. When I had seen several of them in televised interviews, these men had impressed me as genuine. The subsequent troubled lives of some, rather than proving them to be unreliable witnesses, are consistent with having been scarred by abuse as children. Two of these claimants were accepted by the Magistrate's court as worthy of a jury trial, the previously mentioned "Swimmers' Trial". This was scheduled for 2018, but later cancelled because of illness, and the death of one accuser. However there are other credible "swimming pool" accusers, such as Michael Breen, who have not wished to be drawn into the arduous court-room process.[10]

Again, a manager of the Torquay surf-club told how he had in 1986 or 1987 confronted Pell for prolonged self-exposure to young boys in the changing sheds. Still another man claimed that his son, when swimming at a picnic in northern Victoria, had also been molested by the young Father Pell who was then stationed at Swan Hill.[11] Another accuser, interviewed in a televised documentary, claimed that Pell had sexually abused him in a Ballarat children's home. Were all these false accusations? Was someone coordinating a far-flung conspiracy against Pell, stretching over decades? Or was this a pattern, pointing to a different conclusion?

During the sittings of the Australian Royal Commission in 2016, I had watched all of the evidence Pell gave under oath by video link from Rome.

---

9. https://www.theage.com.au/national/sex-abuse-allegations-force-pell-to-stand-aside-20020821-gduijp.html   https://www.smh.com.au/national/pell-exonerated-over-abuse-claims-20021015-gdfq5n.html
Justice Southwell was appointed by Archbishop Wilson and Brother Michael Hill.
10. Milligan, *Cardinal*, Location 5517–19.
11. Milligan, *Witness*, Location 3814.

He was asked about a meeting which he had attended in Ballarat in September 1982, as one of Bishop Ronald Mulkearns' "consultors". Mulkearns told that meeting that he was taking the extraordinary step of moving Father Gerald Ridsdale, not just to another parish in the diocese—which had happened many times already—but to an office job in Sydney. This was a most unusual move for a parish priest, but Pell declared, under oath, that he did not know *why* Ridsdale was being transferred. The Royal Commission did not accept Pell's evidence, for complaints about Ridsdale sexually abusing children were already common knowledge among Ballarat's clergy and lay people. Watching the televised interview, I thought that Pell's claims and denials amounted to perjury. That Pell probably knew more in that meeting than he admitted was confirmed by the British author and journalist Austin Ivereigh when visiting Victoria. Writing about Pell's years in Ballarat, Ivereigh noted that the energetic young priest had been a key player as a "consultor" and as episcopal vicar for education. There were just too many stories to ignore, about him as the "fixer" who would mop up after abusive priests, pacifying parents and keeping the problem "in-house".

In the same video interview from Rome, Pell did admit that he had sometimes recorded "ill health" as the reason for priests' resigning, when in fact it was pedophilia. But further denials followed, when he was questioned about his time as auxiliary bishop in Melbourne (1987–1996). The Doveton parish, which came under his supervision, had endured six abuser-priests as pastors or assistants. Parents were gravely concerned about the current pastor, the notorious Peter Searson, and had complained about him to the Catholic Education Office. The school principal resigned over the church's lack of action against Searson. Pell, still under oath, denied before the Royal Commission that he knew about Doveton's problems, claiming that archbishop Frank Little kept these matters from him.

There is evidence that these denials were not true. The diary of Melbourne priest Noel Brady records that Pell summoned him on July 8 1994, to rebuke Brady for mentioning child abuse in a homily at Dandenong. Pell commanded Brady to keep silent about the matter. Other evidence can be found in the minutes of two meetings of the Melbourne Curia in 1992. Auxiliary Bishop Pell is mentioned in those minutes in connection wihth with Fr Kevin O'Donnell in Oakleigh. The minutes do not mention that O'Donnell was a notorious abuser, but simply state: "Bishop Pell said that Father Kevin O'Donnell is prepared to stay alone in the parish provided adequate supplies [of other priests to provide Masses] can be arranged."

Clerical Errors

The question had been raised because the assistant priest, John Salvano, was most unhappy about O'Donnell's frequent inappropriate behavior with children. The archdiocesan authorities at first proposed to move Salvano, rather than the senior O'Donnell, but Salvano refused to go.[12]

Further evidence that Pell did not tell the truth to the Royal Commission comes from Ms Eileen Piper, whose brother Monsignor Kevin Toomey was violently assaulted by Bishop Pell as he ordered Toomey not to help with the case of Eileen's daughter Stephanie. The archdiocese was contesting Eileen's claim that Stephanie had been raped by Father Gerard Mulvale who was already convicted on other charges. In 1994, Eileen was in her brother's home when Auxiliary Bishop Pell visited and ordered him not to get involved in Stephanie's case. Eileen said that Pell repeatedly banged her brother's head against the wall. She said that the assault was "sickening", and made her cry uncontrollably.[13]

As auxiliary bishop and as archbishop in Melbourne, Pell had acted callously towards parents of abused children when they brought their complaints to him. Chrissie and Anthony Foster's two little daughters had been raped by their parish priest Kevin O'Donnell. In her book *Hell on the Way to Heaven* Chrissie tells of a meeting—the "Melbourne forum"—in October 1996, which was called to launch Archbishop Pell's Melbourne Response. This programme had been hastily drawn up in Pell's first months in office, but would later be described by the Royal Commission as seriously flawed. It will be discussed in chapter 2.

At the forum, which was attended by about 350 people, a strong statement recorded by Chrissie Foster was played. Later in the meeting a challenging letter composed by her was also read out. While the latter was happening, the audience began to applaud. Rather than listen to the tragic complaint, however, Archbishop Pell and the other officials all walked from the stage and out of the meeting.[14]

With the media gag now removed, Pell's conviction could be openly discussed . . . but not by everyone. The Vicar General of the Melbourne archdiocese sent a letter to all clergy, outlining what they could say about the matter in their preaching. I was grateful that the letter did not come to my attention until after I had given a homily on the following Sunday, for the letter seemed to suggest that the situation was not as bad as it seemed.

12. Milligan, *Cardinal*, Location 756–99.
13. Tess Lawrence, *Independent Australia*, April 6, 2020.
14. Foster *Hell*, 139–48.

It noted that the cardinal was maintaining his innocence and had appealed against the verdicts. This last statement appeared to suggest that the jury had got it wrong; that 'J's accusation was false and that the appeal would reverse the guilty verdict.

The letter then advised preachers to "respect" the Australian justice system. The Vicar-General's seventh point, in a list of nine, advised preachers to acknowledge and respect those who come forward with accusations. This advice from the cathedral repeated what had so often been done in the past: it put first the powerful clerics' claim to be innocent, as if this were more important—and more certain—than the cries of the powerless. The scales of justice seemed more than slightly tilted. Was it not time to be honest?

In the homily for that Sunday's Mass, I began by praising the good works done every day by Christians, who *are* the church. But I wondered whether collectively we were making the mistake that Jesus had warned about, with humorous exaggeration, in the gospel we had just read: criticizing others for having a splinter in their eye, but failing to notice the plank in our own? Were we prepared to admit that our church's clerical leaders sometimes commit huge errors?

I challenged Frank Brennan's widely published claim that the jury had got it wrong, pointing out that the witnesses had *not* ruled out all possibilities and that Pell *might* have had opportunity to commit the crimes of which the jury had found him guilty. I reminded the congregation that we often find it incredible that powerful men abuse children; that some abusers conceal their terrible crimes behind a genial and cultured exterior and their high status in society. People can have many faces. My comments were later confirmed by Clare Linane, wife of Ballarat abuse survivor Peter Blenkiron: "Pedophiles can be . . . lovely, intelligent, charismatic people. We know from history they include extremely successful politicians, celebrities, judges, teachers, priests . . . they are from all walks of life and run the whole gamut from stupid to brilliant, charming to repulsive."[15] This point about character may be difficult to accept, but it is confirmed by many victims, such as Georgie Burg, who as a child was raped many times by a popular clergyman. She described his kind as ". . . intelligent, articulate, highly educated. They hold multiple degrees—they're absolutely idolized. They can talk their way out of anything . . . they're fantastic at justifying and going on the attack if they ever feel caught out."[16]

15. *Ballarat Courier*, March 4, 2019.
16. Davey, *Case*, 354.

Clerical Errors

In Pell's case this truth was endorsed by the writer Austin Ivereigh, who remarked that on first meeting Pell he had found him "gracious and hospitable," yet later saw that Pell often dealt with people in confrontational, overbearing, crude, and bloody-minded ways. An experienced observer of Catholic politics, Ivereigh had seen Pell behave "abominably" at the Synod on the Family, baselessly accusing pope Francis of rigging the synod to secure an outcome that displeased conservatives.

In the homily I mentioned Pell's failures as a bishop in responding to complaints of abuse, and my doubts about his evidence before the Royal Commission. I spoke of the inadequacy of his Melbourne Response; and the several prior accusations against him. I concluded that the whole record of abuse and concealment shows that "our church is sick," and that we need to accept this fact if we are ever to change. After the Mass, many people thanked me sincerely, but some objected strongly: a dozen or more people had walked out of the church before the end of the homily and several friars in my Dominican community later condemned it. Some of my friends had already begun to circulate the homily, and it must have been reported to the archbishop, for he telephoned our Provincial Prior requesting that I not publish it. I obeyed, but it continued to circulate, and I received a small flood of emails and phone calls thanking me for having the courage to admit publicly the sickness in our church, and that high-ranking prelates sometimes do commit terrible crimes.

Other voices reassured me that I was not being unreasonable or perverse in criticizing Pell. Soon afterwards John Ellis published an article retelling what he had suffered from the Sydney archdiocese when Pell was archbishop. His story is summarized in chapter 2. Ellis vividly described the barriers that confronted him when he sought redress and expressed his sadness that many commentators were failing to respect Pell's Melbourne accuser. From his own bitter experience Ellis knew how extraordinarily courageous this survivor must be, and how grueling the saga that he and his family must have endured.

Another former victim/survivor strongly challenged the people who could not believe Pell might be guilty. Paul Tatchell, now a town mayor, had been raped when he was at St Patrick's College Ballarat by Brother Edward Dowlan, but had campaigned against his abuser and helped others in their struggles. Tatchell described himself as normally fearless, but admitted that Pell had made him afraid: "... the most intimidating person, and one of the most intelligent I've ever met; and he's calculating."

The Trials of George Pell

On March 13, 2019, I was in the large crowd that packed the Melbourne County court to hear Judge Kidd impose sentence. This time a large media circus had assembled outside the court and the judge's words were to be live streamed to world television. Judge Kidd read the five charges for which Pell had been found guilty "by 12 men and women, randomly selected . . . after almost five days of deliberation." The judge's words were severe, describing the offenses as the "brutal rape of a 13-year-old" . . ."sustained", "brazen" and "breathtakingly arrogant . . . forcible, causing distress, degradation and humiliation." They were committed by Pell when he was "fully functioning" and "lucid." The later offense in the cathedral corridor, was "brazen, forceful re-offending." Refuting QC Richter's attempt to minimize the crimes, Kidd emphasized that Pell had showed arrogance and impunity: "You were prepared to take risks." Where Richter had told the jury: "only a madman would do this," the judge responded that Pell must have thought that he could get away with it. Pell's offences were "intentional." "You *did* reflect," even if only for a moment. Victim impact statements had been presented by the complainant 'J' and the father of complainant 'R'. Pell's counsel tried to argue that the father was not a victim, but the judge rebuked him, saying that although it could not add weight to the sentence, the abuse of a child *can* have an enormous impact on its parents The judge summarized details which increased the seriousness of the crimes: the children were young: they depended on being in the choir to pay their school fees; they cried and pleaded with Pell not to continue; they were humiliated by seeing each other abused; the offending was a grave breach of the archbishop's authority, trust and responsibility; there was a huge imbalance of power between the archbishop, as responsible for the whole cathedral, and choirboys, its most junior members.

Some mitigating factors were noted: the attacks were spontaneous and unplanned; and Pell had no previous convictions. Although ten character references listed his kindness, generosity, compassion and humor and his passion for social justice, the judge said that "good character" is largely about rehabilitation, which at Pell's age was less important. Nor does an otherwise blameless life diminish the seriousness of offending. The fact that Pell did not take responsibility for the crimes or show any evidence of remorse would add to his sentence, but his plea of "not guilty" would not increase it. The judge allowed mitigation for "extra-curial punishments" such as being unable to resume his career, but for the first and second charges the law demanded a prison sentence. The maximum penalty for "penetration" was now fifteen years. Kidd imposed a total sentence of six years, with a non-parole period of three years and eight months. The sentence included surrendering a DNA sample and signing the *Sex Offenders' Register*, which was brought to him before he left the court.

Pell began his sentence at once, but immediately appealed. Four months later the Appeal Court rejected his appeal, two judges against one. The dissenting Justice Weinberg, more experienced in criminal law than the others, did not accept that the jury could have found Pell guilty "beyond a reasonable doubt." The High Court was later to confirm that he was correct on this legal point, but a woman friend pointed out to me that he lacked understanding of the real world of sexual offending. Weinberg could not accept that Pell could have "groped" the choir boy in the corridor with other people present, but my friend remarked that women know from sad experience that men often "grope" breasts, buttocks and genitals, even in crowded public places.

Cardinal Pell was to serve thirteen months in jail, but the High Court of Australia granted him leave to appeal, and in April 2020, when its full bench of seven judges quashed the jury's verdict, Pell walked free from his jail cell. He had been tried before three levels of the court system, and there have been several civil cases against him, with others pending. Have all these processes brought us nearer to the truth?

The High Court exposed serious legal weakness in the earlier trial. But while it dealt justly with the case, did it penetrate the smokescreen by which that power and money can obscure the truth about the crimes of "important people." As already mentioned, professors of law have pointed out that the High Court did not declare Pell to be innocent. Has he been the victim of a gigantic conspiracy involving media, police, and even persons in the Vatican, through more than a quarter of a century? Or is he actually guilty of sexual offences against boys, as dozens of other prelates, and thousands of priests, have been found to be? His trials as a high-ranking cleric have been only a small part of the deep challenges confronting the Catholic church around the world today. The following chapters will summarize these horrific errors, made by clerics world-wide. When cardinals, bishops, priests and members of religious institutes err in this way, no doubt part of the reason is human weakness. But there is also abundant evidence to show that clericalism, and its claim to special privilege, have enabled clerics more easily to commit such crimes, and for church officials systematically to deny and conceal them. It is this culture of clericalism, and the harmful errors it has caused, which are the subject of this book.

2

"... To All Nations"

THE LAST PAGE OF Luke's gospel describes the risen Christ sending out his apostles to take the Good News "to all nations."[1] The first generations of Christians *did* spread the wonderful news that God loves all people and empowers each person to find eternal life through loving and forgiving. Inspired by this Good News, Christian communities soon sprang up around the known world. But within a few centuries those small communities had evolved into a structured institution in which had developed a clergy, a social caste, wielding considerable power. This chapter will examine just a few of the countless cases in which clerics have misused their power by sexually abusing children. It will show the tragic fact that the Christian church has also spread "to all nations" these crimes, committed by men who claimed to be building up the Reign of God. It will become evident that although only a small percentage of clergy have been guilty of abuse, the problem is neither recent, nor confined to the "decadent West." The stories listed here are only a small sample of the clerical failings which we know about. Beyond those, we know that many people have been abused by clerics but have never complained publicly about the abuse. But the cases quoted here are enough to show the tragic truth that abuse of children by clerics has happened, and still happens, in every part of the church. No territory has been exempt. A Vatican spokesperson recently admitted this: that abuse is

---

1. Luke 24:47.

"... To All Nations"

"a universal problem in the ... church everywhere."[2] Even more tragic is the fact that Bishops everywhere have responded ineffectually to the disaster.[3]

There is ample evidence that the scourge of sexual abuse has been present in every era of the church and has always been seen as evil. But before describing the contemporary distribution of the problem, it is useful to look at a brief historical overview. I make no apology for including some unpleasant and shameful details of crimes committed by clerics: euphemisms do not help us to understand the depth or extent of the problem.

One of the earliest Christian documents, the *Didache*, or the *Teaching of the Apostles* (65–80 CE), commands: "thou shalt not corrupt youth."[4] St Justin Martyr (c100–65 CE) and Tertullian (c155–240 CE) also spoke against the enslavement, prostitution and sexual exploitation of children.[5] The earliest church council for which we seem to have records was held at Elvira in Spain around 305 CE. Its 12th Canon condemns the abuse committed by parents who sold their children into prostitution, and its 71st Canon condemns anyone, not specifically clerics, who sexually abused boys. Offenders were to be permanently excommunicated.

When monasteries began to be established, governed by Rules such as those of St Basil (d. 379 CE) and St Benedict (d. 547 CE), the custom arose of enrolling young boys as oblates or recruits—not always voluntarily—for the mutual benefit of their family and of the monastery. Even though the Rule carefully specified how they were to be cared for by guardians, the practice brought problems on a new scale. When abuse inevitably occurred, both abusers *and* victim were punished, on several principles:

1. Boys were viewed somewhat as women in antiquity were viewed: as innocent virgins yet simultaneously as tempters. Hence it was thought that the boys' "evil side" was partly responsible when a senior monk abused or raped them.

2. The abusing older monk, ordained or in vows, was seen as more important than the boy.

3. The boy's passive role was despised as being "female."

4. The young victim was presumed to have taken pleasure in the activity.

2. Fr. Federico Lombardi, SJ, in J. McElwee, NCR, September 27, 2015.
3. Cahill and Wilkinson, *Child Sexual Abuse*, 96.
4. *Didache*, 2, 2.
5. Justin Martyr, *Apologia*, 1, 27, (Migne, Cols 369B–372B); Tertullian, *Apologeticum*, 9, (Hoppe 69, 23).

Clerical Errors

The Spanish rules of St Isidore of Seville (d. 636 CE) and Fructuosus of Braga (d.665 CE) were exceptional in that they saw that the aggressor was more responsible for the abuse. They recognized grooming and saw the child as deserving protection rather than punishment.

Harsh punishments were generally assigned for those who abused boys, as they were for same-sex activity. Typically, it included public whipping; having the head shaved; being imprisoned in chains on a diet of bread and water and even after release, long periods of supervised manual labor. Condemned monks were never again to counsel youths or associate with them in private. A Council of Toledo in 693 CE ordered that any clerics who committed acts "against nature" should be degraded, exiled and debarred from Holy Communion until their deathbed. Other church councils demanded that clergy found guilty must be dismissed from the clerical state then handed over to the civil authorities for punishments. Penalties might be lengthy periods of slave labor in the galleys, or even burning at the stake.[6]

By the mid-eighth century a sizeable body of clerical privilege had been built up, based on Patristic writings, papal decrees, *Acts* of Councils and astute forgeries. Clerics were exempt from public penance because of possible "scandal" to the lay populace if the clerics were forced to repent publicly of their sins. By the eleventh century, clerical corruption was widespread. St Peter Damian (1007–73 CE), the bishop of Ostia, sent Pope Leo IX a comprehensive summary called the *Book of Gomorrah*. It lamented the problem of monks and priests sexually abusing young boys and adolescents, their own "spiritual sons," and it denounced lax bishops who failed to address such abuses because, as in modern times, they were short of priests. Peter Damian stressed the crime's impact on *victims*, but Pope Leo focused on the *clerics'* need to repent.[7] The next pope, Alexander II, suppressed Damian's book.

During these centuries church leadership was struggling against the perceived problem of clerical marriage and concubinage. Hence it has been argued that in the twelfth century there was more concern among reformers to stamp out clerics' relationships with women than with adult males or children. One of the Councils of Toldeo (655 CE) had ordered that the offending priests be punished and their women sold as slaves, with the proceeds given to the poor. In the twelfth century the reforming Pope Gregory

---

6. *RCFR*, 16, 1, 170.
7. Anderson, *Magisterium* 750.

VII was still campaigning to eliminate clerical marriage but did not act with the same energy against same-sex activity among clerics. Bishop Ivo of Chartres (d.1115 CE) also expressed concern about the abuse of boys.

Although some theologians and canonists in the medieval church tacitly tolerated clerical sexual abuse, severe penalties were nonetheless administered throughout that period. We might however wonder why the legal codifier Gratian (d.1140 CE) did not include earlier legislation such as that of Fructuosus—mentioned above—or the severe punishments previously called for by monastic rules. Child abuse seems to have begun to draw less attention than clerical marriage or concubinage. Perhaps this was because the abuse of children seemed ineradicable. Perhaps also it was because the increasing privileges of clergy made punishments less acceptable.

As centuries passed, clerical sexual aberrations continued to be found in the highest places. Pope Julius III (1550–55) gave great scandal by his sexual relationship with a teenage boy Innocenzo, whom he made a cardinal.[8] St Joseph Calasanz, (1557–1648) founder of the Piarist order, knew that one member, Stefano Cherubini, was abusing boys in their Naples school. Concerned to protect the reputation of his new institute, Calasanz stressed the importance of not allowing the matter to become known.[9].

Between 1561 and 1741 four popes decreed that any priest trying to commit abuse during the sacrament of confession must be reported, and around forty cases per year can be found in the records of the Spanish inquisition.[10] In 1770, when the cleric and repeat offender Johannes Figulus of Prum abused two ten-year-old boys, he was condemned to perpetual imprisonment.[11] This severe punishment was typical, but by the late nineteenth century the church began to treat this grave problem in a radically different way, allowing more lenience and demanding secrecy. Church laws began to hide it from public sight, as we shall see in more detail in chapter 6.

There follows a sampling of clerical abuse from the five continents, with the countries within them listed in alphabetical order. The list necessarily includes a degree of repetition, for diocese after diocese presents a sadly similar picture. The list includes only a few cases per country, but gives more detail from my own country, Australia. It is a mere sample of the crimes that are known about, and we need to recall that probably only

8. Kelly, *Dictionary*, 263.
9. MacCulloch, *Silence*, 204–5.
10. RCFR, 16, 1, 174.
11. Lehner, *Monastic Prisons*, 78–79.

10 percent of child sexual abuse is reported. A large proportion of victims/survivors never report their suffering, and those who do report wait for an average of twenty-three years. So "absence of evidence is not evidence of absence."[12]

Africa

The church in Africa maintains a culture of silence over child abuse. Few cases are reported, for most African clerics view the issue as too delicate and sensitive for the public. Lay people keep quiet because they fear the institution. Some people claim that there is less abuse than in Europe and America; others affirm there is strong cover-up. Most attention has so far been focused on expatriate missionaries, whose crimes draw attention in their homelands, but a significant problem is emerging of African priests fathering children, often to mothers who are under-age.

Kenya

In 1989, sixteen-year-old Sabina Losirkale bore a child to Italian missionary priest Mario Lacchin, who had employed Sabina to cook and clean at the priests' quarters. Lacchin was transferred but continued in ministry. A catechist was chosen to marry Sabina, whose light-skinned son became an outcast from his black family. Such stories have been common in African missions, where there is a wide gap of wealth and power between expatriate clergy and the people they are meant to serve.[13]

Tanzania

In the 1960s, Rosminian Fr Kit Cunningham and three other priest-teachers abused many pupils in the school at Soni. Cunningham returned to London and became a popular pastor. When he died in 2010, one of his victims/survivors noticed his obituary and angrily spoke out. The Rosminians

---

12. The cases listed are mainly from the Royal Commission's *Final Report* and from the internet, particularly from the Australian *Broken Rites* website: http://www.broken-rites.org.au/drupal/. The specific sources of all cases are too numerous to detail.

13. Nicole Winfield and Khaled Kazziha, NCR, October 9, 2019; *Malta Independent*, December 8, 2019.

at first refused, but later, in a civil case, awarded twenty survivors almost UK£2 million. No priest was ever convicted.[14]

South Africa

Archbishop Tlhagale of Johannesburg admitted that the child sexual abuse crisis "affects us all." Thirty-five cases have been reported since 2003; one offender has received a life sentence. In 2019, three South African priests were laicized.

North America

Canada[15]

First Nations People

Countless incidents of abuse were revealed among the 150,000 Indigenous children who, since the 1860s, had passed through Canada's Residential Schools. By 2015 almost 40,000 former students had made claims of physical and sexual abuse.

Newfoundland

Media attention to the Irish Christian Brothers' Mount Cashel Orphanage led to the 1989 Winter Commission. Nine Christian Brothers were convicted, and the orphanage closed. The Commission found that there was "a general poor sense of ecclesiology in the Archdiocese, whereby the People of God are kept powerless," so that Catholics were reluctant to report abuse to Church officials. Archbishop Penney resigned.

Ontario

Twenty-eight De La Salle brothers were charged with offences committed at their training schools between 1930 and 1974. Former students received C$8.5 million compensation.

---

14. Peter Stanford, The Guardian, June 19, 2011.
15. *RCFR*, 16, 1, 186–91.

Clerical Errors

United States

Louisiana

Abuse by Catholic clergy first drew world-wide attention when in 1984 the priest Gilbert Gauthe (ordained 1972) was sentenced to jail for twenty years for abusing eleven altar boys. Pope John Paul II was given a detailed report on Gauthe's crimes.[16]

Boston

In January 2002, the *Boston Globe* published evidence that led to Fr Geoghan being sentenced to ten years in jail. More than a thousand victim/survivors of other priests came forward with complaints dating from the 1940s[17] The Attorney General found that the widespread child abuse in Boston was due to "institutional acceptance . . . a massive . . . failure of leadership."

It was pointed out that some diocesan leaders had denied under oath that they had known of the abuse, and that the church's responsibility for the harm wrought on victims needed to be recognized.[18] Just before Cardinal Bernard Law's concealing of abusers was made public, he fled to the Vatican, where he was given a prestigious appointment, and took part in the next papal election.

Philadelphia

In 2005 a Grand Jury exposed many hundreds of cases of abuse. In subpoenaed files it found complaints of "countless acts of sexual depravity against children" committed by many priests but systematically concealed during four decades by Cardinals Krol and Bevilacqua. The accused priests had been allowed to continue in ministry. Euphemisms were used when recording offences: the oral, anal and vaginal rape of children was described as mere "touching." One priest "shared the same bed" with a twelve-year-old altar boy and "there were touches." In fact, the priest had taken him to a motel, repeatedly tried to penetrate him anally and manipulated his penis for hours.

---

16. *RCFR*, 16, 1, 180; Kaiser, *Whistle*, 21–45.
17. *RCFR*, 16, 1, 183.
18. Cahill and Wilkinson, *Child Sexual Abuse*, 71.

"... To All Nations"

Cardinal Bevilacqua's degrees in canon law helped him to conceal the crimes. He did not record his decisions; often ignored allegations or took a priest's denial as proof of innocence. Therapists at the archdiocesan hospital dealing with accused priests understood their role was to protect the archdiocese from legal liability. Philadelphia priests had an unwritten rule against "ratting" on fellow priests. Seven of the most abusive priests had been seen routinely taking young boys, alone, into their bedrooms, yet none was reported by a fellow-priest. Some priests were complained about again and again—the abusive priest Chambers was transferred seventeen times in twenty-one years—but because of Pennsylvania's statute of limitations, many escaped prosecution.

The Grand Jury noted several times that Bevilacqua lied in claiming that no accused priests were still in active ministry. It described that cardinal's calculated indifference to victims' lifelong shame and despair as no less immoral than the abuse itself. But the church's lawyers attacked the Grand Jury's *Report*, calling it a "vile, mean-spirited diatribe." So as to leave no doubt about the scale of the evil perpetrated by these cardinals and the church-institution which they led, some more cases are included here.

Father McCarthy was accused of taking high school students to his beach house, plying them with liquor, sleeping nude in the same bed with them and masturbating the boys and himself. Bevilacqua transferred him to lead a different parish. In 1971 Bevilacqua heard complaints that Fr. Kostelnick had groped a teenage girl immobilized in a hospital bed. Similar complaints continued for thirty-two years, yet Kostelnick was continually appointed as a pastor. Father Dunne once paid $40,000 to silence a victim. Diagnosed as an untreatable pedophile, he was allowed to remain active for seven years then retire on a pension to his rural cabin. It was known that he continued to take boys there for sleepovers.[19]

Washington

In February 2019, eighty-eight-year-old Cardinal Theodore McCarrick was removed from the priesthood. He had been archbishop of Washington for nineteen years, and previously bishop in Newark, Metuchen and New York. He was found guilty of "solicitation in the sacrament of confession" and sexual offences with minors and adults. Abuse of power was an aggravating factor. As early as the 1980s, Newark seminary staff were seriously

19. Ralph Cipriano, *NCR*, October 7, 2005.

concerned that McCarrick regularly took seminarians to share his bed at his beach house, but no seminarian reported McCarrick, for he controlled their futures. When a bishop abuses his power over seminarians, a pattern of institutional abuse is being established. From 1993, multiple complaints about McCarrick's conduct with seminarians had reached the Vatican, and in 2005 and 2007 the church had privately paid large amounts of compensation to two men whom McCarrick had abused as *minors*. But it was only in 2018—twenty-five years after the first complaints were made to the Vatican—that McCarrick's sexual abusing became public.

One of the children whom McCarrick abused was James Grein, who was eleven when McCarrick befriended the family in the early 1970s. McCarrick began by sexually abusing James while hearing his confession before celebrating Mass in the family's home. The abuse continued for the next twenty years, and Grein struggled for decades with immense shame and guilt, and with alcoholism. His marriage broke up, and he attempted suicide many times. Even when laicized, McCarrick maintains his innocence, as bishop abusers invariably do. Was it merely coincidental that McCarrick was renowned as a fundraiser? As will be seen below in the tragic story of Marcial Degollado, the Vatican is inclined to ignore reports of sexual misconduct if the accused cleric is adept at bringing in donations and "vocations."

The Jesuits

Ninety-two Jesuits in their Oregon province were accused of sexual abuse, committed mostly in Indigenous communities. The charismatic and outgoing—but narcissistic—Father Poole was found guilty of abusing at least twenty women and girls, one only six years old, at a mission in Alaska. He impregnated one girl when she was sixteen, forced her to get an abortion and to claim that her father had raped her. The girl's father went to prison. Poole's superiors knew of his crimes for more than three decades but did not stop them. After paying $166 million to settle almost 500 lawsuits, the Jesuit's Oregon province declared itself bankrupt in 2009.[20]

In 2013 the Jesuits in Chicago paid $19.6 million to settle a civil lawsuit against Fr. Donald McGuire (ordained 1961). A spiritual director and leader of retreats, McGuire persuaded the mother of an eleven-year-old boy to let the boy be his personal assistant. For five years the boy lived and

20. https://en.wikipedia.org/wiki/Sexual_abuse_scandal_in_the_Society_of_Jesus.

travelled with McGuire, who sexually molested him more than 1,000 times. In 1983 McGuire became spiritual director to Mother Teresa's *Missionaries of Charity,* who strongly supported him at his trial. Mother Teresa herself wrote to support McGuire, saying that McGuire "admitted imprudence in his behavior" but that the sisters would do all in their power "to protect him and the priesthood of Jesus Christ which he bears." McGuire was eventually laicized and died in prison in 2017 while serving a twenty-five-year sentence. For thirty-eight years six Jesuit Provincials had been receiving complaints about McGuire but had lied and destroyed documents.[21]

Central and South America

The *Third Wave* report summarized sexual abuse by clergy in eighteen countries. The Church had tried systematically to suppress complaints and scandals by transferring abusers. Victims were hindered from taking legal action. They and their families were sometimes blamed for the abuse or bribed to keep silent. Complaints have increased sharply in the past twenty years, because reporting is easier, and six countries have abolished time limits on reporting.

Argentina

In 2019, two priests were sentenced to forty years in prison for sexually abusing deaf children at the Antonio Próvolo Institute. When the church had failed to act, survivors appealed to the UN committees against Torture and for the Rights of the Child.

Chile

Jesuit priest Renato Poblete (died 2010, aged eighty-five) was venerated and widely admired for decades of work among vulnerable children, the poor and the addicted. An enquiry found that Poblete had sexually abused at least twenty-two women, including minors, over forty years. Another charismatic priest and leader, Fernando Karadima, was at last exposed as a serial abuser in 2010. Pope Francis at first did not believe Karadima's

---

21. https://abcnews.go.com/US/wireStory/lawsuit-famed-jesuit-abused-boy-1000-times-world-67994009. Kaiser *Whistle,* 256.

accusers, but later admitted his mistake. Francis also laicized two retired Chilean bishops for abusing minors.[22]

Colombia

Cardinal Alfonso López Trujillo (1935–2008) was fabulously wealthy and highly influential in the Vatican. He was found to have been seducing seminarians and using prostitutes.[23]

Asia

In the Asian Catholic church sexual abuse cases were not openly spoken about, and rarely reached the level of formal charges, but this is changing. A conference of Asian bishops in 2011 was titled: The Impact of Pedophilia—Crisis for the Church in Asia. The bishops admitted publicly: Bishops all over Asia receive letters from different quarters of the Church that pedophilia has already become a considerably serious problem in Asia. "Let us not be complacent that pedophilia is a problem of the West . . . it is equally prevalent in many countries of Asia."[24]

India

Tellicherry

In 2014, four priests in Kerala were arrested on various charges of raping minors. In 2017, another was arrested on the charge of repeatedly raping a 15-year-old girl, who gave birth to a child which was taken to an orphanage without the mother's consent. The priest was sentenced to 20 years in prison.[25]

---

22. https://en.wikipedia.org/wiki/Karadima case
23. Martel, *Closet*, Location 5510.
24. http://www.fabc.org/. Cahill and Wilkinson, *Child Sexual Abuse*, 92.
25. *India Today,* May 5, 2014.

Jalandhar

In 2018, five Missionaries of Jesus sisters accused bishop Franco Mulakkal of raping many times the former leader of their congregation. Her complaints had been ignored by the Bishops' Conferences of Kerala and India and by the Vatican. Bishop Mulakkal retaliated aggressively against the sisters by a lawsuit and by pressuring the complainant's superiors to expel her from the congregation. Mulakkal was acquitted in January 2022, but the sisters have appealed the decision.[26]

Japan

Japanese culture is reserved about sexual assaults of women and girls, although these are rife on public transport. The statute of limitations period is quite short, and many sex-abuse victims choose not to come forward. Japan's 500,000 Catholics are only .4 percent of the population of 127 million. No stories of sexual abuse by Japanese clergy have been publicized, but there have been reports of abuse by overseas missionaries which have not been adequately dealt with.

Phillipines

In July 2002, archbishop Quevedo, president of the Catholic Bishops Conference, apologized for sexual misconduct, including child abuse, homosexuality and affairs, by various offenders over the past two decades. About 200 (2.8 percent) of the country's 7,000 priests were involved.[27]

Europe

Austria

In 1995 Benedictine Cardinal Hans Groer was forced to step down as archbishop following allegations that he had harassed and sexually abused seminarians and priests. One former seminarian claimed that when the seminarian was fourteen, Groer had caressed him; massaged his genitals;

---

26. Saji Thomas, https://www.ndtv.com/india-news/bishop-accused-of-kerala-nun-rape-prays-in-church-before-court-appearance-2035671 May 10, 2019.

27. *RCFR*, 16 1, 206.

harassed him into giving "French kisses," lain in bed with him and washed him in the cardinal's shower. Many Catholics expressed solidarity with Groer, and his close friend Pope John Paul II remarked that Christ also had faced "unjust accusations." In 1998, after thirteen more young men lodged additional charges, the Austrian bishops accepted the accusations as essentially true. The cardinal retired but kept his title and died in 2003 without undergoing a canonical trial. The Austrian Church has faced hundreds of other accusations involving priests sexually abusing minors.

Belgium

In 2000 the Episcopal Conference established a commission to investigate more than 300 complaints of abuse in almost every Catholic school from the 1950s to the 1970s.[28] From the 1990s a number of priests or former priests were convicted and jailed for raping minors. In 2010 Bruges' bishop Roger Vangheluwe resigned. For thirteen years, even as a bishop, he had sexually abused two of his nephews. In 2006 several clerics and ex-clerics were arrested through Operation Falcon, a worldwide investigation of internet child pornography.

Croatia

Before 2000 no Catholic priest had been jailed in Croatia for sexual abuse. In that year Ivan Čuček was convicted of the sexual abuse of 37 young girls; and in 2007 Drago Lubičić was sentenced to three years for molesting five teenage boys. The first priest to be convicted of pedophilia by a *church* court was Fr Ivanov, in 2014.

France

Serious cases of abuse have occurred, and clerics jailed for long terms at *Bayeux, Besançon, Chambéry, Evreux, Meaux, Orléans, Paris, Perpignan, Rouen, Seine et Marne*. The retired judge leading a commission investigating sexual abuse in the French Catholic church since 1950 estimated that it would find "at least 10,000 cases" by the time it finishes its work.[29]

28. *RCFR*, 16 1, 200–201.
29. *Tablet*, March 3, 2021.

Tragically, this figure was found to be grossly underestimated. In 2022, the results of an inquiry revealed that 216,000 children had been abused by clergy over seven decades,

In *Lyon*, in 2020, the priest Bernard Preynat was sentenced to five years jail for sexually abusing seventy-five boy scouts and many other offences too long ago to prosecute. For forty years bishops knew of complaints by parents. Archbishop Cardinal Barbarin received a six-months suspended sentence for concealing Preynat's actions. Barbarin then resigned but declared that he had "followed Vatican instructions."

Germany

In 2018, a report commissioned by the church revealed that since 1946, 3,677 children or adolescents were victims of sexual abuse by more than a thousand members of the clergy. Most of those responsible for these crimes were not sanctioned.[30]

In 1979 Archbishop Joseph Ratzinger of *Munich and Freising* (later Pope Benedict XVI), accepted the priest Peter Hullermann into Munich archdiocese "for therapy." Ratzinger knew that Hullermann had admitted demanding oral sex from an 11-year-old boy. The priest was assigned pastoral work. Despite strict warnings, he again abused minors, was sentenced and eventually suspended in 2010.[31]

Regensburg

When bishop of *Regensberg*, Gerhard Müller—later cardinal and prefect of the CDF—had reassigned Peter Kramer to parish work, although Kramer had been previously jailed for multiple abuse of a minor. In 2015 it was claimed that at least 547 members of the prestigious Regensburg boys' choir were physically or sexually abused between 1945 and 1992. From 1964, the choir's conductor was Georg Ratzinger, whose brother became Pope Benedict XVI. It was credibly alleged that Cardinal Müller blocked investigation of the abuse.[32]

30. *Pledge Times*, March 8, 2021.
31. *NYT* March 15, 2010.
32. https://www.dw.com/en/regensburg-domspatzen-choir-more-than-500-boys-abused/a-39731018.

Ireland

From the 1990s, television documentaries about harm to children led to a series of government-sponsored reports about the dioceses of Ferns, Dublin (the *Murphy Report*) Cloyne, and the *Ryan Report* about children's institutions. The Reports showed that bishops had often focused on secrecy, avoided scandal and protected the church's reputation and assets. They had failed to exclude unsuitable candidates from the priesthood or to protect children from abusive priests.

In 2002, religious institutes combined to pay more than €128 million to compensate victims of child abuse but asked recipients to waive their right to sue, and to keep abusers' identity secret. By 2018, over 1,300 Irish Catholic clergy had been accused of sexual abuse, but only 82 were convicted.

Among the most infamous cases were Sean Fortune, who killed himself before coming to trial; and Norbertine priest Brendan Smyth (1927–1997), who in Belfast and Dublin, from 1945 to 1989 indecently assaulted or raped over one hundred children. In 1995, when Ireland's Attorney General did not immediately extradite Smythe to Belfast, the controversy led to the government's collapse. In 2003, Dominican friar Vincent Mercer, former headmaster of Newbridge College, was jailed for sexually assaulting thirteen boys in their dormitory and in 2012 faced thirty-nine other charges. His superiors had concealed the allegations.[33]

The *Ryan Report* (2009) examined institutions that cared for children and found that, between 1914 and 2005, of the 25,000 children who had attended the institutions, around 1,500 made complaints of physical, emotional or sexual abuse. Such abuse was endemic in boys' institutions, and in some girls' institutions there had been predatory sexual abuse by male employees or visitors. When detected, perpetrators were often transferred. Religious orders commonly placed the interests of the institution ahead of the good of the children, in efforts to conceal sexual abuse or "to avoid scandal."

The various Irish reports show that institutions often betrayed their own purpose and allowed their religious ideals to become debased by systemic abuse. Members came to tolerate crimes and failed to respond appropriately when abuse was discovered. The Irish bishops admitted that the reports disturbingly showed "a culture prevalent in the Catholic Church."[34]

33. Healy, *Perfect Heart*.
34. *RCFR*, 16, 1, 195.

Italy

In Italy the issue of Catholic sexual abuse had been largely buried. If priests are found guilty by a Vatican court, most end up being transferred to a new diocese rather than being defrocked or jailed. Of those found guilty by an Italian civil court, few are imprisoned. Whereas the recent inquiry in France found that 216,000 children had been abused by clergy over seven decades, Italy has 52,000 priests to France's 21,000, so it is feared that the number of victims in Italy could be many times greater. A group of religious and lay associations is now calling for an independent inquiry into abuse, but some bishops are resisting this, or asking that it be conducted by the church itself.

In 2012 the priest Mauro Inzoli was dismissed from the priesthood by a church court for abusing dozens of children over ten years. A cardinal interceded for Inzoli with the newly elected Pope Francis, who ignored the advice of the Prefect of the CDF and returned Inzoli to the priesthood, directing him to receive psychiatric treatment. When a civil court later jailed Inzoli, Pope Francis again dismissed him from the priesthood.[35]

The Netherlands

In 2011 a comprehensive investigation identified 800 Catholic clergy and other church employees who had sexually abused children since 1945. One newspaper claimed that 20 Dutch cardinals and bishops were involved in concealing those crimes. Four senior clerics were themselves found to be abusers.[36]

Poland

The documentary film *Tell No One*,[37] strongly divided national opinion. Viewed online more than eighteen million times in its first week, it exposed decades of official concealment of clerical child abuse, especially during the 1980s, when John Paul II was pope.

---

35. *NCR* June 28, 2017.
36. https://en.wikipedia.org/wiki/Adrianus Johannes Simonis.
37. Director: Tomasz Sekielski, 2019.

The Vatican

Frederic Martel's well-researched book[38] confirmed that in the Vatican the "clerical closet" of secretly homosexual clergy is active and influential. The truly shocking corruption that Martel exposes at the center of the church-institution would seem seriously to undermine its claims to be a moral authority.

In 2002 Pope John Paul II stated that there is no place in the priesthood or the religious life for those who harm the young, but for decades he had himself enthusiastically supported the notorious Mexican abuser Marcial Maciel Degollado. It seems impossible that the pope did not know of Degollado's crimes.

Degollado had suffered abuse as a child. In his youth he had been expelled from two seminaries and treated for morphine addiction. In 1944, as a charismatic 21-year-old, he had founded the Legionaries of Christ. Although accused in the 1940 of sexually abusing minors, he avoided charges, seemingly because he had access to enormous wealth. Bribes to cardinals were to define his long career.[39] In 1956 the head of the Congregation for the Religious suspended him as Director of the Legionaries, but he was somehow re-instated after the death of Pope Pius XII. The Legionaries, who claimed to be saving the church from the liberal "abuses" of Vatican II, grew to have 800 priests and 2,500 seminarians; fifteen universities, fifty seminaries, 177 schools, and were said to have untaxed "offshore" assets of US40 billion. Degollado controlled the members of his organization by including in their Constitution a vow never to criticize him or other leaders, but to inform on those who did. This extraordinary Constitution was approved in 1983, with the intervention of Cardinal Pironio and Pope John Paul II. Was it coincidental that Maciel had paid for expensive renovations of Pironio's residence?[40]

Degollado was one of the church's greatest fundraisers, and in 1992 gave a large cash gift to Cardinal Somalo, head of the Congregation for Religious, and won the support of Cardinal Sodano, Secretary of State. The Legion also steered streams of money to Msgr. Dziwisz, secretary of Pope John Paul II, but Dsiwisz's autobiography makes no mention of Maciel or of

---

38. Martel, *Closet*.
39. Main site used: https://en.wikipedia.org/wiki/Marcial Maciel.
40. NCR March 4, 2022.

the Legion's donations.[41] Former Legionary and sociologist Stephen Fichter described Degollado as a consummate con-artist who would use any means to achieve his end.

After Degollado's death it became known that he had sexually abused more than sixty minors, mainly seminarians. From long-term liaisons with two women, he fathered probably six children, and abused several of his own sons. In 1997 eight ex-Legionaries tried to prosecute Marciel for abusing them as seminarians, but Cardinal Ratzinger, head of the CDF, was pressured not to proceed. The complainants were told that the process had been halted on orders from Pope John Paul II, who had praised Degollado as an "efficacious guide to youth." Soon after Ratzinger became pope, he did continue the investigation and found Maciel guilty of "very grave and objectively immoral actions; [his life] devoid of authentic religious meaning." Marciel died, still a priest, in 2008.

Oceania

Australia

The problem of clergy abuse is not new: Australia's first bishop, John Bede Polding (1835–1877), received allegations that deacon John Caldwell was sexually abusing boys. Polding, short of clergy for his 181 far-flung churches, instinctively did what generations of church leaders after him would do: he moved Caldwell to work elsewhere, hoping he would overcome "his strange propensity." Another of Polding's priests, Dom Garroni, was "habitually unchaste; very dangerous among young men."[42]

In Kapunda, South Australia, sisters in Mary McKillop's new congregation reported in 1870 that the Franciscan priest Patrick Keating was committing sexual offences in the Confessional.[43] The Vicar-General found Keating guilty and ordered him to return to Ireland, but Keating's friend, Fr Horan, took revenge against the sisters. Shortly afterwards, they were dispersed when Bishop Shiel excommunicated Mary MacKillop. But within two years, a Roman investigation found Horan had been at fault and reinstated Mary. These early grim reports of clerical crime and its concealment were a sad presage of things to come.

---

41. Dsiwisz, *Life with Karol.*
42. *RCFR*, 16, 1, 178.
43. *RCFR*, 16, 1, 179.

Clerical Errors

The Catholic Social Welfare Commission's 1999 report *Towards Understanding* claimed that the rate of offending by priests was no different from that of the general population, but this is manifestly not the case. The later solid research of the Australian Royal Commission found that among 9,025 priests who ministered in Australia through sixty-one years (1950–2010), 507 were alleged perpetrators.[44] Taking into account their respective lengths of ministry, this was 7.9 percent of diocesan priests, and 5.7 percent of religious priests. In Aotearoa-New Zealand the rate of offending among diocesan clergy—between the 1950s and 2020—was found to be 14 percent, and among religious priests and brothers it was 8 percent.

In Australia, the rate of alleged perpetrators varied among dioceses, from 15.1 percent (Sale) to 2.4 percent (Adelaide). Among religious orders of priests and brothers it ranged from 21.5 percent (Benedictines, New Norcia) to 2.1 percent (Dominican Friars). Among congregations of brothers the highest rate was 40.4 percent (St John of God Brothers) and in the Christian Brothers and Marist Brothers the rates were higher than 20 percent.[45] One obvious conclusion that can be drawn even from these rough figures is that higher rates of offending occurred among those priests and religious who worked in schools—particularly boarding schools—and as resident carers. Few offenders are found among Australian women religious:[46] e.g., 0.6 percent among Sisters of St Joseph of the Sacred Heart, and 0.3 percent among the Brisbane Sisters of Mercy.

Ballarat

Under bishops James O'Collins (1941–1971) and Ronald Mulkearns (1971–1997), the leadership of this diocese had been a "catastrophic failure." The Royal Commission placed responsibility for this on the hierarchical structure and culture of the Church. O'Collins and Mulkearns received many allegations against priests John Day and Gerald Ridsdale but often moved them to different parishes. For over twenty years Mulkearns did nothing effective to restrict Gerald Ridsdale's access to children. As parish priest of Mortlake, Ridsdale persuaded a recently separated father to allow his son to stay at the presbytery, where for six months Ridsdale sexually abused him almost daily. Mulkearns ignored strong complaints about

44. *RCFR*, 16, 1, 296.
45. *RCFR*, 16, 1, 35.
46. *RCFR*, 16, 1, 329.

the situation and left Ridsdale in the parish for nine months longer.[47] The bishop referred to the complaints as: "... vague rumours of a very general kind."[48] Mulkearns also failed to deal with the notorious Christian Brothers Best and Dowling and the priest David Ryan. Mulkearns accepted Ryan into the seminary despite serious doubts, and Ryan was abusing boys in the week he was ordained.

Maitland-Newcastle

Bishops failed here also to prevent notorious abusers, neglecting to act on complaints for many years. The priest Denis McAlinden abused more than 100 children, being moved in that time to New Zealand, Geraldton, Bunbury and twice to Papua New Guinea. The NSW Special Commission found "a disturbing story of repeated inaction and failure" by church officials.[49] James Fletcher (ordained 1968) sexually abused boys, particularly altar servers, for more than 25 years.[50] Vincent Gerard Ryan was one of Australia's worst pedophiles, preying on children for more than 20 years, and abusing one boy more than 200 times. He would encourage groups of altar boys to masturbate him and themselves, and to attempt anal intercourse. Ryan was sentenced to three periods in jail, but not stripped of his status as priest. The Maitland-Newcastle diocese has spent at least $20 million in compensation and legal expenses, and the deeper cost to the church's repute has been incalculable.[51]

Melbourne

The Royal Commission concluded that for decades Melbourne's archbishops had failed catastrophically as leaders.[52] They had tried to protect the church from scandal by a culture of secrecy, rather than caring for abuse victims. Archbishop Frank Little accepted a knighthood from the state, but he devastatingly failed to bring justice to victims of abusive priests. When

---

47. *RCFR*, 16, 1, 466.
48. *RCFR*, 16, 2, 519.
49. *RCFR*, 16, 2, 127, 146.
50. *RCFR*, 16, 2, 145–46, 241.
51. http://brokenrites.org.au/drupal/search/node/vincent%20ryan.
52. *RCFR*, 16, 2, 127–28.

seeking justice, victims were often further traumatized.[53] There were many infamous priests: Victor Rubeo, "Billy" Baker, Desmond Gannon, Peter Searson, Kevin O'Donnell, Michael Glennon,[54] and Ronald Pickering,[55] who in 1993, when police were preparing to arrest him, fled back to England, where he continued to receive a stipend.

It is part of the deep ambiguity of human life that each of these men may have done much good for people and were rightly thanked for it. But they also left behind them a trail of damaged persons. The evil they did was compounded by the lies which church authorities told about them. For instance, when Archbishop Little withdrew Gannon's faculties in 1993, he announced that it was "on health grounds". He honored Gannon with the title *Pastor Emeritus* and publicly thanked him for giving "the highest standard of pastoral care" over thirty-seven years. Parishioners, unaware of Gannon's crimes, presented him with a gift of $3,500. Two years later Gannon was in jail, and died, still a priest, in 2015.

Peter Searson, as parish priest in the 1970s, sexually abused a boy for six months. Despite a young woman's accusation that Searson had raped her, and many later complaints by various groups, Searson served as a parish priest for another two decades. The Royal Commission called this "institutional paralysis". In 1997, as new Archbishop, George Pell at last put Searson on "administrative leave", but then restricted the activities of the Diocesan Pastoral Office with regard to the Doveton parish so that it was prevented from helping the victims and their families that Searson had traumatized.[56] Searson was charged with physical, but not sexual abuse of children, and remained a priest.[57]

For fifty years, (1942–1992) under four archbishops, Kevin O'Donnell committed sexual crimes against children in many Melbourne parishes.[58] A shrewd businessman, O'Donnell helped to develop a Priests' Retirement Fund. In 1995 he was jailed, but only for fifteen months. Having unquestioned access to children at the Oakleigh primary school, he was able to rape Emma and Katie Foster when they were five and six years old. Emma remained silent for years, knowing she could not say anything negative

53. *RCFR*, 16, 2, 428.
54. Broken Rites website: http://www.brokenrites.org.au/drupal/node/97.
55. *RCFR*, 16, 2, 131.
56. Personal correspondence with a former Diocesan Pastoral Worker.
57. *RCFR*, 16, 2, 134–35.
58. Mannix, 1942–63; Simonds, 1963–67; Knox, 1967–74, Little, 1974–96.

about clergy, but as a teenager she became disturbed and attempted suicide several times. After a troubled, drug-affected life she died at 26. Katie turned to alcohol to numb her pain, and in 1999 was hit by a car and left with disabilities, needing full-time care.

Not long after Emma's death, the Fosters went to Sydney, hoping to speak with the visiting Pope Benedict about their daughters' abuse. At a press conference bishop Anthony Fisher referred to the Fosters' complaint as "dwelling crankily on old wounds".[59] Even if the archbishop was accusing reporters rather than the Fosters, his words, though spoken under pressure, reveal a typical clericalist disregard for victims of clerical crimes. The "old wounds" were the recent death of one daughter and the permanent disabilities of another. The Melbourne Response scheme offered the Fosters trivial compensation, which they rejected "in the interests of all victims". They sued the archdiocese in a civil case, and despite strong opposition from the church's lawyers they eventually received a settlement of $750,000. O'Donnell was never laicized, but retired as *Pastor Emeritus* and was buried as a priest. His estate was not used to help victims.[60]

The Melbourne Response was a program for dealing with abuse complaints. It was launched by Archbishop Pell in 1996, two months after he became archbishop and when all the other Australian bishops were preparing their collaborative scheme Towards Healing. The Melbourne Response was criticized by the Committee for Professional Standards and later by the Royal Commission as being heavily dominated by lawyers and lacking compassion and support for victims/survivors. Complainants were expected to pay for their own lawyers; were often confused about their right to go to the police and were sometimes warned about probable negative outcomes if they did go.[61] Compensation payments included a demand for confidentiality that covered the complaint and the payment.[62]

Sydney

Cardinals Gilroy and Freeman, like most other bishops, were good men and effective leaders, but they too failed to deal justly with victims of sexual abuse. In 1951 Gilroy ordained the Irish-born Denis Daly, who served in

59. Davey, *Case*, 41.
60. RCFR, 16, 2, 132–33, 482–83.
61. RCFR, 16, 2, 446.
62. RCFR, 16, 2, 321–22.

Sydney until, in 1963, police agreed not to prosecute him provided that he left the state of New South Wales. He was sent to Western Australia, but Catholics there were not told why. After returning to Sydney, police again wanted him removed so he returned to Ireland where the Limerick diocese accepted him, not knowing of the demand by the police. Daly continued to abuse boys. One victim, having become an adult father of three daughters, sought but was refused help from both Limerick and Sydney dioceses. He then committed suicide.[63]

Cardinal Freeman accepted the Benedictine monk Aidan Duggan, even though he had been accused of serial child-abuse when teaching at a monastery-school in Scotland. From 1974 Duggan sexually abused John Ellis, a 13-year-old altar boy, and continued until 1987. Like many victims, Ellis could not understand the abuse, and suppressed the memory of it, but in 2001 he began the Towards Healing process. The archdiocese was blatantly untruthful to John, telling him—and later swearing in the courtroom—that no other complaints had earlier been received about Duggan, when in fact there had been. The archdiocese deceived Ellis in other matters, falsely claiming that a psychiatrist had declared Duggan unable to be interviewed. Ellis' mother, who visited Duggan, knew this was false. The "psychiatrist" was merely a general practitioner.

Ellis was further traumatized when he tried but failed to sue the archdiocese to cover his psychiatric and medical expenses. The church successfully argued that its trustees were not accountable for crimes committed by individual priests who abused. This "Ellis defence" was subsequently used by church lawyers until, following the Royal Commission, several Australian states changed their laws to abolish it.[64]

Wollongong

This diocese too was plagued by horrific abusers. Peter Lewis Commensoli, chaplain to Wollongong College, abused students during overnight stays at his presbytery. Sometimes Christian Brother Michael Evans shared in the abusing. Despite accusations from victims in 1984, Bishop Murray took no action. The two abusers were at last charged in 1994. Commensoli was jailed for eighteen months, but Evans killed himself.

63. http://brokenrites.org.au/drupal/node/85.
64. *RCFR*, 16, 2, 447–48.

"... To All Nations"

Christian Brothers (CFC) and Marist Brothers (FMS)[65]

These large congregations, which each conducted a network of schools across Australia, also both shared the burden of having a number of serial abusers in their communities. The Royal Commission found that both congregations had poorly handled the problem of abuse. Their superiors had seen abuse as a "moral lapse" or "weakness" that was likely to be repeated, but out of loyalty to colleagues and because of the shortage of staff, superiors used secrecy to keep offenders functioning as teachers. They kept few written records of their transfers, and most accusations and admissions of sexual misconduct were treated as highly confidential. They were known only to Provincial leaders, who often did not pass on the information to their successors.

Abuse was rampant at two Christian Brothers' Boys' Schools in Ballarat, where several brothers—Stephen Farrell, Edward Dowlan and Robert Best—were notorious pedophiles. Many early deaths among ex-pupils have been attributed to suicide. The Royal Commission found it to be "inexcusably wrong" that Dowlan, after abusing boys at both St Alipius and at St Patrick's College, was appointed principal of St Vincent's Special School in South Melbourne, where he was the only adult living with the troubled boys. Dowlan and Best were eventually jailed for crimes against dozens of victims. The Christian Brothers also conducted orphanages in Western Australia which were the subject of the 2001 *Lost Innocents Report* to the Australian Senate. Ex-residents of those orphanages told of systemic crimes of sexual assault and predatory behavior by many brothers over a long period, but as happened elsewhere, the powerful aura of "religious" persons and the prestige of the Church prevented the boys' allegations from being believed or investigated.[66] Among the Marist Brothers, Kostka Chute admitted to abusing a child in 1962, but because no records were kept of his repeated offending, he was twice appointed as school principal. Only in 2008 was he convicted of 19 sexual offences—from among dozens more similar claims.[67]

---

65. *RCFR*, 16, 2, 162–68.
66. *RCFR*, 16, 2, 158–59.
67. *RCFR*, 16, 2, 177–87.

Clerical Errors

Salesians

This order of priests conducted a school in Sunbury, where in 1987 David Rapson, the Coordinator of Religious Education, was accused of abusing a student. The Principal, Julian Fox, sent Rapson for counselling, but also appointed him as deputy principal. Rapson was later convicted of multiple offences and jailed, and in 2015 Fox was himself convicted for earlier child abuse. Another notorious Salesian offender was Frank Klep, who served a total of ten and a half years in jail, and there were at least ten other Salesian offenders. Some were jailed, but one died before being convicted.

Dominican Friars

In 1960 an Adelaide schoolboy made allegations against Father Albert Davis. The Provincial Prior moved Davis to Melbourne, giving confidential instructions that he was not to work among children. However, under subsequent Provincials, Davis worked in parishes and as university chaplain in Melbourne, Newcastle and Canberra. When Davis died in 2007, he was about to stand trial for historic offences in Adelaide.[68] The Dominicans paid compensation to a youth whom Davis had raped in the 1960s; to a claimant against Dominic Fitzmaurice for an offence committed when Fitzmaurice was suffering from dementia; and in Aotearoa New Zealand to three victims/survivors of Michael Shirres.

Jesuits

Among the 453 Jesuit priests ministering in Australia and Aotearoa New Zealand between 1950 and 2010, the known rate of abusers was 5.7 percent. Credible allegations have been made against twenty-one priests and thirteen brothers or scholastics. Brother Victor Higgs, (b.1930s) committed sexual offences against boys at the Jesuits' Adelaide college and was then appointed night-time supervisor in the boarding school at St Ignatius College Riverview. He was later made spiritual director for 12- and 13-year-olds at Xavier College. The Jesuits paid modest compensation to Higgs' victims, asking that the matters be kept confidential. In 2016 Higgs was jailed for one year without parole, then at age eighty-one jailed again for a minimum of seven and a half years, for sixteen other offenses. Another offender jailed

68. *RCFR*, 16, 2, 191.

in late life was David Rankin, (ordained 1970) who had been chaplain in Hobart University then had charge of two parishes in Canada.

Treatment

In 1997 the Australian Bishops' Conference established a national program, Encompass, to help priests and religious with "psycho-sexual and related disorders", although it was becoming apparent, world-wide, that psychological treatment for these problems was not effective. By the late 1990s Encompass accepted that although treatment might reduce recidivism, abusers could not be returned to ministry. The bishops closed Encompass in 2008.[69]

In summary, the Victorian Parliamentary Inquiry (2012–2013) and the Australia-wide Royal Commission (2012–2017) found that through many decades, leaders in the Catholic church, like leaders of many other institutions, knew that some clergy and religious had sexually abused children. Many church leaders did not believe or accept complaints, even in the face of evidence, and sometimes they hindered allegations from being disclosed. Their failure to respond adequately enabled many more children to be abused.[70]

Guam

In the northern Pacific the church in Micronesia suffered trauma because its leaders were seriously abusing their power. In April 2019, the CDF rejected the appeal of Capuchin Archbishop Anthony Apuron, leader of Guam's only diocese of Agaña. He had been found guilty of sexually abusing boys, even his own nephew. He did not go to jail but was deposed and forbidden to dwell within the archdiocese, which found itself with $45 million in liabilities and filed for bankruptcy protection. Like other prelates accused of such crimes, Apuron had steadfastly denied the accusations.[71]

---

69. RCFR, 16, 2, 336.
70. RCFR, 16, 2, 202.
71. *NCR* April 4, 2019.

New Zealand

The tragic case of Dunedin priest Magnus Murray (b.1927) is a blight on the New Zealand church. In 1958 Murray won the trust of a Catholic couple and often visited their home. He abused their seven-year-old son for fourteen years. The young victim did not know that what Murray was doing to him was abuse, but at age 69 was still living every day with its consequences: mental illness, a collapsed marriage and a "disturbed" son. Nothing was done about Murray's crimes until in 1972 two angry fathers confronted the Dunedin bishop John Kavanagh, who sent Murray to Sydney for counselling. While ministering in Woollahra, Murray groomed seventeen-year-old "Paula". The friendship became sexual, and Murray kept contact with "Paula" after she married. He baptized one of her three sons and babysat all of them. When staying with their family in Dunedin, Murray had sex with "Paula's" husband.

In 1976 Bishop Kavanagh refused to let Murray return to work in Dunedin but offered him a choice of any other diocese. Bishop Mackey of Auckland accepted Murray "on professional advice" even though he knew of Murray's offending. Murray worked in five parishes within four years before moving to the Hamilton diocese, where Bishop Gaines appointed him parish priest in Waihi. Murray was moved to yet another parish, but after four years Bishop Gaines was prompted by police to retire Murray. The families of two Waihi boys were later paid compensation. In 2003 Murray was jailed for less than three years and laicized in 2019. At ninety-four he was living in an aged-care facility.[72]

The Cost

This chapter has shown only a sample of the tragic stories of priests and bishops who have committed or concealed sexual crimes against children. The samples show that such abuse has indeed spread "to all nations". Each crime caused serious damage to a child, and was also a sacrilege, for priests and bishops are ordained in a ceremony which dedicates them to God's service and calls them "holy".[73] The total tsunami of abuse is a catastrophe which has gravely wounded children and their families and continues to weaken the entire church.

72. *Sins of a Father*, Chis Morris, *Otago Daily Times* August 1, 2018.
73. *CCL Canon* 1012; *CCC* 1538.

". . . To All Nations"

These clerical crimes also bring huge financial burdens. By 2010 the church in USA had paid $2 billion to victims, including $US700 million in Los Angeles archdiocese alone. By 2017, fifteen US dioceses and some provinces of religious orders had filed for bankruptcy.[74] In Australia—population 25.9 million—the totals were smaller. From 1980–2015 the church there had already made payments of $268 million in response to 3,057 claims, but *Catholic Church Insurance* expects to pay out much more. Civil suits will everywhere multiply these amounts. Far more important has been the incalculable cost to the church's credibility as an institution, for the crimes indicate "massive failure on the part of the worldwide Catholic church to protect its own children" and "a corruption of the gospel which the Church seeks to profess".[75]

How could bishops who were otherwise good men and long-serving Christian leaders, systematically choose to favor criminals before children? We may not know the motives of individual bishops, but we will later see their admission that they were trying to save friends and colleagues from disgrace and jail, and to prevent their institution from being discredited. Had the church developed a culture of putting clerics before children? Or worse, did bishops make those fateful decisions because the laws of their institution compelled them to? The following chapters will continue to show how bishops' decisions were substantially influenced by the clericalism that permeates their institution, and by its defective laws.

---

74. Kaiser, *Whistle*, 281.
75. Francis Sullivan, *RCFR*, 16, 1, 288.

3

A Lifetime Sentence

THE PREVIOUS CHAPTER SURVEYED some of the tragic crimes of child sexual abuse by clergy in all nations. Before we look at specific causes for the flood of abuse, this chapter will examine the lasting effects of being abused, especially when the abuser is a cleric. It will show how every story of abuse is a profoundly human tragedy whose victim/survivor needs compassion and help, which their church's leaders too often have failed to provide.

The overwhelming number of these tragedies might tempt us to think the problem is in some perverse sense "normal", and therefore insurmountable. Cardinal Castrillon Hoyos, head of the Congregation for Clergy, appeared to lean towards this opinion when he lamented that lawyers and media were unduly focusing on the sexual abuse of children. He referred to it as an unavoidable fact of life, and asked why people were so outraged by it, when society also promotes sexual liberation.[1] Most people respond with more understanding and compassion than the cardinal, and strongly condemn the sexual abuse of children. Mercifully, we no longer demand the appalling punishments of earlier times, but our knowledge is increasing about the psychology of those who abuse children, and about the effects of abuse on children: consequences which often affect them for the rest of their life.

Until the 1980s, even in countries with developed health systems, victims/survivors of sexual abuse were usually left without professional help. Now, as a result of more open public discussion and increasing involvement

1. *NYT* July 1, 2010.

by doctors and psychologists, victims' suffering is better understood, and they have more access to support. At the Australian Royal Commission bishops tried to defend their lack of response to complaints by claiming that in earlier years they and their predecessors did not understand how serious was the damage that sexual abuse caused in children. This may have been partially true, but in no case were those church leaders unaware that sexual abuse was a *crime* that would normally lead to a jail sentence.

Sexual abuse almost always has serious effects on the victim's physical and mental health. One immediate effect is to damage the person's view of themselves. This self-description, by a woman who had been raped, might equally be spoken by a victim/survivor of child sexual abuse: "I fight every day to prove that I am worth something". She felt that she had been "trashed", and subconsciously believed she *was* trash. When she was again treated poorly she did not defend or assert herself, but accepted it without complaint. Rather than stepping out to reach her potential, she took on menial roles. It was only years later that she began to understand how the abuse had affected her whole attitude to herself and her direction in life.

Childhood abuse can confuse the person's sense of right and wrong. Many recall that as children, knowing nothing of sexuality, they did not recognize at first that what their abuser was doing to them was wrong. Because it is a primal invasion of the child's privacy, abuse shakes the young person's sense of safety and security and plants deeply in their heart the fear that privacy and safety might never again be possible. The impact of the invasion may affect their own sexual behavior as a child and adult; their sexuality and gender identity; their relationships with parents and their social well-being. Not uncommonly, the recurring distress that they suffer leads them to seek relief in substance abuse, which can lead to them commit crimes and become enmeshed in the prison system, where they are further damaged.

One of the first noticeable outcomes of abuse is poorer performance in school. This tends to impact further on the person's employment and economic security. Another outcome is that abuse tends seriously to damage their trust of institutions and authority. Many victim-survivors of child sexual abuse have been clinically diagnosed as having post-traumatic stress disorder (PTSD) similar to that suffered by war veterans or first-responders at disasters involving violent death. Even when PTSD is not diagnosed, most abuse victims endure some of its symptoms.[2] In addition to all this, when the abuser is a "religious" person, sexual abuse can also cause deep

---

2. *RCFR*, 16, 1, 484.

spiritual harm. Children raised in Catholic families were often taught that priests were much more than human officials: they were God's representatives on earth. When children from such backgrounds are sexually abused by a priest or a religious brother or sister, the impacts are often profound. Some child-victims experience a kind of toxic transference, feeling that they have been abused by God or that God must have willed the abuse to happen. For them sexual abuse can be a form of spiritual death.[3]

Some perpetrators actually exploited the victim's religious beliefs and their own religious status and authority to prevent victims from disclosing. David Owen gave evidence that for years at Neerkol orphanage, Father John Anderson sexually abused him. On many occasions he was threatened with "the fires of hell" if he did not do what was required of him. "I would succumb in fear and let him have his way with me. I complained to many of the nuns, . . . but each time I was punished for being 'evil'. On one such occasion, Sister Anselm shaved my head in punishment."[4]

A person abused by a priest or religious can experience long-lasting spiritual confusion. This may lead to loss of faith not only in the institution, but in the Transcendent God. Some survivors have reported that in later life they could not walk through the door of a church even to attend a parent's funeral or a sibling's wedding. Others could not celebrate religious holidays such as Christmas or Easter because it would trigger memories of sexual abuse.[5] "Arnett" told the Royal Commission that after being sexually abused by a religious brother during his first few weeks at boarding school in the mid-1970s, his belief system was undermined and he turned away from religion. Before the abuse he had had a strong faith, but after it his belief in right and wrong, Christianity and Roman Catholicism was totally turned upside down. He became an atheist, seeing no way that a God could have allowed such things to happen to him.[6] One victim of the Jesuit Brother Higgs said that because of the abuse he lived for more than thirty years without any self-esteem; his trust in people had been shattered and his marriage had fallen apart. His parents were also "broken" and "destroyed".

Stephen Woods' family was heavily involved in the Catholic Church. In 1972 he was sexually abused at St Alipius Boys' School in Ballarat by his Grade 6 teacher Brother Robert Best. When he moved to high school at St

3. *RCFR*, 16, 1, 488.
4. *RCFR*, 16, 1, 472–73.
5. *RCFR*, 16, 1, 496.
6. *RCFR*, 16, 1, 488.

A Lifetime Sentence

Patrick's College he was again sexually abused by Brother Edward Dowlan and by the parish priest Father Gerald Ridsdale. A few years later two of his brothers were also abused by people in religious ministry. His parents were utterly shattered to learn that their three sons had all been abused. They had entrusted their most precious gifts to the church, but now their faith in the church was destroyed. Mrs. Woods, a devout Catholic for nearly seventy years, lost her belief in the church, and Stephen's sisters and brothers absolutely despise it: a tragic result for a family that had been strongly involved in the church for three generations.[7]

"Bridget" strove to explain to the Royal Commission how, for the children of "strong Catholics", the priest was a figure wielding powerful authority, even inspiring fear. The Catholic child knew that a priest's word was sacred. "They hold the truth . . . but "when they treat you like Fr. X treated me, you do feel like you are the ultimate dirt because this is the man of God doing this to you. You are nothing. . . . it takes away . . . everything."[8]

These examples only begin to show how difficult it can be for victims/survivors to analyze and deal with what has happened to them. The evil actions of their attacker can distort or destroy the mysterious faith-bond that links them to God. Unless they can later make the necessary distinctions between the abuser and the God whom the abuser is himself betraying—distinctions which are quite difficult to realize—the result is profound confusion.

Many people who as children were sexually abused in a religious institution, in later life experience suicidal thoughts or actually try to end their own life. Some—even as children—do kill themselves. Suicides can occur in clusters, as happened among ex-pupils of St Alipius in Ballarat. One abuse victim told the Victorian Parliamentary Inquiry that while any abuse is dreadful, and sexual abuse is among the worst, when it happens within the context of the Christian community it "damages your soul". When people are deeply embedded in the church, it becomes like a family to them, so abuse by a church leader is like an attack by one's own family and deeply destructive to one's "meaning of life."[9] As a result of being sexually abused at St Alipius School in Ballarat, Mr. Paul Auchettl described his lasting "hatred for authority and men who dress up in the name of the clergy."[10]

---

7. *RCFR*, 16, 1, 489–90.
8. *RCFR*, 16, 1, 444.
9. *VPI* 2, 439.
10. *RCFR*, 16, 1, 501.

"Patrick" tried to express the fears he had felt in childhood as a pupil and altar boy in the parish led by Father Desmond Gannon. As a young priest in the 1960s Gannon abused many boys. "Patrick" told Broken Rites: "I felt particularly vulnerable, terrified and traumatized, particularly whilst serving early-morning Masses by myself during weekdays, and at other times during the day because our school was so close to the parish church. On several occasions Father Gannon called me over to the presbytery and the school hall to molest me. He would ask me to remove my underclothing, sit me on his knee and grope me". Aged about eleven at the time, "Patrick" was too embarrassed to discuss the abuse with anyone else.

"Patrick's" family was relatively poor. His devout Catholic mother had separated from his father when the boy was only two, and "Patrick" remembered his mother making big sacrifices to give money regularly to the church. He saw Gannon betraying her trust, gratifying his lust by molesting her son, and asked: "How much more despicable can it get?" This led to inner conflict, confusion, fear, trauma and anxiety. "I lost my faith, my respect for the church, my confidence and self-esteem. The on-going effect on my life, [my] prospects and those of my children, is immeasurable. The damage has . . . contributed to my inability to have lasting relationships, [and to] other problems . . . that are hard to quantify, problems I have tried to forget."

Like "Patrick" many other survivors told the Royal Commission that after they were sexually abused they felt betrayed and lost their former unquestioning trust in the church. This feeling of "institutional betrayal"— when a trusted and powerful institution harms the people who depend on it for safety and spiritual well-being—exacerbates the trauma of child sexual abuse.[11]

Professor Chris Goddard told the Royal Commission that we still do not fully understand the impact of abuse on victims. He quoted the example of one woman now in her 60s, who would still describe herself as a hostage to the religious abuser. Her abuse caused a catastrophic spiritual disorientation. According to Goddard the scientific literature supports the claim that abuse of children and young people in religious organizations is truly diabolical because of the lasting and terrible spiritual damage it causes. "While the abuse of children by adults always rests on a power imbalance, the large number of offences by Catholic priests reflects an extraordinary power imbalance. The religious authority they possess allows them even to

11. RCFR, 16, 1, 500.

turn parents and families against their own children. This has meant that many victims have had to attempt to deal with the abuse on their own, magnifying the impact."

Although sexual abuse can do terrible damage to the faith of a little one, sometimes, in apparent contrast, that faith is strengthened by having to cope with awful experiences at the hands of a church leader. Some kind of instinct—or grace—helps the victim/survivor to make the valid distinction between their relationship with the Transcendent God and the religious institution through which they learned about the mystery. Paul Tatchell survived sexual abuse at St Patrick's College in Ballarat, but his faith in God has endured: "I'm still a Catholic, believe it or not... Catholicism is a human element that has lost its way. I still follow the principles of Catholicism. I don't go to church; I just choose to cut out the middleman and go straight to the boss."[12]

"Darlene" told the Royal Commission that in Queensland in the 1960s, when aged sixteen, she tried to tell "Father Murphy" that she was being sexually abused by her parish priest, "Father Murphy" agreed to meet her alone to discuss it with her. When she arrived, he immediately suggested they have sex. She refused, but he forced her down onto a kitchen table and raped her. She conceived a child from the rape and "Father Murphy" gave her money to procure an abortion. She refused, and her mother and other priests then took her to a home for unwed girls run by religious sisters, who put her to work in a commercial laundry "right up until my waters broke". The baby was taken from her and adopted out. Despite everything, "Darlene" believes her religious faith has helped her to cope. "Even though I have no faith in the Catholic church... I still will not let them cheat me out of my belief... that there is a loving God who one day will call me to himself".[13]

Strong bonds to the church can make it almost impossible for some people to believe that a religious person could abuse children. So when abuse does happen, it can cause painful divisions in Catholic families. In the 1970s and 1980s Andrew Collins was sexually abused in Ballarat by a priest and several religious brothers. When the media first interviewed him about the abuse, his horrified family accused him of shaming them and the church. They did not believe the abuse could have happened; but if it did, they said, it was so long ago that he ought to "just get over it".[14] When

12. RCFR, 16, 1, 510.
13. RCFR, 16, 1, 502.
14. RCFR, 16, 1, 495.

Andrew became a spokesperson for other survivors, his family severed ties with him. His mother said he was a liar and was destroying their family's reputation. She told the police that they shouldn't listen to anything he said. Other survivors have described similar alienation from their families.

Philip Nagle recalled how he and his brother were both sexually abused by Brother Stephen Farrell at school and in their family home. Their family's door was always open to Farrell as a "man of God". When Philip revealed the abuse, it drove a wedge between him and his family for many years. Only years later, when Farrell admitted in court that he *had* committed the abuse could Philip feel they finally believed him.[15]

The family of "BAV" was very involved in the Catholic community in Ballarat. When he told his mother that he had been sexually abused at St Alipius Boys' School, she did not believe him. Because he had spoken out against the Catholic church, their relationship "was broken and it never really healed". In addition to the family rift, he was bullied, excluded from social events and lost work opportunities.[16]

Accusing a popular cleric can lead to the victim/survivor losing their job, and all future job-opportunities. This happened to Georgie Burg in Canberra,[17] and to the whistle-blower Graeme Sleeman in Melbourne.

During the investigation of the Philadelphia archdiocese, one seminarian victim of Fr Gana, revealed that the priest had abused him as an altar boy, but he could not tell his family because he knew that their respect for priests could not allow them to believe that a priest would forcibly and painfully rape their son. Two other young boys tried to tell their devout father that Gana had abused them, but he replied: "Priests don't do that" and beat them so severely that one was rendered unconscious.

When abuse is revealed, it can divide and fracture a whole community. This is particularly true when the perpetrator is well liked, trusted and respected, for abusers are often popular, charismatic personalities, and remain so even after being convicted. While some people in the community are disgusted by the crimes, others are unable to believe the abuser is guilty, and remain loyal supporters. An unfortunate result of this phenomenon is that abused persons often have to face hostility from many in their church community. Such ostracizing can cause additional feelings of devastating isolation and betrayal.

15. *RCFR*, 16, 1, 495–96.
16. *RCFR*, 16, 1, 496.
17. Davey, *Case*, 354.

A Lifetime Sentence

"KO", the mother of a Toowoomba victim/survivor, told the Royal Commission that when it became known that her child had been sexually abused by the Catholic primary teacher Gerard Byrne, her local school community and the Catholic Education Office were torn by divisions. In the courtroom there were always people supporting the school, but she felt it as a serious lack that neither the school nor the Education Office contacted her personally.[18]

The survivors of child sexual abuse who spoke to the Royal Commission took an average of almost twenty-four years to tell anyone about their experience.[19] Why does it take so long? In addition to the deep pain and shame that the abused person feels, the victims of clerics are psychologically trapped in a structure that holds great power over them. This power is spiritual, sometimes stronger than the bond between parent and child. It can confuse the victim as deeply as can the "double bind" by which the parent's power and the child's love can keep the victim of an incestuous father trapped within the home.

Survivors of clerical sexual abuse find it difficult to disclose because they find the gap between the "holy" person and their confusing actions is too great to understand. Most poignantly, many children who lived in an institutional environment can come to believe that abuse is "normal". More than 500 survivors told the Australian Royal Commission that they did not disclose their abuse because they thought it was "a part of life".[20] Some who have been abused by religious persons never tell anyone at all, for every victim/survivor faces some of the barriers mentioned: fear of their family's reaction; fear of speaking openly about sex and sexuality; fear of being ostracized by their religious community; or just confusion about the "holy" person who has done wrong. Survivors are often reluctant to "bring shame" on their church. Perpetrators often psychologically manipulate their victims. They may use the victim's religious beliefs to deter them from speaking out or threaten and punish them if they do.[21]

On top of the child's intense pain and confusion when abused by a religious person, they are often further betrayed when church authorities disbelieve or dismiss their claim. The authority may challenge the victim by such comments as "This is a pillar of the community you're attacking.

18. *RCFR*, 16, 1, 505.
19. *RCFR*, 16, 1, 508.
20. *RCFR*, 16, 1, 536.
21. *RCFR*, 16, 1, 484.

Clerical Errors

Is this really something you want to do?" Some authorities may not only fail to believe or support the complainant: they may comfort the abuser instead. After Father Thomas Shea of Philadelphia had confessed to abusing several boys, the cardinal's priest-secretary comforted Shea, suggesting that he had been "seduced" by his eleven-year-old victim.

When the priest Kevin O'Donnell was on trial in 1995, having by that time abused children in Melbourne for more than fifty years, Father John Brosnan appeared as a character witness for O'Donnell, and described the predatory behavior as "a great affliction" which caused the abuser "great suffering". No doubt it was, but as we have seen, he brought incalculably greater suffering to countless families, in shameful contrast to the loving service that as their pastor he was meant to offer them.

Abuse in Catholic residential institutions was made worse because the young victims were confined there, with no access to outside help. When abused children did sometimes cry to the authorities for help, they were rebuffed. This extra betrayal stripped them of what seemed to be their last hope and opened the way to complete despair. Some of their stories are difficult to hear, but again are included here, to underline how the church as an institution has done enormous harm to children under its care; harm that is magnified by the religious context of the abuse.

In the orphanage at Neerkol, Rockhampton, one victim told the Royal Commission that violence was used to maintain discipline. ". . . they put the fear into you with the stick, the whips, the bamboo canes".[22] Another recalled that in the 1950s: "We did not wear shoes and lived in worn, thin clothing. My feet were regularly sore, cracked from the cold in winter. We had to walk approximately half a kilometer to Mass every morning at 6am."[23]

Boys Town, a residential institution managed by the De La Salle Brothers in Beaudesert, Queensland, was identified in 219 claims of abuse, more than any other Australian Catholic institution.[24] Boys Town is not necessarily the institution where the following abuse occurred.

"Mick" told the Royal Commission that in the 1960s he was sent away at the age of twelve to an institution run by brothers: "The first week I was there I think I was bashed if not every day, every second day because I wouldn't kneel down and give "Brother Patrick" a head job [oral sex]. The bashings were to shut me up and not talk to anyone about it". The abuse

22. *RCFR*, 16, 1, 400.
23. *RCFR*, 16, 1, 403.
24. *RCFR*, 16, 2, 97.

by "Brother Patrick" continued over the next three years, with other boys as well. Few of the boys dared to report the abuse. "... someone did try to speak out. Before two weeks were up, he was in hospital. And that was just "Brother Patrick" letting us know what can happen".[25]

Many children in these institutions suffered psychological abuse, with some staff calling them "scum of the earth", "slut" or "filthy pig", and telling them that that no one cared about them. This degrading treatment gave perpetrators and institutional leaders greater power over the children and caused the children to see themselves as powerless, thus lessening their resistance to further abuse.[26] Possibly the worst examples of abuse in Catholic institutions came from the residential institutions in Western Australia which housed many orphans from overseas. "VV" was a British child migrant who was brought to Australia in 1954 at the age of nine and lived at Bindoon Farm School until he was 16. He gave evidence that he was sexually abused there by no less than nine different perpetrators. He was the youngest child at Bindoon and reported that within two weeks of arriving there he was raped by Brother Christopher Angus. When he reported this to Father William, a Benedictine chaplain, the priest took "VV" to his room and sexually assaulted him again. "VV" was also sexually abused by older boys and by a regular male visitor to Bindoon who would take the boys out on picnics. "VV" reported that his abuse was sexual, physical and mental in every manner possible and often with sadistic delight. He felt perpetually debased, betrayed and shamed.[27]

These real-life horror stories told by victims/survivors before the Australian Royal Commission and to enquiries in other countries tell how institutions within the Catholic church can wretchedly fail to serve the vulnerable persons they are meant to assist. As we will see in chapter 7, such failures are made possible by elements intrinsic to every kind of institution: workplaces; the military; prisons; parishes; communities of vowed religious men or women and even the Vatican. When a privileged group of people holds power without sufficient accountability or independent oversight, there is real risk that they can cause grave and systemic harm to vulnerable people. When this happens, even Christian institutions become mechanisms that allow evil to flourish. The way to avoid such failures would appear to lie in radically reshaping the institution, so that power is shared

25. *RCFR*, 16, 1, 400.
26. *RCFR*, 16, 1, 401.
27. *RCFR*, 16, 1, 338–39.

more equally, and those who hold power are accountable. In the case of the church, such radical reshaping seems necessary if it is to be faithful to the gospel which it claims as its foundation: the gospel whose essential principle is love.

4

How Could It Come to This?

MOST CATHOLIC CLERGY AND religious are rightly respected for what they contribute to society. In their hundreds of thousands, they have served their communities as pastors, teachers, nurses and friends. However, as the world now knows all too well, a substantial minority of clerics and religious in every land have sexually abused children at a rate which appears to be higher than for other professional groups.

No studies have been done that would enable exact comparisons between Catholic clerics and other professions, but a comparison with Catholic lay teachers shows a significantly lower rate of offending by them. If male Catholic school staff in Victoria had sexually abused at nearly the same rate as priests (greater than 5 percent), then over the past twenty to thirty years, 279 male staff in Catholic schools would have been credibly accused, if not convicted, of child sexual abuse. This is far from being the case.[1]

A finding by the Australian Royal Commission supports this. In private sessions, 4029 survivors from diverse institutions were interviewed. Of these, 52.9 percent alleged that they were abused by persons in religious ministry, while only 29 percent alleged abuse by lay people.[2]

It is hardly consoling to know that among thirteen religious denominations in Australia, the Catholic clergy had the fourth highest rate of clerical sexual offending against children, after the Seventh Day Adventists,

1. Cahill and Wilkinson, *Child Sexual Abuse*, 185.
2. Davey, *Case*, 69.

Salvation Army and Jews. Since these three have much smaller populations than the Catholics, a percentage extracted from such small samples gives a less reliable picture of the reality.

Nor are "higher" clergy exempt. More than a hundred cardinals and bishops from many countries have been credibly accused of sexual crimes against children or adults. These are profound failures. How can it be that men who profess to be holy and to lead others towards God have so often harmed vulnerable children or concealed the harm done to them? This chapter will look at possible causes for these failures. Much background is needed, to answer the question: "How could it come to this?"

In 2004 the US bishops commissioned the John Jay College of Criminal Justice to conduct a survey of sexual abuse of minors by United States clergy. The *Report*, (revised in 2011) found that from 1950–2002, among 109,694 ordained priests, deacons or members of male religious orders, 4,392 priests—about 4.4 percent—had been credibly *accused* of offending. It must be added that the researcher and psychiatrist Richard Sipe and other authorities find that the true percentage is more likely between 6 percent and 9 percent, with some US dioceses reaching 20 percent and more.[3] The John Jay survey also found that the number of alleged abuses in the US increased in the 1960s, peaked in the 1970s, declined from around 1985, and by the 1990s had returned to the level of the 1950s.

That survey has been criticized for not acknowledging that the level of abuse was already substantial in 1950; and for relying on the integrity of all US dioceses to provide accurate information. When we consider how strongly many bishops resisted the investigation of clerical abuse, this was a remarkable act of trust. Nor was enough allowance made for the fact that many victims do not disclose their abuse to authorities for up to 20 or 30 years; or that the base number of clergy and of children increased substantially during the period measured. In the USA, as in Australia, the number of priests and religious increased dramatically after World War II, peaked in the late 1960s and then markedly declined. The John Jay College specializes in the analysis of "ordinary" crime, so its *Report* may also be criticized for failing to notice, or for underplaying, the effects that Church cultural factors had on the rate of abuse within the church: a policy of secrecy; the legal requirement to maintain a secret archive; and obedience to "Rome".[4]

---

3. http://www.awrsipe.com/Dialogue/Dialogue-12-2007-07-25.html.
4. Cahill and Wilkinson, *Child Sexual Abuse*, 76.

How Could It Come to This?

What might account for the temporary increase in child sexual abuse from the late 1950s? Priests' lives were then changing in significant ways: their activities were less monitored than previously and less accountability was expected of them. Now they more often lived alone, and—like the general population—used the car to a greater extent than before. Almost half of the offending happened in the priest's own home, and much of it took place in the car or at places to which the cleric had driven the child.

After World War II, in the "baby boom", the Catholic population grew by natural increase and by massive immigration into Australia, Canada and USA. Many new parishes were opened, and more vulnerable children— many of them migrants or orphans—filled the expanding Catholic schools. Boarding schools were flourishing, as were orphanages and other Catholic institutions for children. Priests still had a high social standing, and the prestigious role of the cleric attracted altruistic young men from the growing Catholic population to join seminaries and religious life. There was little screening of seminarians, and bishops sometimes ordained unsuitable candidates.

The Second Vatican Council's necessary reforms did indeed cause turbulence in the Catholic Church. Its reforms and the unprecedented cultural, technical and professional developments of a globalizing world challenged priests and religious, many of whom re-considered their position and resigned. Some of those who remained were unsettled and stressed. In the social revolution of the 1960s, with its greater openness about sex, clerics who were psycho-sexually immature may have felt freer to experiment, even to abuse children.

Perhaps the increase of child abuse was distorted by an increase in the amount of abuse that was being brought to light in those years. It is important to recall that reported abuse is only a fraction of the actual abuse committed. During and after the 1960s, society was becoming more forthright about sexual matters, putting aside shame and secrecy. Longer Statutes of Limitations and other improvements to legislation made it easier to prove abuse in court, and successful prosecutions encouraged others to come forward.

However, since the mid-1980s the incidence of abuse has declined. This may be attributable to the increase in public discussion, which has made the public more alert and cautious, thus lessening opportunities for offenders to groom and abuse children. There has also been considerable activism by victims of clerical abuse. Child protection has improved; help centers, female police, and children's tribunals have been established, and more credibility given to children's testimony.

Clerical Errors

In some aspects of prevention, the Catholic Church has become a leader. Parents and church personnel are trained to be more aware and vigilant. Altar-servers, less numerous now, are better-monitored, as are Catholic schools, which now restrict access to their students. Society's view of institutional care has changed, and many Catholic residential institutions have closed. Offending priests and brothers have been dismissed, and the overall number of priests has greatly declined.

Many causes have been proposed to explain clerical sexual abuse of children. Because in our time widespread sexual abuse of minors by clergy was first publicly acknowledged in "Western" countries, some have assumed it to be a problem only in "decadent", affluent societies. However, we have seen sufficient evidence to know that abuse occurs extensively in poorer countries too. Perhaps it earlier became public in more affluent countries because higher levels of education enabled victims/survivors to speak out and to expose offenders more effectively. In richer countries people also had easier access to lawyers and legal aid to help them seek redress. There too it was easier to establish support groups like Survivors' Network of Those Abused by Priests (SNAP) and Broken Rites; just as it was more possible for the "Me Too" movement to evolve among them. In wealthy lands, pressure developed to set up inquiries and Royal Commissions, which are expensive but have helped to plumb the depth and extent of this corruption.

Other attempts have been made to explain the abuse. Some people, trying to minimize the tragedy, have described the perpetrators as a "few rotten apples". Others blame the Second Vatican Council (1961–1965) or liberal theologians for sowing confusion in the church and weakening strong, clear Christian principles. Some people blame homosexual priests, while others again see a huge conspiracy by the media against the Catholic church. Some simply see the crisis as an inexplicable disaster, akin to a tsunami.

These suggestions are mostly naive, for clerical sexual offending can be found throughout the history of the church and its rate was already significant long before the 1960s. Approximately half of known priest-abusers, including many notorious ones, were ordained *before* the Vatican Council, having been educated in seminaries that instilled the morality and piety of the pre-Vatican Church. There was an increase in offending from the late 1950s until the 1980s, but this had begun before the Council and before the "permissive 60s". It is quite inaccurate to blame an increase of abuse on the teachings of the assembled bishops of the world, advised by their theologians. Their expressed aim was to assess the state of the church and

How Could It Come to This?

strive to return to the sources—*resourcement*—and commit to serious modernization—*aggiornamento*.

We need to look beyond individual abusers and seek generic causes. If many people in a population are falling sick with the same novel symptoms, medical scientists do more than treat sick individuals. They also study the environment in which the sick people live. Devastating plagues have been eradicated by finding that they came from sewage-polluted water or were borne by mosquitoes. Endemic brain-damage among children has been traced to the lead in paint and petrol.

Aberrant sexual behavior by clerics must be looked at in the same way. Sexual crimes do stem from deficiencies within the *individual* perpetrator: perhaps their genetic make-up; their personal immaturity, aggravated by their inadequate formation and selfish lack of restraint. But we can also reasonably assume that their abusing is made more likely by *social* influences: the culture in which they have been formed and the institution to which they belong. Environmental forces can powerfully affect us. Hence in attempting to understand the tsunami of sexual abuse by Catholic clerics which has spread "to all nations", we need to look at the clerics' specific environment: the church-institution which formed and continues to guide them.

Causes within the Person

Is there a typical profile of abusers? We will focus here only on men, for they commit more than 90 percent of abuse, and this study is of clerics and religious brothers. Unsatisfying as it may be for those who want simple solutions, experienced therapists affirm that there is no typical profile of an adult who engages in the distorted behavior of sexually abusing a child. Much is known, however, about factors within the person that can contribute to this deviant behavior.

Some of these factors have been labelled *biogenetic*. Therapists note that many priests and religious who abuse children grew up in families where emotional relationships were cold; the father was emotionally absent, perhaps alcoholic; the mother dependent and emotionally too close to the children. The family environment generated poor self-esteem and reluctance to trust others or to admit that one needed help. Sex was a largely taboo subject, around which there was suppression, guilt and a vacuum of knowledge. Knowledge about "boundaries" was inadequate. Those who later became offenders lacked experience of intimacy and continued to be deprived of it in their seminary or novitiate. If, as was common, such youngsters entered the seminary aged 13-18, when after seven years they eventually left its protective environment their need for intimacy had only increased. They were now immature adults, committed to celibacy, and tended to gravitate to young people in search of the physical affection they craved. They "felt safe" with children, imagining that children liked them and sought their company and affection.

Factors known as *psychodynamic* include having suffered sexual abuse in childhood. This applies to 66–80 percent of men who offend against children. Such victims are more likely to offend as adults, but it is by no means inevitable that they will.[5] Biogenetic and psychodynamic factors can combine to result in an adult man still being immature in many respects: he may lack peer relationships; be excessively passive, dependent, and too inclined to conform. He may be confused about power, obedience and sacrifice; may lack masculinity and be confused about his sexual orientation.

While a few abusers may give indications of being abnormal, the majority do not appear as "monsters" or psychopaths but are often much-admired public figures who serve people generously. In Australia, the priest Vincent Kiss was described by society women as "utterly charming" and "like Jesus Christ ... not just priestly, ... saintly." Kiss was eventually jailed for six years for stealing $1.8 million, and for "diverting" another $2.5 million from charities. He had been deported from Vanuatu for "offences of gross indecency" and was later sentenced in Australia to ten and a half years for sex crimes against four teenage boys.

The Irish *Ferns Report* too, noted that most abusers appeared kind, pleasant and capable of warmth, affection and generosity. They are often described as impressive, affable personalities with a charming manner; perceived as "pious and holy", "gentle and inoffensive", friendly and easily accepted by the families of their victims. Their persuasive manner, added to their clerical status, gave them extraordinary access to children, whom they could call from the parish school's classrooms without causing suspicion; take them on holidays or even invite them to stay at the presbytery, and so abuse them undetected over long periods. Some of the most notorious abusers became expert fund-raisers, cultivating wealthy and famous people and indulging expensive tastes in dining and accommodation. Like Cardinal McCarrick and Marcial Degollado, some reached elevated positions in the clerical hierarchy.

5. Cahill and Wilkinson, *Child Sexual Abuse*, 244.

How Could It Come to This?

The experienced Catholic reporter Peter Stanford published a glowing obituary of Father Kit Cunningham, who had celebrated the Stanfords' wedding and for many years had impressed Peter as a "good priest". After Cunningham's death, one of his many victims read that obituary and angrily wrote to Stanford: "he was a sexual, physical and mental abuser . . . a deviated creep; let him rest in peace."[6]

Researchers have created "models" to explain offending.[7] These overlap considerably, and variously combine the factors already listed. Most models attempt to classify offenders by lumping them into three general categories: Fixated, opportunistic and situational.[8]

1. The fixated are properly called pedophiles. They are sexually attracted only towards children and may commit countless offences against them. They comprise less than 10 percent of clerical or religious offenders. Australian examples have been Robert Best, Kostka Chute, Kevin McAlinden, Kevin O'Donnell and Gerald Ridsdale. In Ireland, Brendan Smythe; in Aotearoa New Zealand, Magnus Murray, and in the USA, Gilbert Gauthe.

2. The opportunistic type have an inclination to abuse and will assault a child when an opportunity arises. They are usually older when they first do so. They are less likely to groom children, and may not prefer children over adults, but will use children opportunistically for sexual gratification. They are likely to abuse females, including members of their own extended family.

3. The situational abusers tend to abuse in response to the stresses caused by a lack of positive adult relationships; by social isolation or low self-esteem. They are usually older when they first abuse, their victim is often a female and they tend to have fewer victims, over an extended period.

Narcissism is a common characteristic in abusers. Every balanced person needs to achieve a level of independence and self-confidence, but if these qualities are magnified until they become a sense of superiority and entitlement, they can become narcissism, which can reach dangerous pathological levels. In Catholic communities, being ordained a priest

6. Peter Stanford, *The Guardian*. London, June 19, 2011.
7. These include Drewermann, Finkelhor, Hogen, Keenan, Ranson, Rosetti, Sipe, Winship, the Boston model and the Ulm-Rome model.
8. *RCFR*, 16, 1, 336.

automatically gave a man honored status and adulation. In their clinical and pastoral work Sipe, Benkert and Doyle saw notable examples of narcissism in some clerics, and even described a narcissistic spirituality.[9] Narcissistic people have an intense need to be admired and loved. They can be charismatic but grandiose and feel entitled to attention and admiration. They may lack empathy and can devalue, bully, intimidate and exploit those "under" them. When manipulating people, they fail to grasp the devastation they cause in victims, families and the community.[10]

Narcissists seek power, and it is well-recognized that sexual abuse is as much about a lust for power as it is about sexual pleasure. The cleric's pastoral relationships already involve an inherent power imbalance, for people often come to the pastor when they are vulnerable, seeking help or spiritual guidance. The power of a narcissistic senior cleric can seem unassailable. James Grein had been abused since childhood by Cardinal McCarrick. When, as an adult, he told the cardinal that he was going to "go public", McCarrick told him: "No one's going to believe you. You're a drunk; an idiot. Do you know how important I am?"

The clerical world includes elements that appeal to narcissists: liturgical rituals appeal to the cleric who enjoys being "center stage". Clerical dress, impressive robes and elaborate public ceremonies draw attention to prelates as symbols of the institution. These trappings express power and can tempt the wearer to vanity and arrogance.[11] Strong personalities may be able to avoid being affected by this and may function maturely within the clerical system, but they cannot easily alter it. Sipe suggests that many priests, especially those who aspire to episcopal and Vatican appointments are deeply narcissistic beneath a veneer of altruism and holiness. Affected by elitism and careerism they may fail to listen to the people over whom they have power, and even morally disengage from them.

Some clergy insist that laypeople always address them by their clerical title. Even if their personal achievements are unremarkable, some presume that clerical status automatically entitles them to respect and deference. This presumption can attract inadequate personalities or those seeking refuge from the serious demands of being an adult in the world. Dr Gerardine Robinson, a clinical psychologist who observed many priests participating in Encompass Australasia, saw narcissism as one personality trait that

9. *RCFR*, 16, 2, 595, 605.
10. Ronson, *Psychopath Test*.
11. *RCFR*, 16, 2, 627.

the Catholic church tends unintentionally to select and reward in clergy.[12] Seminary formation has been inadequate to identify narcissism, much less heal this trait, which is prominent in priests and religious who sexually abuse children.[13]

Although some try to blame homosexuality for the abuse crisis, this view is naive in the extreme. Research suggests that heterosexual men are just as likely as homosexual men to commit child sexual abuse.[14] Research also shows that 20–50 percent of Catholic priests and religious brothers are homosexual, a percentage considerably higher than in the general population. There is a gay culture within seminaries and in a sector of the priesthood. But being gay is an orientation within which persons can be healthy and life-giving, whereas pedophilia is a psychiatric disorder.[15] Church proclamations in the 1990s linking clerical child sexual abuse to homosexuality were fundamentally flawed and had the serious negative result of increasing shame and a desire for secrecy in homosexual men. Both responses can put the gay person under pressure, which actually increases any tendency to abusive behaviors.[16]

Homosexual *orientation* is not directly correlated with the sexual abuse of children but being confused about one's sexual orientation beyond the age of twenty-five *has* been found to indicate that a priest may be at risk of abusing. Marie Keenan's study found that all gay clerical offenders had difficulties coping with sexuality and celibacy; they feared and denied their homosexuality and were emotionally lonely.[17] The Australian Royal Commission heard from therapists that most sexual offences committed by priests and religious can be described as instances of homosexual ephebophilia: a sexual preference in adults for adolescent partners.[18] The church's official position is that homosexual persons, even if they are healthy and functioning well, are suffering from a "grave objective disorder" which makes them unsuitable for the priesthood. Despite the large numbers already ordained, in 2016 the church was still officially prohibiting gay men from entering seminaries.

12. *RCFR*, 16, 2, 627.
13. *RCFR*, 16, 2, 595.
14. *RCFR*, 16, 2, 599, 766.
15. *RCFR*, 16, 2, 610
16. *RCFR*, 16, 2, 611.
17. Keenan, *Gender, Power and Organizational Culture*, 98.
18. *RCFR*, 16, 2, 611.

Gay priest James Allison commented that one effect of this teaching is to destabilize and confuse every young gay Catholic man as he tries to understand his sexual orientation. If he enters a seminary, he does so with a huge disadvantage in comparison to others. Allison points to the "cognitive dissonance" about homosexuality that is prevalent in the Vatican and the church generally, by which gay clerics keep, in a separate section of their mind, all knowledge of their own or other clerics' homosexuality, lest it force them to contradict the church's official teaching. Alison concludes that the real problem about homosexuality is not the individual's efforts to be continent; nor is it pedophilia; but public honesty about gay priests.[19]

Institutional Causes

In addition to *individual* qualities or deficiencies that might predispose a person to sexually abuse children, the church institution also creates many situational and contextual factors. These interact with personal weaknesses, increasing the individual's tendency to exploit and abuse.[20] Sexual abuse becomes rife in situations where there is inequality of power. This is found in the various branches of the military; in refugee camps; in prisons and boarding schools or in remote and isolated locations. It also occurs in workplaces where women and children are vulnerable employees, afraid of losing their job.

The abuse committed within the church is surely linked with the severe imbalance of power that is commonly found there. As mentioned, Catholic clerics have power of several kinds. They are appointed leaders in one of history's oldest and largest institutions, which has evolved out of the simple but profound teachings of Jesus of Nazareth. Every cleric's spiritual power is based on people's belief that the cleric is a channel by which to access the Transcendent, and the power of bishops is augmented by their control of priests' work-assignments and of church wealth, which if it is not theirs personally, is often immense.

Clerical power is linked with sexual offending against minors through the church's organizational structures, governance processes, institutional culture and some of its theological beliefs.

---

19. https://www.abc.net.au/religion/fr%C3%A9d%C3%A9ric-martel-and-the-structure-of-the-clerical-closet/10843678.

20. John C Gonsiorek, *RCFR*, 16, 2, 608.

How Could It Come to This?

Church *structures*, only slightly modified by recent reforms, expect clerics to be accountable only to those "above" them, not downwards to those over whom the bishop or priest is said to "rule". Sometimes there was hardly any accountability.[21] Although priests are encouraged to have personal supervision, among all professionals they probably make least use of it.

The report of the 2013 Victorian Parliamentary Inquiry, *Betrayal of Trust*, claimed that over time a Church culture had been allowed to develop whereby senior Church leaders were able to trivialize the problem of sexual abuse by clerics. This contributed to its not being disclosed or appropriately responded to. The report saw this as a culture of inaction, disavowal, and avoidance of the problem, driven by theological and pastoral realities.[22]

The church's teaching about the human body and its sexuality has often been misunderstood or distorted. Drawn from the Scriptures, Christian teaching deeply respects the dignity of sexuality and marriage, but from the early days of the church this teaching has been tainted by strong traces of Manichaeism. This can be seen in early writers such as Origen and St Augustine—a dualism which tends to see the material world and sexuality as suspect, if not evil, in contrast to the "good" spiritual dimension. Through the centuries, when promoting celibacy as a path to sanctity, the mistake has been made of seeing sexuality as dark and troublesome. When clerics committed sexual crimes, church leaders were sometimes led by this distorted theology to dissociate these individual failures from the "perfect" church institution. Perfectionism led clerics and laity alike to conceal the failures, so as to preserve the public image of the "holy church".

Does obligatory celibacy—being commanded not to marry—lead to sexual abuse by clergy? Despite assertions even by popes, celibacy is *not* an essential dimension of the priesthood, yet in the Catholic Roman Rite it is demanded of most candidates for ordination. Exceptions are now made for married clergy who transfer from other Christian churches and wish to be re-ordained. For men and women who choose to join a religious order, the question is different. They accept celibacy as an essential part of the community life to which they commit themselves by vows. It is naive and simplistic to blame celibacy alone for sexual abuse, for most child abusers in the population are *not* celibate, and only a minority of those who *are* celibate become abusers. The Royal Commission found no causal connections

---

21. Cozzens, *Faith that Dares*, 13.
22. Cahill and Wilkinson, *Child Sexual Abuse*, 242.

between celibacy and child sexual abuse.[23] Nevertheless, it needs to be noted that celibacy may in some way contribute, if only from the fact that in Eastern rite churches where priests are allowed to marry before ordination, the offending rate is much lower than in the Roman rite.[24]

Through the centuries, vast numbers of Catholic clergy and religious have successfully and happily lived celibate lives, devoting themselves to the education and protection of children; caring for the sick and doing many other community works. As committed celibates they find peace and wisdom through their life of prayer and service, but among today's Roman rite diocesan priests, about half believe that the church's demand that they be celibate is an unnecessary imposition. Among Catholic *laity* in many countries, the percentage wanting change would be considerably higher.

Many diocesan clergy, knowing that celibacy is not essential to being a cleric, find it burdensome to be obliged to live without a marriage partner. Research has found that diocesan priests suffer from significantly greater levels of emotional exhaustion, stress, depression and burnout than religious and monastic clergy who live in community. The same burden of loneliness can trouble a religious priest or brother if his community is not healthy and happy. Any celibate who is maladjusted can become lonely, frustrated or unfulfilled; given to anger and hostility. If one in this situation lacks maturity or sound motivation, or if he has opted for the celibate state because he has repressed or denied his sexual appetites, then failure can be expected. He may typically become secretive and take to drinking heavily; to gambling; to bullying others; having physical relationships with a "consenting" adult or using internet pornography.[25]

There are other indicators suggesting that the celibate cleric may become an abuser: a rigid way of viewing the world; being too passive and deferential towards church authority figures; complying externally and rigidly with rules rather than maturely internalizing them. Research suggests that in the past the Catholic Church's hierarchical system actually chose and rewarded this kind of personality.[26] Some celibates in this position, especially if they have few intimate peer friends, are at higher risk of abusing children, but often seminaries and novitiates were—and probably still are—unable to detect such persons during their training years.[27]

23. *RCFR*, 16, 2, 738.
24. Cahill and Wilkinson, *Child Sexual Abuse*, 260.
25. *RCFR*, 16, 2, 608.
26. *RCFR*, 16, 2, 606.
27. *RCFR*, 16, 2, 607.

5

Clericalism[1]

MANY ENQUIRIES INTO SEXUAL abuse by clerics have concluded that the phenomenon of clericalism has contributed substantially to the abuse and to its concealment. Clericalism can be defined as *attitudes and culture that excessively idealize the role of clerics, and give them preference as persons,* as if clerics are superior to other members of the church.

This phenomenon is not unique to the church. Analogues of clericalism can be found in other institutions, whose officials are often tempted to be jealous of their power, striving to increase it and sometimes abuse it. Chapter 7 will look more closely at this intrinsic tendency within institutions. But—as Bishop Geoffrey Robinson warned—a singular danger arises when spiritual power is claimed, because it *magnifies* the ordinary human temptation to dominate others.[2]

This belief in clerical difference comes originally from clerics' claim that they alone have the power to consecrate the Eucharist; to celebrate Mass. We will see later that their claim over the Eucharist was an early historical development and that in medieval times there developed the further belief that at his ordination a priest is changed substantially or "ontologically". This basic claim to spiritual power was augmented by the fact that clerics were

---

1. For a comprehensive analysis of clericalism see Wilson, *Clericalism, Death of Priesthood.*

2. Geoffrey Robinson, *For Christ's Sake.*

commonly, but by no means always, better educated than most of the people they served, and so were in the middle to upper strata of society.

Contemporary Canon Law states: "By divine institution [clerics] . . . through the sacrament of order, [are] marked with an indelible character and are . . . constituted sacred ministers . . ."[3] The current *Catholic Catechism* says that "Baptism, Confirmation, and Holy Orders confer . . . a sacramental character or "seal" by which the Christian shares in Christ's priesthood."[4]

Since baptism is the primary sacrament of initiation and is always received first, the "seal" that it confers must change the person in the most radical way by making them a Christian, a member of the "body of Christ". Being ordained later to lead the ceremony of the Eucharist appoints the person for a particular service. It does not elevate them to a superior status, yet this appointment—ordination—has come to be called '*Holy* Orders', while baptism is never honored in the same way. If, as is claimed, the later sacrament changes the recipient *ontologically,* then surely Baptism does the same. The validity of this claim about ordination will be discussed with priesthood, in chapter 8, where we will see that among the earliest Christians there was no special ordination of the person who led prayer at the eucharistic ceremony. Christians of the first two or three centuries would be baffled by the idea of elaborate ordinations or the claim of an "ontological change" in the ordinand. They would likewise be horrified by the suggestion that "priests" be regarded as a kind of superior caste to whom special deference is due.[5] It is a main contention of this book that clerics, by claiming and promoting this monopoly status, for males only, have created clericalism and betrayed what Jesus taught in the gospel.

The Second Vatican Council's *Constitution on the Church* emphasizes that all Christians are equal: "There is . . . in Christ and in the Church no inequality . . . all are called to sanctity and have received an equal privilege of faith."[6] The Council also stresses that ". . . the faithful, in virtue of their royal priesthood, join in the offering of the Eucharist." While the Council does mention "the distinction *which the Lord made* between sacred ministers and the rest of the People of God," [emphasis added] it gives no

---

3. Canon 1008.
4. *CCC* 1121.
5. *RCFR,* 16, 2, 638.
6. *LG* 32. Abbott, *Documents,* 58

Clericalism

reference to support that distinction, nor does it say that ministers are superior, but stresses that these different roles mutually depend on each other.[7]

Those who analyze Vatican Council documents point out that they often include pairs of statements that seem to differ but were both included in order to obtain the agreement and vote of two groups who interpret the tradition differently. This would seem to apply to statements that emphasize a difference *in kind* between the roles of minister and others participating in the Eucharist, when numerous alternative statements by the Council stress the equality of the two groups.

The historical claim about clerics' being different has created a power structure in the church and resulted in the church becoming a hierarchical pyramid of several strata: bishops, priests, deacons and laity. Clericalism maintains that an essential distinction between the ordained and the non-ordained was established by Christ. Pope Pius X, now canonized as a saint, committed an astounding clerical error when he declared in a 1906 encyclical letter: "The Church is essentially an unequal society ... comprising two categories ... pastors and flock ... So distinct are these categories that ... the one duty of the multitude is to allow themselves to be led, and, like a docile flock, to follow the pastors."[8]

This is a basic error. It creates inequality between church members, in conflict with the New Testament description of the church as a community of equals who all share the Spirit of Christ. "There is no longer Jew or Greek, ... slave or free, ... male and female; for all of you are one in Christ Jesus."[9] The error also discourages independent thought and initiative in all who are not clerics: surely a policy that has contributed to the decline of the church as a living part of society.

The clerical power based on this distinction has often been used in ways that clash with Jesus' clear advice about the use of any power: ". . . whoever wants to be great among you must be your servant."[10] Jesus exemplified this by washing the feet of his followers, and by eventually enduring torture and execution on behalf of those abused by both religious and secular power.

Clericalism—as attitudes within the clerical culture—originated in the patriarchal cultures of the early Mediterranean church, where women

---

7. *LG* 10. Abbott, *Documents*, 27.
8. *Vehementer Nos.* 221.
9. Gal 3:28.
10. Mark 10:42–45; Matt 20:29–34; Luke 18:35–43.

occupied inferior social positions. Clericalism still thrives in societies where patriarchy strongly differentiates the roles of the sexes. But in "Western" societies, since the mid-twentieth century, women have contributed to political life and to practically all trades and professions, even if they do not always receive the same wages as men for doing the same work. In the Catholic church, not much progress has been made in accepting the equality of the sexes. A clerical monopoly on control of the Eucharist has spilled over into a monopoly on authority which effectively keeps women marginal and denies them any real power in the church-community.

It has become official Catholic teaching that women cannot be priests or perhaps even deacons, although a large proportion of Catholics believe the contrary. The prohibition is based on the belief that women are unsuited to "represent Christ" by leading at the Eucharist. Clergy, even bishops, who dissent from this teaching are ruthlessly suppressed. Such clericalist discrimination against women is bad enough; but the idea of women's "unsuitability" has spread like a contagion. For centuries, church law also forbade them from serving at Mass, preaching, or even reading during the liturgy. As late as 1997 this clerical monopoly was officially extended to adult Catholics who serve in jails and hospitals, forbidding them—quite ineffectively—from using the titles of pastor, chaplain, coordinator or moderator.[11] Bishop Geoffrey Robinson told the Royal Commission that because sexual abuse has been an overwhelmingly male problem, "a true equality between male and female in the Church would—by itself—change the entire culture dramatically."

It was clericalism that underpinned the swarm of child abuse that chapter 2 summarized. In order to emphasize the outrageous criminal corruption that clerical "privilege" can lead to, the example of Monsignor Day is given here. In Mildura, Victoria, the serial child-abuser Day exploited the deference shown him by Catholics among the local police. Besides protecting him from investigation, the police arranged that every Saturday the monsignor received the amount that would have been won by a $10 bet on the horse that won the last race. The police extorted this "donation" from an illegal SP bookmaker, whom they would otherwise have prosecuted. The police could not consider prosecuting the cleric, despite the complaints they were receiving from local parents. The special status given to clerics could thus result in a "clericalist pathology".

---

11. *Instruction on Certain Questions Regarding the Collaboration of the Non-ordained Faithful in the Sacred Ministry of Priest.* Vatican City, 1997. Quoted in Armour, *Call*, 8.

Clericalism

This status led many to assume that priests were nearer to perfection than "ordinary" Catholics. If a cleric showed weaknesses or failures, these were hushed up, denied, and too readily forgiven. Such idealistic assumptions about clerics were self-deceiving and dangerous, for confidential surveys of clerics' lives have revealed that they are typically human. Even allowing for inaccuracy in the anonymous responses, one USA survey of 2,776 active and former priests from 1960–2002 showed that despite professing celibacy, up to 50 percent were sexually active: 20 percent with women; 10 percent with adult men; 8 percent admitted to heterosexual and homosexual "experimentation"; 5 percent to "problematic masturbations"; and ominously, 6 percent with minors.[12]

The great majority of clerics have served their communities faithfully. In their important pastoral roles, they are uniquely placed to help people, who often entrust clerics with access to their inner lives. This trust is largely justified, but clericalism often idealized and distorted the picture to the extent that until recent times, most parents would have found it totally impossible to believe that any priest could sexually abuse a child. As the stories already quoted abundantly show, this delusion gave clerics unfettered access to children, and a minority of clerics used this to groom parents as well as children, with tragic consequences.[13]

Children, who naturally look up to adults' wisdom and power, became easy victims of clericalism. Victims/survivors of clerical abuse have reflected on this: "to a child in a Catholic primary school . . . the priest was the closest thing to God . . . When he said, 'I need helpers' . . . everybody puts their hand up, saying 'Pick me, pick me'".[14] Some clerics abused their role as spiritual teachers to manipulate their victims, for instance by threatening them with hell if they resisted or disclosed the abuse.[15]

Clericalism can give rise to the most extraordinary excesses. It is laughable, but also sad, to see a few cardinals still parading in a fifteen-metre satin train, and not just because in 1952 the regulation length was reduced to *seven* meters. It is far more sinister to hear of the corruption and immorality entrenched among some clerics at the Vatican, as Frederick Martel's careful research has disclosed.[16] Clericalism breeds triumphalist attitudes, leading

---

12. Sipe, *RCFR*, 16, 2, 743.
13. *RCFR*, 16, 1, 23.
14. *RCFR*, 16, 1, 453.
15. *RCFR*, 16, 1, 456.
16. Martel, *Closet*.

some to believe that the church does not change, despite the abundant examples of practices and teachings that have shifted over time.[17] The upper ranks of the hierarchy can find it particularly difficult to admit being wrong. They try ruthlessly to suppress internal dissent, for they consider that the church is superior to the rest of society and has little to learn from the outside world. Leaders affected by clericalism can be in thrall to status, titles and insignia; prone to narcissism and entitlement, and be psychologically distant from human intimacy and the sufferings of "ordinary" people.

Despite the obvious conflict with the gospel, clerics have for centuries been addressed by titles indicating their different levels in the hierarchy, which were learned from the Roman empire and later royal courts: "My Lord", "Monsignor", "Your Grace", "Your Eminence". This practice is now being challenged. At least one cardinal asks that even the honorific title "Father" be dropped.[18] Although not all clerics "get it", many priests and bishops are seeing through these ancient aberrations and doing their best to transcend them. Not least is Pope Francis, who has often condemned "the disease of clericalism"; but any cleric who listens to perceptive lay people is readily made aware of the damage that this sickness is still doing to the church. Professor Eamonn Conway has noted that the exclusively male monarchical model of priesthood, in which priests are seen as "sacred personages" has been bankrupt for some time; a destructive model of Church leadership that is crumbling.[19]

Esprit de Corps

Most institutions develop a strong corporate spirit among their members. This is found in the military, the police, in sporting clubs and in the various trades and professions. Mutual loyalty can have obvious positive benefits, for camaraderie and team spirit help to bind an institution together. But the corporate bond can also have ambiguous or negative consequences: it can lead to people being unfairly excluded from the group; to outsiders being treated unjustly; to crimes and corruption being concealed. Pride in belonging to the group can easily develop into an excessive sense of privilege and entitlement. The fact that the clerical profession involves dealing with the sacred does not prevent them from succumbing to all of these.

17. See Gary Wills, *Papal Sin*.
18. Cardinal John Dew, *Helder Camara Lecture*, Melbourne July 17, 2019.
19. *RCFR*, 16, 2, 627.

Clericalism

Perhaps more than most professional groups, dedicated clerics develop positive bonds among themselves, for they are engaged in promoting love and peace by word and example. Bishops have a special care for their priest colleagues, who have always been fewer than needed for the work. Priests are seen as valuable co-workers, brothers or sons. But this good relationship has sometimes inclined bishops to be too merciful in dealing with the terrible faults of the few criminal priests.[20] In such situations decision-making can be complex. The bishop naturally wants to protect and heal the offender, even though it is always immoral to value the criminal cleric above the person whom he has gravely harmed. Bishop Michael Malone of Maitland-Newcastle, who had worked hard against clerical opposition to bring justice to victims of abuse, admitted that in the past it had been considered best to cover up scandal, rather than publicize it. "Loyalty to the Church goes very deeply." [sic].[21]

Between priests themselves there is usually a bond of friendship and brotherhood. This too is good in itself, but dangerous if it tends to limit their friendships only to other clerics, or to consider that being loyal to those friends is more important than justice. *Esprit de corps* has led some clergy to suspect that anyone reporting sexual abuse is falsely attacking a colleague. It can make them resist admitting that a colleague may be guilty.[22] Disastrously, the camaraderie between clergy has sometimes led several abusers to collaborate in the same crimes, as happened, for instance, in Ballarat, Sunbury, Philadelphia and the diocese of Guam.

Obedience and loyalty are virtues that bring strength and unity, helping a community to achieve its common task. But they too can become vices, for to obey without question can cause serious harm. True obedience involves a patient and intelligent conversation between leader and members to reach good, moral decisions. In contrast to this are the unquestioning obedience of the military, or the extraordinary vow never to criticize their superiors, that until recently was demanded of all members of the Legionaries of Christ.

The gospels frankly record Jesus rebuking his own followers when they succumbed to rivalry and power-seeking—incipient clericalism. He condemned James and John when they asked for high status in the coming kingdom.[23] He also reproached his followers when they bossily prevented

---

20. *RCFR*, 16, 2, 233.
21. *RCFR*, 16, 2, 235.
22. *RCFR*, 16, 1, 531.
23. Matt 20:21–23.

children from approaching him.²⁴ Even in the deeply personal matter of praying to God, Jesus warned of clerical arrogance and exceptionalism, in his parable of a religious leader who thanked God that he was "Not like other people".²⁵

It was reported to the Australian Royal Commission that the cultural environment in many seminaries and religious communities sometimes hindered the emotional and sexual development of the men who later wielded power in the church. Clinicians who treat clerical sexual abusers have found that these offenders had not mastered self-understanding; were unskilled in the art of critical engagement; and had learned merely to conform to what was expected of them to become "good" priests or brothers. It was suggested that some young men who join seminaries of religious novitiates may still, as in the past, be seeking a safe place and career into which they can escape; where they expect to do good and "not worry about" sexuality with its normal temptations. Such men are likely to be strict rule-keepers; docile, obedient subjects, fearful and anxious to fulfil the duties dictated by the rule book. They become "systems men" who do not sufficiently question what the institution demands of them.

Living in an environment that lacked tenderness and mainly excluded women, these men—at least in examples known from the past—were not helped to develop emotionally or relate deeply either to men or women in healthy adult, generative ways. If the seminary and later clerical environment did not provide them with opportunities for development, their need for intimacy might seek expression in ways that were covert, distorted and sexualized. Without self-knowledge and genuine interior reflection, such candidates did not develop as persons, but were inclined to find their identity chiefly in their role and work. They became molded by a clericalist worldview, where individualism is overshadowed by obedience. In such an environment, it was highly unlikely that a young man struggling with sexual challenges or even a sexual disorder, would be inclined to reveal this to the authorities who were to decide whether he was suitable to be ordained. Although balanced personalities may have been able to surmount such an environment, it is now evident that many unsuitable candidates remained undetected and unchallenged.²⁶

---

24. Mark 10:13–14, 19:13–14; Luke 18:16.
25. Luke 18:11.
26. *RCFR*, 16, 2, 775.

Clericalism

The experienced therapist Dr Marie Keenan has treated many priests who have sexually abused children. She has sketched their typical path: emerging from the seminary without sufficient maturity, they found their work as a priest disappointing. Although they had been taught that ordination had changed them "ontologically", they felt personally powerless within a governance system that was neither transparent nor accountable. They had to obey their bishop or superior, on whom they depended for their house and income, but in contrast, their pastoral work often gave them much independence and power. They were virtually unsupervised, unsupported and unchallenged. Confusingly, they were powerless and yet powerful.

These men lived on their own or with just one other priest or were brothers in a dysfunctional community. Emotionally lonely and isolated, they were immersed in secrecy and silence. Their situation was made worse by regular moves to a new parish or school. When put in charge of children or adolescents they tended to develop particular friendships with a few, gravitating to children who were also deprived of love through family break-up or poverty. They had no idea of children's vulnerability and undeveloped sexuality and were blind to the vast difference in power between themselves and the child, falsely imagining that he or she was capable of saying "yes" or "no" to their sexual advances.[27] We may better understand the abusers' destructive behavior if we hear some of the distorted thinking by which they try to excuse it:

- children really want to have sex, for they do not physically resist my advances
- having sex with children is a good way for me to teach them about sex
- children do not tell others about it, because they really enjoy our sexual activity
- merely fondling children's genitals is not really having sex with, so no harm is being done
- when children ask me questions about sex, it means they want to see my sex organs
- my relationships with children are enhanced by having sex with them.[28]

---

27. Keenan *Gender, Power* 118.
28. Abel, Becker and Cunningham-Rathner, quoted in Cahill and Wilkinson, *Child Sexual Abuse*, 294.

Eventually the self-deluding clerics would cross sexual boundaries, but striving to remain good and faithful priests or brothers they would try to resolve their conflicts by surrendering to God in faith and prayer. When these failed, they engaged in a complex web of psychological and moral bargaining but could find no escape.

It is by no means certain that the culture in which future priests are being formed has overcome the difficulties of the past. Several experienced witnesses at the Royal Commission pointed to a resurgence of clericalism in seminaries in Australia and worldwide. They reported that it is not uncommon for seminary students and young priests to be seduced by the trappings, power and sense of entitlement that clericalism can bring them. Many candidates assume that the hierarchical class structure is original and valid and presume their own right to priestly privileges. They have rigid attitudes and see themselves as set apart by God and essentially different from the laity.[29] At the time of the Royal Commission there was no course in Australian seminaries that looked at the ethics of priesthood or the use of power it wields.[30] Dr Doyle maintained that among such candidates "Catholic clericalism is alive, malignant and prospering."[31]

The Sacrament of Reconciliation—Confession

This sacrament is important in the tradition of the church, for it has evolved as an excellent instrument for spiritual growth. It offers a personal encounter in which a person can admit their faults to a compassionate listener; receive advice about their inner lives and be assured that God forgives them. Of necessity it implies complete confidentiality, the "seal of confession," for no third party has a right to know what is shared by confessor and penitent about the latter's encounter with God.

Usually the church has severely punished any priest who sacrilegiously abuses the confessional by sexually exploiting children or adults. But confessors have failed in other ways. When they heard abusers confessing their sins, seeking to be absolved of their crimes, most confessors in the past were far too lenient. Even if they recognized that child abuse was a crime, many confessors deceived themselves into thinking that it was enough to absolve the abuse "in God's sight." Although confessors would routinely

---

29. *RCFR*, 16, 2, 795.
30. *RCFR*, 16, 2, 798.
31. *RCFR*, 16, 2, 639.

Clericalism

demand restitution in lesser matters such as theft, they seemed inexplicably unaware of the immense need for restitution in cases of abuse. Nor did they consider how the offender could be prevented from committing further crimes or recognize the offender's own urgent need for deeper healing. In view of the "sacramental seal" it was rightly unthinkable that the confessor report the penitent to the police, but it ought *not* have been unthinkable to demand that he report himself.[32]

Another serious mistake that the church needs to recognize is that confessors did not warn each other or their bishop—which they could have done without "breaking the seal"—that abuse by priests was a widespread, destructive problem that needed urgently to be dealt with. Once again, the cult of excessive secrecy damaged the Christian community. This is no reason for states to legislate, as many are now doing, that confessors must report to police any penitent who confesses abuse. Such legislation blatantly infringes on the freedom of conscience and of religion. To obey such a law would immediately destroy all trust in the sacrament and remove one of the few avenues that can be used to help both the offender and his victims. Instead of destroying the sacrament, confessors need to use it wisely, demanding, *before they give absolution*, that the penitent show evidence of having reported themselves to police and of receiving therapy.

Much of what is described in this book will be incomprehensible to those clergy and laity who have not yet recognized the clericalism that has been their environment since birth. Such a lack of comprehension is not surprising, for we commonly fail to recognize what has surrounded us all our lives. But there may be hope in the fact that we understand most complex situations by stages. Various researchers have listed the successive steps by which we learn the diverse skills needed for mature life: our sense-perception; psycho-social skills; faith and moral understanding; and the process of grieving.[33] It has been reasonably suggested that only by similar stages do we come to comprehend the truth that the church as an institution is corrupt, and urgently needs to be reformed.

For example, when Catholics hear that a respected cleric has committed sexual abuse, at *first* they are likely to disbelieve the news and deny what they are hearing. A *second* stage in the struggle to understand includes a tendency to allocate blame, often in the wrong places. The accusers of clerics are often presumed to be lying, or "just after the money." They may

---

32. Keenan, *Gender, Power* 164.
33. As expounded by Piaget, Erikson, Fowler, Kohlberg and Kubler-Ross.

Clerical Errors

be dismissed as "disreputable characters, alcoholics, criminals," or at least suffering from "false-memory syndrome." This denial is similar to clerics "explaining" the stark decline in church attendance by blaming people for having "lost their faith" or their "sense of sin"; or that society is becoming increasingly "secularized," as is proved by its allowing Sunday sport and shopping and passing laws that conflict with Christian principles. Such blaming excuses the cleric from looking at the church's own faults.

These attitudes of denial and blame were strikingly evident in the Australian bishops *Statement of Conclusions* (1998), which purported to describe the current state of the Catholic church in Australia. Although numerous cases of clerical sexual abuse were already public knowledge, the *Statement* did not once mention the topic. The same attitude was evident when a Royal Commission was first proposed to examine child sexual abuse in institutions. The Australian Catholic Bishops' Conference defensively stated: "talk of a systemic problem of sexual abuse in the Catholic Church is ill-founded and inconsistent with the facts." Cardinal Pell considered that "the faults overwhelmingly have been ... personal failures, rather than structures."[34] The same attitudes of denial and blame were exhibited earlier by the US bishops. From the 1980s, when the extent of child sexual abuse by clerics began to emerge, and it began to be evident that the institution itself might be a principal cause of the crisis, the attitude of those bishops was typically one of denial.[35]

The findings of the five-year Australian Royal Commission showed convincingly that church structures are at fault. The Commission gathered evidence from thousands of survivors of clerical sexual abuse and heard expert research. It concluded that major causes of the abuse committed in the Catholic church, and of the church's inadequate responses, were historical, cultural and theological factors in the *structure and organization* of the church itself. A central factor, underpinning and linked to all others, was the *status* of people in religious ministry.[36]

The Commission collated a clear picture of clericalism and how it contributed to clerical sexual abuse. Well-qualified witnesses told the Commission that there is a "culture of impotence" in the leadership of the church, from top to bottom, and "the dominant culture of our Church *remains* that

---

34. *RCFR*, 16, 1, 88.
35. Thomas Doyle, in Kaiser, *Whistle*, 306.
36. *RCFR*, 16, 2, 586; 16, 1, 28.

Clericalism

of a dysfunctional, autocratic clericalism".[37] Some of the Australian bishops were brave enough to confirm this conclusion.

The Royal Commission is not the only group that has pointed this out. The following comments from a range of investigating bodies deserve examination. As early as 1983 a conference report of male religious orders in the USA recognized a "conscious or unconscious concern to promote the particular interests of the clergy and to protect [their] privileges and power".[38] The Canadian Winter Commission (1989-90) criticized the patriarchal nature of the Catholic Church, whereby clergy rule "by virtue of position and not by capacity or service." It noted that there is no separation of powers: "executive, legislative and judicial aspects of governance are combined in the diocesan bishop and ultimately in the pope. The clergy's elevated position gives them unquestioned and unsupervised access to male children."[39]

Many other bodies have reached similar conclusions. These are merely listed here by name: The 1992 Canadian Catholic Bishops' Committee on Child Sexual Abuse.[40] The report *Towards Understanding*, by the Australian Catholic Social Welfare Commission, in 1999;[41] in 2002, the Massachusetts Attorney General and in 2004 the US bishops' *National Review Board Report* each noted "a causal relationship between clericalism and sexual abuse on many levels," and said that clericalism led bishops into massive denial of the extent of the problem.[42] In 2010, in Ireland, the Murphy Commission pointed out that *by his status alone* a priest has more opportunity to have access to children and hence to abuse them. In 2010 Pope Benedict XVI himself, in his *Pastoral Letter* to Irish Catholics noted, among factors which had contributed to clerics' sexual abuse of children, "*a tendency in society to favor the clergy*, a misplaced concern for the reputation of the Church and [to avoid] scandal."[43] The Victorian Parliamentary Inquiry report of 2013 criticized the "combination of unquestioning trust, absolute authority and lack of supervision."[44] The 2013 *Whitlam Report*

---

37. Professor Ormerod: RCFR, 16, 2, 631; Dr O'Hanlon: RCFR, 16, 2, 622.

38. *In solidarity and service: reflections on the problem of clericalism in the Church.* (1983).

39. RCFR, 16, 2, 650.

40. RCFR, 16, 2, 626.

41. RCFR, 16, 2, 334.

42. RCFR, 16, 2, 644.

43. *Pastoral Letter of Pope Benedict XVI to the Catholics of Ireland.* (2010).

44. RCFR, 16, 1, 258.

into the actions of the notorious abuser John Joseph Farrell in Armidale diocese exposed "clericalist solidarity" and a bishop's hubris in refusing to accept the informed advice that he not ordain the pedophile. In 2019, a paper *Confronting the Systemic Dysfunction of Clericalism*, was produced by the Association of US Catholic Priests.

To return to analyzing the stages by which we process difficult news: when we are eventually forced to accept that there is a serious problem, a *third* stage of the response is often to *minimize* the problem. It is common to hear clerical crimes blamed on "a few bad apples," or that clerics are no worse than other professional groups. Another common response is that: "We were on a learning curve *then*, but *now* we have the problem under control." This last response was decisively rejected by several official enquiries,[45] but in 2019, Cardinal Pell could still naively claim that "the bishops broke the back of the pedophile crisis nearly twenty-five years ago with Towards Healing and the Melbourne Response. Offences fell radically from the 1990s."[46]

A *fourth* stage in comprehending and accepting is to *admit the truth*, in this case that a primary responsibility for clerical abuse lies with generations of clerics who, although only a small percentage have abused children, have claimed privileges and shaped laws that protect themselves. Some responsibility for this clericalism lies also with lay people who have been persuaded to accept the false inequality in their church community. Only when we have reached this fourth stage of accepting the evidence, no matter how shocking, can the truth make us free.

A *fifth* stage will bring us to make decisions towards transforming the church. Some good administrative changes have already been made towards creating child-safe parishes and schools and making clergy more accountable, but these modifications do not reach the heart of the problem. As chapter 10 will show, the basic structure of the church needs to be transformed from a pyramid to a circle, in which power and responsibility is more widely shared. It needs to become a "communion of communities", in which all persons are recognized as equal before God.

These two chapters have sought answers to the question "How could it come to this?" We can ask further to what extent bishops and religious superiors bear responsibility for the crimes of those who owed them obedience. Many bishops and superiors have claimed that before the mid-1980s

---

45. *Ryan Report* (2009); Victorian Parliamentary Inquiry. (2013).
46. *Prison Journal*, Vol. 2, 195.

Clericalism

they did not understand the nature of pedophilia and the incurability of pedophiles. Bishop Connors, for instance, acknowledged to the Royal Commission that by not acting quickly against abusers he had personally failed, but he explained that at that time he was to some degree ignorant of the depth and consequences of pedophilia.[47] Bishop Bede Heather also claimed that in the 1980s he did not recognize its gross consequences on the victims; or that it was compulsive and addictive in the offender. He saw it as a *moral* failing from which the offender could, with guidance, recover.[48] Prior to 1984 there *was* a common belief that clergy sexual misbehavior could be cured by psychological treatment and by recourse to prayer. But how much did that ignorance excuse? Did the bishops who pleaded ignorance really not know that raping a child was a crime that used to carry the death penalty, and so must have been known to cause real harm? If they "did not understand", were they not obliged to do some basic research and take steps to prevent their clerics from ever causing such harm again?

In 1947 a new religious order, The Servants of the Paraclete, was founded in New Mexico to treat errant clergy, including sexual abusers. It focused on "spiritual healing based on intense prayer". In 1948 the order's founder, Fr. Gerald Fitzgerald, resolved *not* to receive priests who had sexually abused minors. He firmly believed that no priest who had violated a minor "should ever be allowed back in ministry but should be dismissed from the priesthood." He stated this belief to bishops; to the prefect of the Holy Office in 1962, and to Pope Paul VI in 1963, but was ignored.[49] Under pressure, the New Mexico center continued to treat pedophiles. Gerald Ridsdale, one of Australia's worst, was sent there by his Ballarat bishop in 1990. Bishops' pleas that they "did not know" need to be accepted with some reservations.

Bishops may have shared the general ignorance about the depth of harm that sexual abuse does to a child; they may also have failed to trust children to be reliable witnesses. But when they received barrages of complaints from parents and other loyal Catholics, it was not possible that they failed to know that what some of their clergy were doing was criminal. Otherwise, why did they take such care to conceal it from police—and sometimes themselves conspire with police to hush it up?

---

47. *RCFR*, 16, 2, 231.
48. *RCFR*, 16, 2, 232.
49. *RCFR*, 16, 1, 180-81.

Clerical Errors

Long after it did become clear that most offenders could not be cured, bishops and provincials continued to deal internally and secretly with complaints about what they knew were crimes. Bishop Hilton Deakin told the Royal Commission that as late as the 1990s he would not have reported Father Peter Searson's notorious behavior to the police, so as "to avoid scandal to the church".[50] This common attitude and the decision to conceal crimes was based on a terrible choice, which deserves to be called a heresy: to see "the good of the church" as involving only that tiny portion who are clerics, and not the victims, their mothers and fathers and every baptized person from whom the truth was being concealed.[51]

The bishops' decisions to conceal crimes were ultimately self-serving and did little credit to them as the moral leaders that they claim to be. Bishop Robinson gave evidence that clericalism also affected police, leading them to suppress cases involving clergy, and sometimes judges, magistrates, politicians and senior public servants. Proper legal processes were omitted, and publicity was minimized so as to hide the moral corruption among so-called pillars of the community.

But there were always people of conscience who could not condone this corrupt elitism. In Mildura in the 1970s Detective Denis Ryan lost his job through trying to stop the depredations of the pedophile Monsignor Day. Ryan's superior officers removed him from the investigation. By assigning him away from Mildura they effectively forced him to leave the police force, for he was not willing to pull his children from their Mildura schools. As recently as 2012 Detective Chief Inspector Peter Fox also faced enormous opposition when trying to expose the police cover-up of abuse in Maitland diocese. Police had silenced victims, hindered investigations, alerted offenders and destroyed evidence, thus enabling bishops to move priests elsewhere to "protect the good name of the church."[52]

In its closing stages the Royal Commission questioned a panel of five Australian archbishops. In what must have been for them an excruciating interview, Archbishop Fisher of Sydney admitted that in some cases it was "a kind of criminal negligence" when bishops failed to deal with ". . . problems that were staring us in the face. In other cases, [bishops] . . . were just like rabbits in the headlights, [having] no idea what to do . . ."[53] But can

50. *RCFR*, 16, 2, 237–38.
51. Thomas Doyle, *RCFR*, 16, 2, 236.
52. ABC interview: *Lateline* November 8, 2012. *RCFR*, 16, 1, 262.
53. *RCFR*, 16, 2, 231.

it truly be claimed that these men, well-educated in moral theology and appointed to lead hundreds of thousands of Catholics, were unaware that sexually abusing a child is a crime and needed to be dealt with as such? Did they really have "no idea what to do"? Or did they choose, time after time, following church custom and Canon Law, to judge the reputation of clerics who had committed such crimes as more important than the suffering of the abused children? Since they *did* make the latter choice, again and again, rather than being like "startled rabbits", were they not were more like foxes shrewdly manipulating victims much less powerful than themselves?

Bishops failed to protect children because the culture of clericalism had come to assume that the institution should be protected even if it meant concealing grave crimes. Fisher admitted this: "you didn't want scandal, [or] ... people to think less of the clergy or the bishops or religious ... *they just wanted to protect the name or the institution* ..." [emphasis added].[54] Yielding to clericalism is bad enough, but behind it there is an even more shameful dimension. When bishops concealed crimes of abuse, they were obeying instructions from their superiors in Rome. As will be seen in the following chapter, the Canon Law which guided them was, in this matter, itself corrupt.

---

54. *RCFR*, 16, 2, 632.

6

The Failure of Canon Law[1]

> *More hideous crimes have been committed in the name of obedience than in the name of rebellion.*
>
> —C. P. SNOW

THE PREVIOUS CHAPTER SHOWED that clericalist attitudes within the church have contributed to clergy child sexual abuse and to concealment of the crimes by church leaders. Many authorities were quoted in support of that finding. This chapter will show that clericalism has distorted even the Canon Law by which the church is governed. The pope and the papal *curia* gradually became more powerful through the centuries, and today govern the church with a high degree of central control. This centralization often breaches the principle of *subsidiarity,* an ancient principle that was clearly formulated in the 1938 encyclical *Quadragesimo Anno*. The principle states that decisions about any issue ought to be made by the people closest to, and most affected by, those decisions. Higher authorities must intervene only when necessary.[2] The principle derives from the gospel statements that those in authority should not dominate.

  1. On June 1, 2021 a revision was released of Book 6 of the *Code*, amending some of the serious faults listed by the Royal Commission. On December 8, 2021 a new version of Book 6 of the *Code* entered into force.

  2. *Quadragesimo Anno* 79: ". . . it is an injustice . . . to assign to a greater and higher

The Failure of Canon Law

The Second Vatican Council tried to restore some of the authority that properly belongs to local bishops, but since that Council, popes and the papal *curia* have often neglected to respect this. They have demanded—for example—unnecessary uniformity in liturgical practice everywhere in the world. In totalitarian fashion, this deprives particular peoples of their right to *inculturate* the gospel: to explore and worship God creatively via their own local traditions. Insisting on uniformity ignores the obvious truth that the natural world is continuously developing new forms in rich variety. Many initiatives in local churches have been stifled by the erroneous claim that uniformity is necessary for the "welfare of the church", when in truth the church's welfare takes quite different forms in different places.[3]

If the Vatican had followed the principle of subsidiarity, the church in Australia and in other countries may not have suffered from the "moral paralysis" which Melbourne Archbishop Denis Hart admitted had "crippled it" and prevented it from responding effectively to the pedophilia crisis. Bishop and canon lawyer Geoffrey Robinson, who for many years dealt professionally with cases of abuse, reinforced what Archbishop Hart had told the Royal Commission: that the Vatican has been a major obstacle to dealing with abuse. Dr Michael Leahy put it succinctly by saying that any governance practice which produces moral paralysis in an institution has to be called dysfunctional.[4]

Through the centuries, church synods and councils have produced laws and regulations to meet local needs. In 1917 this complex mass of historical decrees was edited into one code, to which additions and adjustments are often made. As already noted in chapter 2, from the mid-nineteenth century, the church's law began to respond to sexual abuse by treating clerics quite differently from lay people. This claim may sound extreme, but its practical end-result was summed up crudely by a police commissioner at the 2013 Victorian Parliamentary Inquiry: "If a child was raped on Catholic Church grounds it would be reported by officials to police . . . unless the offender was a member of the clergy".[5]

---

association what lesser and subordinate organizations can do." See also Pope Benedict XVI. 2009 *Caritas in Veritate*, 57–58.

3. Schillebeeckx, *Church with a Human Face*, 235. The principle is also convincingly argued by Donovan, in *Christianity Rediscovered*, based on his experience among the Masai.

4. *RCFR*, 16, 2, 658.

5. *VPI* 2, 493.

Clerical Errors

The origins of this privileged position for clerics can be traced to the early fourth century, when the emperor Constantine astutely lent his support to the expanding Christian church. The church's officials were granted privileges such as exemption from taxes and from being judged in civil courts. Erring clerics were tried by the church's own legal system.

By the sixth century the influence of the emperor in distant Byzantium was waning, and the Bishop of Rome, as its largest landholder, was growing in religious and political power. The role of the clergy developed, in step with the growing material strength of the church.

From earliest times, church leaders punished the crime of child sexual abuse with severe penalties. From the fourth century, offending clerics were tried mostly in Church courts, and when found guilty were often handed over to the state. Sometimes they were executed. In the seventh and eighth centuries punishments meted out to clerics who sexually abused were even more severe than for lay persons. In 1551 the Council of Trent still recognized that some crimes committed by clerics were so grave that the offenders should be deposed from sacred orders and handed over the secular court. Pope Pius V named child abuse as such a crime, and during his reign, when in 1570 the cleric Fontino was found guilty of sodomy of a choir boy, that cleric was handed over to the state and beheaded.

This severe attitude continued through the eighteenth century but from the mid-nineteenth century the severity began to lessen. The church became more defensive about clerical crimes, and authorities became reluctant to dismiss priests, even for the sacrilege of soliciting within the sacrament of confession.

Christians had always known opposition and persecution, but from the end of the eighteenth century, troubles were coming from new sources and from many sides. During the French Revolution many clerics and religious were massacred or exiled; then Napoleon captured and imprisoned two successive popes. By 1870 the church had lost the Papal States and was under additional pressure in the new nations of Italy and Germany. It was becoming more sensitive to opposition from secular powers, which could now expose its weaknesses to a world-wide public by mass-circulation newspapers. This happened in 1858, in the notorious case of Edgardo Mortara, a baptized Jewish boy who was "kidnapped" by the pope. In the 1920s the introduction of radio increased the possibility of even more rapid exposure and criticism.

The Failure of Canon Law

An 1866 instruction from the Holy Office had urged restraint in demoting priests, and imposed absolute secrecy on proceedings that followed allegations of solicitation in the confessional.[6] In 1890 a detailed instruction from Pope Leo XIII required witnesses in such cases to swear an oath of secrecy, and procedures were designed to keep hidden not just the evidence, but also the fact that the trial was being held, because these cases could be "a source of... scandal to the faithful."[7]

The increasing reluctance to "degrade" clergy accused of serious sexual crimes, or to hand them over to civil authorities was continued in the 1917 *Code of Canon Law*. This compendium discarded many old decrees which had demanded that priests guilty of sexually assaulting children be handed over to the state.[8] The *Code* still dealt severely with abusers of minors: they were to be suspended from clerical duties; declared infamous; deprived of office and in more serious cases, dismissed, but this was to be done "in house".[9] Priests were being treated differently from ordinary folk because, as Pius X had pointed out, they had quite a different status in the church. Clerical privilege was alive and flourishing.

Crimen Sollicitationis

Five years after the *Code*, in 1922, the *Holy Office* (later named the Congregation for the Doctrine of the Faith) issued the instruction *Crimen sollicitationis*, whose norms dealt with priests accused of any kind of sexual misconduct. Like its nineteenth-century predecessors, this document demanded secrecy about the procedures. It did *not* forbid the victim/survivor to report the crime to the police, but *once a church process had begun*, it bound all participants to secrecy. If church personnel breached this secrecy, they incurred the automatic penalty of excommunication from which only the pope could absolve. The penalty for breaking secrecy about the trial had become more severe than the penalty for abusing a child!

---

6. *Sacred Congregation of the Holy Office*: Instruction, February 20, 1866.

7. "these procedures ... are to be completed in absolute secrecy, and after ... sentencing, are to be completely suppressed by perpetual silence. All ... must submit oaths of maintaining secrecy...." *(Fontes,* IV, 990, 14, 267.)

8. E.g., the decrees of Celestine III, Innocent III, Leo X, Pius V, the 4th and 5th Lateran Councils, and Trent.

9. *Codex*, Canon 2359 §2.

Clerical Errors

This strict secrecy had the honest aims of protecting the accused until proven guilty, and of protecting confidentiality, when cases involved the sacrament of penance. Perhaps it was also meant to protect the privacy of the accuser. It was definitely not a conspiracy to do *nothing* about clerics' crimes, as some have misinterpreted it, but it was nonetheless highly questionable: a somewhat misguided attempt to avoid "scandal" by keeping clerical crimes from public view. Misguided, because concealing the crimes has eventually caused far greater scandal. This secrecy was a left-over from the ancient tradition of the "Privilege of the Forum", which exempted clergy from being tried in civil courts or jailed in civil prisons. Perhaps it was an attempt to reclaim the privilege,[10] which had long since lapsed in most parts of the world, but in 1929 the church persuaded Mussolini to include it in the concordat which also established the Vatican as church territory. The privilege still exists in other Vatican concordats, for instance with Colombia, where bishops are exempt from being tried in civil courts.[11]

Secrecy is sometimes necessary in human dealings. It protects the privacy and dignity of persons when, for instance, they consult doctors and lawyers. It is sometimes required during legal trials. But laws that demand secrecy influence our way of thinking and our culture. The secrecy demanded by these nineteenth- and twentieth-century documents contributed to building *expectations* of secrecy around clerical crimes. The Vatican tried increasingly to conceal clerical misconduct from public view, and twentieth-century bishops, almost universally, failed to report offences and sometimes strongly resisted police investigations.

The very existence of *Crimen Sollicitationis* was highly secret. It was never published in the official Vatican records, and bishops were told to keep it in their secret archives. Academic discussion of it was forbidden. In short, secretiveness, obfuscation and denial became an entrenched part of the governance of the Catholic Church. When powerful organizations use secrecy to protect their privileges, they are acting against justice, for by hiding the truth, the powerful can gravely harm those without power.

The 1922 document made it very difficult for a cleric to be dismissed. This could happen only when there was no chance of his reform. If an offending priest promised convincingly "not to do it again", no further action would be taken against him. If he were tried before a church tribunal, the

---

10. Tapsell, *Potiphar's Wife*, Location 1743.
11. *RCFR*, 16, 2, 700–702. Tapsell, *Potiphar's Wife*, Location 2015, 2483.

records of the case were to be sent to the CDF.[12] The accused could then appeal against the verdict, and the CDF had authority to overturn any local tribunal's decision.[13] Even after being convicted in a church court, the priest could be transferred to another location "to avoid scandal". *Crimen sollicitationis* was reissued, with additions, in 1962 and in 1974 its secrecy norms were maintained in the document *Secreta Continere*.

Secreta Continere

This document demanded that *pontifical secrecy* be observed about any allegation, investigation or trial of clergy accused of child sexual abuse, from the time when an allegation was first received by the superior of the accused.[14] The penalty for breaking secrecy was again automatic excommunication. Although the victim was not forbidden to take the matter to the police, the secrecy clause would mean that when a priest was being tried for a sexual crime by *a church enquiry*, if he was found to have committed other crimes, no one involved in the enquiry could take that additional information to the police without breaching canon law and being excommunicated. The judgement of the canonical court had to be kept secret, although the accused was allowed to know the details of the denunciation and the name of his accuser.[15] This continuing, strict insistence on concealment might have given conscientious bishops the further impression that information should also be concealed from civil authorities even when civil laws demanded it.

The reason constantly given for secrecy was that if these matters were revealed they could damage the "building up of the Church", "destroy the public good" or "offend the inviolable rights of individuals and communities." Such concern for the reputation of the church seems utterly unreal today, now that an avalanche of clerics' crimes has been appearing on the front pages of newspapers for many years. It is also difficult to know whose "inviolable rights" would be put at risk by making a trial public. It could not have been the rights of the complainants, for name suppression is available for those who want it; and many victims/survivors, having found the courage to come forward, *want* their story to be told. When cases of abuse are made public, it actually helps others who have not yet dared to speak

12. *Codex,* Canon 2162.
13. RCFR, 16, 2, 66.
14. RCFR, 16, 2, 55.
15. RCFR, 16, 2, 56.

about it. Nor can it be the accused whose "inviolable rights" are offended, for it is part of an open justice system that when any person makes a credible accusation against another person, it is the role of public courts to test the truth of the charge. Or was the Vatican document still claiming, in the 1970s, that clerics have rights that other people do not have?

These official demands for secrecy certainly seem to rank the status and reputation of "the church"—meaning clerics—above the care and safety of its children, who are just as much part of the church as any cleric. The rules imposing secrecy put severe obstacles in the way of victims' struggling for justice, but those rules were not fully repealed until 2019, by Pope Francis.

As an example of how things worked, bishops Ronald Mulkearns of Ballarat, and Archbishop Francis Little of Melbourne were extremely secretive in dealing with abusers. They kept no notes of accusations. Why? We can presume that they desired to protect accused priests, and to "prevent scandal". But canon law also "justified" them for not starting canonical proceedings, because that step would create documents that could be obtained by police and courts under a warrant or subpoena. This was actually the advice given to canon lawyers at the Australian-New Zealand canon lawyers' conference in 2006: that in sensitive cases, "for the good of the Church" it would be best *not* to start canonical proceedings.[16] The actions of Bishops Mulkearns and Little were even more zealous than demanded by *Crimen Sollicitationis* or the revised 1983 *Code*, whose Canon 489 required only that documents about clergy sexual abuse be destroyed after ten years.

When Canon Law was revised in 1983 under Pope John Paul II, it did not make things easier for victims of abuse. The new *Code's* language about priests who committed sex crimes against children was much milder than that of the 1917 *Code*. It was now even more difficult to dismiss those priests.[17] The Vatican was clearly favoring clerics over laity and seemed reluctant to submit clerics to justice. Church thinking appeared to have moved a long way backwards since the beheading of the unfortunate Fontino.

The 2013 Parliamentary Enquiry in the state of Victoria recognized these serious flaws in church law.[18] Later, the Australia-wide Royal Commission also demonstrated that the church's laws were inadequate in dealing with clerical child abuse. By a gross distortion, the law's goal had become more the good of the abusing priest than the pastoral care for abused

16. Personal correspondence from one who attended the conference.
17. Cafardi, *Before Dallas*, 62.
18. *VPI*, 1, 169.

The Failure of Canon Law

children and their families.[19] Canon 1341 of the 1983 *Code* commands bishops to "repair the scandal" of a cleric's crime against a minor first by "fraternal correction, reproof or by methods of pastoral care"—for the *cleric*. The *Code* contains no solicitous command that the bishop give "pastoral care" to the victims/survivors of child-abusing clerics, or to their families. Only if a canonical trial follows might they obtain the right to claim damages, but such canonical trials are complex and unlikely to happen.

In the 1983 *Code* even the definition of sexual abuse of minors was still seriously flawed. Clerical crimes as grave as rape were dealt with in the section on clerics' sins against the sixth commandment, i.e., in the context of sexuality, rather than as crimes against the victim's "human life and liberty".[20] Moreover, it is astonishing that Canon 1321 can actually be used to *protect* a pedophile from being convicted or dismissed from the clerical state. This canon allows that if the offender is diagnosed as a pedophile, the judges at a canonical trial can find that his crimes were not imputable because of his diminished responsibility. This classic Catch 22 means that a priest cannot be dismissed for acts of pedophilia *because* he is a pedophile. The result was that, if church law alone was followed, there might be no consequences for his crimes. The Grand Jury investigating the church in Philadelphia found that the archdiocese had in fact used this legal escape clause.

In the 1983 *Code* there is no mention of reporting a cleric's crimes to the civil authorities. Only if the bishop perceives—by what kind of subjective judgement?—that his own persuasion has failed to reform the offender, only then may he start a judicial or administrative procedure involving penalties. This instruction hugely favors the child-abuser, not least because of the inbuilt conflict of interest. The bishop, who is the priest's "spiritual father", must conduct the preliminary investigation and decide whether the priest must submit to a canonical trial. Canon law professor Nicholas Cafardi stated that in the 1980s and 1990s it would be improper to use Canon 1341 in cases of child sexual abuse by clergy, because it would be quite ineffectual.[21] Most canon lawyers would agree.

Most decent people would expect that anyone knowing of a despicable crime against a child would report it to police, but most bishops around the world thought otherwise. They interpreted Canon Law to mean that they could *not* take allegations to the police. When complaints were made

---

19. *RCFR*, 16, 2, 232–33.
20. *Code*, Canon 1395.
21. *RCFR*, 16, 2, 713.

Clerical Errors

against Dublin priest Tony Walsh in 1978, canon lawyer Monsignor Sheehy advised that because of the 1922 instruction *Crimen Sollicitationis*–repeated in *Secreta Continere* (1974)–it would be extremely difficult to dismiss Walsh, and that to inform the police would breach "pontifical secrecy." In 1993 the Vatican was still refusing to dismiss Walsh, and only in 2016 was he was jailed for sixteen years.

Many governments make it mandatory to report crimes, but the Vatican has steadfastly resisted this. In 1984 the Congregation for Clergy told Archbishop Moreno of Tucson: "Under no condition . . . should the files be surrendered to any court or judge." In 1997, when the Irish bishops proposed to make reporting mandatory, the Papal Nuncio, Storero, wrote to them expressing serious "moral and canonical" reservations about their proposal. Was he claiming that it was *immoral* for a bishop to report a priest who is active as a serial pedophile? The bishops of England and Wales too, on legal advice, asked the Vatican to approve mandatory reporting, but again the Vatican refused. Clearly, this was treating priests more leniently than the common herd. The words and actions of many contemporary cardinals also show that they are still, today, demanding secrecy to protect the criminal cleric and the public image of the church. In 1996, when the drafters of the Australian bishops' program Towards Healing proposed mandatory reporting, "Rome" would not allow it. In the following sixteen years, Victorian dioceses dealt with 620 cases of abuse, but did not report any of them to the police. It was only victims who reported to civil authorities.

In 2001 Cardinal Castrillon Hoyos, Prefect of the Congregation for Clergy, congratulated the French bishop Pecan for *not* reporting a priest-abuser to police. Claiming that Pope John Paul II had authorized his letter, Castrillon Hoyos wrote: ". . . the relationship between bishop and priest is . . . a sacramental relationship, a very special bond of spiritual paternity." The cardinal argued that civil laws sometimes dispense family members from testifying against their relatives.[22] In 2002, Cardinal Herranz, head of the Council that interprets legal texts, criticized bishops for asking that Canon Law be changed to allow reporting. In 2004 Cardinal Rodriguez of Honduras—once regarded as a possible candidate to be pope—claimed he would be prepared to go to jail rather than "harm one of my priests.". Other cardinals, including Maradiaga and Bertone, have also emphasized the "special nature" of the relationship between bishops and priests, and

22. *RCFR*, 16, 2, 704.

The Failure of Canon Law

claimed that bishops should not report accused priests to civil authorities.[23] With the same clericalist mind-set, Irish canon lawyer Monsignor Maurice Dooley said in 2010 that bishops could not report allegations without breaching Canon Law, adding that as a parent you are entitled to protect your children, or even conceal them from punishment.

The Vatican has been slow to change its official position. In 2010 it did allow reporting, but only where the civil law of the place demanded it. In Australia, this would currently apply only in the state of New South Wales. In 2016, at last, the new Pontifical Commission for the Protection of Minors agreed that the whole Church will comply with relevant civil authorities,[24] but even then, if civil authorities did not demand that cases be reported, neither did the church.[25]

In civil society it is common that a person accused of a serious offence stand aside from their duties until the case is resolved. In 1971, under Pope Paul VI, the CDF allowed that bishops could petition for an "administrative laicization" to dismiss a priest for living a "depraved life", which included the sexual abuse of children.[26] In 1980 however, the new Pope John Paul II, alarmed at the number of priests leaving the priesthood, abolished this procedure. The priest himself had to *ask* to be laicized. If a bishop wished to dismiss a priest, he had to use the earlier convoluted judicial procedures laid down by the 1917 *Code* and in *Crimen Sollicitationis*. The "reformed" Canon Law of 1983 entrenched John Paul II's changes, so that bishops, even if certain of an accused priest's guilt, often had no choice but to restrict his ministry or to move him elsewhere. Obeying this law seems to be part of the reason why so many bishops moved and re-appointed priests whom they knew to be notorious offenders.

Towards the end of John Paul II's reign, in 2001 and 2003, the procedure was modified again, making it somewhat easier to dismiss a cleric. In some cases, the Vatican did deal helpfully with such applications, but not always. When Australian Archbishop Coleridge made eight requests to dismiss priests who had been already convicted by civil courts, the CDF refused to dismiss five of them, requiring only that they "live a life of prayer

---

23. http://natcath.org/NCR_Online/archives/053102/053102h.htm and *RCFR*, 16, 2, 705.

24. *RCFR*, 16, 2, 708.

25. Tapsell, https://johnmenadue.com/kieran-tapsell-pope-francis-abolishes-the-pontifical-secret-over-child-sexual-abuse/.

26. *AAS* 72, 1132–37.

Clerical Errors

and penance".[27] An Irish case also illustrates this difficulty: a Dublin tribunal dismissed Patrick McGuire from the priesthood in 2002, but McGuire appealed to Rome. His dismissal was overturned, and he was merely suspended for nine years because he had been diagnosed as a pedophile. When later he was again arrested and charged, the Vatican did suspend him, but still would not dismiss him.

In Wollongong Bishop Wilson found that complaints against Fr John Nestor were credible and forbade him to minister. Nestor appealed to the Congregation for Clergy, which required that he be immediately restored to full priestly ministry. Only when Wilson appealed to the higher Apostolic *Signatura*, did it overturn the previous decision and in 2006 dismissed Nestor from the priesthood. Something must have been learned, for regulations were then changed, making the CDF the body to determine such matters. In 2010 Pope Benedict XVI further simplified the dismissal process.[28]

As long as the church's law protected priests in these ways, favoring them over their victims, it obviously created an unacceptable risk of more children being abused. The writers of the Australian protocol Towards Healing sensibly included the concept of *unacceptable risk* in that program, but the Vatican rejected this innovation, again favoring accused priests above the rights of children. The US bishops had made many similar requests to the Vatican, but officials rejected these too, and only in 2010 allowed a priest to be stood down while he was being investigated. The 1983 *Code*'s process to dismiss a priest from the priesthood was a complicated judicial process involving three judges and could take as long as seven years. Canon lawyers learned that even this process was not likely to end in dismissal. A variety of bishops admitted to the Australian Royal Commission that the chances of dismissing a priest were "close to hopeless"; "very, very difficult"; "extraordinarily difficult" and "unworkable".[29]

Quite apart from the difficulty of using Canon Law to dismiss a priest, the notorious case of Marcial Degollado, already discussed, demonstrates how a serial offender could evade Canon Law's limited powers by bribery and other corrupt practices. Through his long career he was often accused, but Degollado had the support of Cardinal Sodano who in 1998 pressured Cardinal Ratzinger not to prosecute him. When Ratzinger, as Benedict

---

27. *RCFR*, 16, 2, 400.
28. *RCFR*, 16, 2, 718.
29. Tapsell *Potiphar's Wife*, Location 608.

The Failure of Canon Law

XVI, at last took action, he still did not dismiss Marcial from the priesthood, nor was he reported to the police.

One of the most serious defects in the 1983 *Code* was that it introduced a new law which after five years automatically "extinguished" all crimes of sexual abuse of minors.[30] Since the average victim/survivor does not disclose their suffering for more than twenty years, this law effectively silenced them permanently, so that nothing could be done to bring their abusers to justice. "Extinction" also left abusers free to commit any number of further crimes. Only in 2001, after urgent requests from the US bishops, was this statute of limitations extended—but only for that nation—to ten years beyond the complainant's eighteenth birthday. In 2010 it was further extended to twenty years beyond the eighteenth birthday. Australian civil law never had limitation periods for sexual crimes, and many other civil codes have now abolished such limitations.

It is astonishing that when the new *Code* became law in 1983, even competent canon lawyers were unable to be sure whether this five-year extinction had come into force. This was because legislation—e.g., *Crimen sollicitationis*—contained no such prescription. Had those previous laws been abolished? Believing that they had, the US bishops struggled through six years of negotiations with the Vatican to extend the five-year prescription period, as mentioned above. But in a 2001 *Motu Proprio*, Cardinals Ratzinger and Bertone stated that *Crimen sollicitationis* had *not* been abolished but was still in force. This meant that there was *no* five-year time limit on reporting child sexual abuse. It is hardly surprising that the Irish Murphy Commission described Canon Law as lacking basic features of a coherent legal system.

Bella Figura

Notoriously, the Vatican tries to pretend that such egregious mistakes did not happen. This is known as *bella figura*, the Italian way of keeping up a good appearance, a good look. It is common in Vatican institutions, but no amount of *bella figura* could conceal the many defects in the church's legal system. These deficiencies for long hindered the exposure of clerical crimes and largely explain why, if offenders were brought to justice at all, it was only after long delay. Once again, it must be stressed that the tragic consequence was that abusers were free to commit crimes against many

---

30. Code Canon 1362: 1, 2.

more children. It must also be admitted that these faulty laws came from the heart of the institution, the church's central government, and at least six recent popes were involved in creating and maintaining them.

Many bishops have been condemned for handling pedophiles' crimes incompetently. Besides the Boston exposures and Philadelphia Grand Jury's condemnation of its cardinals, the Australian Royal Commission unequivocally blamed bishops Ronald Mulkearns of Ballarat and Francis Little of Melbourne for protecting notorious serial abusers. But all those bishops were legally obliged to follow the directions of Canon Law, which suffers from all the defects just described. It is claimed that in recent times bishops have generally been selected for loyalty to the institution rather than initiative, leadership or independence of thought. When bishops are appointed, they must promise on oath to adhere to the teachings of the pope and College of Bishops "with religious submission of *will and intellect* . . ." This demand is seriously problematic, and a short digression is needed to explain why.

The demand conflicts both with common sense and with psychology, including the psychology and philosophy of Thomas Aquinas, favored by the church. Aquinas pointed out that it is our will that moves—commands—our intellect to *start* thinking, and which directs it to focus on a particular topic. But our will cannot compel the intellect to *understand* or *accept* a particular truth, for the mind is moved or convinced by truth alone.[31] So, if a bishop does not understand a particular teaching or command of the church, he may indeed choose—with his will—to obey that command and pass on the teaching to others. But if he cannot see with his intellect—that it is true, or actually disagrees with the teaching, he is not being truthful if he *pretends* to see it as true. No authority can command us to accept, intellectually, something with which we disagree. So the command to bishops, and their promise to obey it, is fallacious.

Despite the above, during the pontificate of Pope John Paul II no candidate would be accepted as a bishop, who openly disagreed with the papal teachings that artificial contraception is against the Divine Law; that priests cannot be allowed the option of marrying; that women cannot be ordained priests; or spoke of homosexuality differently from Vatican documents. One witness told the Royal Commission that selecting bishops in this way limits open debate within the Catholic Church on fundamental issues[32] and results in intellectual mediocrity and institutional blind-spots.

31. *S Th* Ia 82 4: "Does the will move the intellect?"
32. Dr Gerry O'Hanlon, SJ, *RCFR*, 16, 2, 688.

The Failure of Canon Law

Another witness even more bluntly said that the policy produced a church full of obedient episcopal clones who were managers and administrators, rather than leaders in teaching the Christian Gospel.[33] The Commission recommended that the Vatican allow wider consultation before appointing bishops, so as to overcome the tendency to appoint men who will not "rock the boat"; men who fail to speak out against blatant social injustice; who often block from speaking in church venues, scholars who might challenge aspects of the church that need to be changed.

To return to Bishop Mulkearns: while we cannot condone his failures to seek justice for the victims of pedophiles, we might better see his terrible failures in their human context if we examine more closely how the institution had shaped him, as it shaped many others.[34] After his catholic schooling and isolated seminary training, Mulkearns went directly to Rome for further studies, then worked in the *Curia*. He was made a bishop at forty-one, having had virtually no parish pastoral experience by which to gain empathy for the everyday life of ordinary families. Formed in a deeply clericalist milieu, he was extremely deferential to Roman authorities and accepted without question the institution's anachronistic trappings and pomp. Even in the 1990s, for example, he would insist that people meeting him must kiss his episcopal ring.

When Mulkearns was appointed to Ballarat and had to deal with several notorious abusers, he would have been terrified of the scandal that would explode if the crimes became public. Unswervingly obedient to Canon Law, he could not imagine reporting priest-abusers to the police. In fact, Catholic police are known to have collaborated with Mulkearns to cover up at least the crimes of Monsignor John Day. Even if Mulkearns had wanted to remove such abusers from the priesthood, he knew that under Canon Law this could almost never happen. As the law commanded, he treated the pedophiles with "pastoral care," sending Gerald Ridsdale and other abusers to treatment centers, for it was believed at the time that they could be cured. It is heart-breaking to read the statements of victims' parents, who vainly sought justice from Mulkearns;[35] but like other bishops of the time, he saw his role as doing strictly what "Rome" wanted. This meant giving clerics and "the church"—as they narrowly saw it—a much higher

---

33. *RCFR*, 16, 1, 45.
34. Michael Morwood, *The Swag*, Winter 2016.
35. *RCFR*, 16, 2, 482–83.

priority than the welfare of victims. Clericalism prevented them from going against the institution by treating victims with real compassion, or justice.

From the late 1980s, more crimes by priests emerged into public knowledge and the law's deficiencies became more apparent, but official denials continued. In Ireland, soon after the *Murphy Report* in 2010 had shown that the church's own structures and rules had facilitated the cover up, Pope Benedict XVI wrote a pastoral letter to the Irish bishops. He did not acknowledge what the *Murphy Report* had just pointed out about Canon Law's deficiencies. Nor did he admit that the Vatican curia had protected abusive priests from civil prosecution or dismissal. Instead, Pope Benedict accused the Irish bishops of "failure of leadership" and "grave errors of judgement". He condemned them for using a "pastoral approach" towards their priests, blatantly failing to recognize that it was Canon Law itself which *demanded* they use that "pastoral approach". Nor did he give any hint that the law is riddled with defects that seem designed to protect clerics instead of bringing justice to the children they have gravely damaged.

Two years later the Australian Bishops' Conference showed a similar blindness. They submitted to the Victorian Inquiry their report: *Facing the Truth,* which wretchedly *failed* to "face the truth" since it pretended that the church was *now* "coming to grips with the problem", when any adult had *always* known that the sexual abuse of children was evil. Nor did the *Report* mention any of Canon Law's deficiencies that favor clerical offenders rather than help their victims. But the Victorian Inquiry was not naive. It found that senior representatives of the Catholic church and of other religious bodies—had tried directly to conceal wrongdoing, and were not frank even about the church legislation that commanded that concealment.[36] Many other writers, such as the experienced canonist Tom Doyle, point out that official excuses are hollow, and that secrecy and cover-up have long been part of the nature of Catholic institutional culture. What normal person, Doyle asked, doesn't comprehend that *any* sexual assault against a child is harmful? What Catholic, cleric or lay, cannot understand that when a priest or bishop sexually abuses a devout Catholic child, the effects will be disastrous? If any cleric—from deacon to pope—does not grasp this, then there is something drastically wrong with the culture that formed and sustains him.[37]

The United Nations Committee on the Rights of the Child recommended that the Holy See undertake a comprehensive review of Canon

---

36. Tapsell, *Potiphar's Wife,* Location 160.
37. Tom Doyle, *NCR* October 13, 2006.

The Failure of Canon Law

Law, with a view to ensuring that it complies fully with children's rights to be protected against discrimination, violence, and sexual exploitation or sexual abuse.[38] In particular, the UN Committee recommended that Canon Law redefine child sexual abuse as a crime, and that reporting abuse be made mandatory.[39] The Holy See replied that it would consider the Committee's recommendations, but disingenuously objected that "Rome" did not have the capacity to impose the UNCRC's principles on local churches in the territory of other States. In fact, "Rome" constantly imposes its own principles in those territories. The Australian Royal Commission, after hearing abundant evidence of bishops mishandling clerics' crimes, recommended substantial changes to Canon Law and strongly advised that the Holy See establish a process for appointing bishops which is transparent and includes the direct participation of lay people.[40]

The insights and complaints of good people are gradually bringing about much-needed change in the church. In 2003 the Pontifical Academy for Life organized a conference on sexual abuse of children by clerics, where eight psychiatric experts, who were not Catholic, identified a list of factors contributing to such abuse, such as failure by the hierarchy to grasp the seriousness of the problem; overemphasis on the need to avoid a scandal; use of unqualified treatment centers; misguided willingness to forgive, and insufficient accountability.

In 2014 Pope Francis instituted the Pontifical Commission for the Protection of Minors, and in 2019, convened a Vatican summit on sexual abuse, and as mentioned at the beginning of this chapter, the much-needed changes in Canon Law have begun to be addressed.

All this demonstrates that since the mid-nineteenth century the church's laws have been slanted towards concealing the crimes of its clergy from public knowledge, with the underlying aim of protecting the priests themselves and the Church's public image.[41] This conclusion is consistent with the findings in another area of legal studies, the study of racism. Critical Race Theory is showing that laws are constructed, perhaps half unconsciously, to serve the interests of the dominant white society and to retard the progress of people of color.[42] We will see this again in chapter 7, where clericalism is shown to be a form of caste.

38. Cahill and Wilkinson, *Child Sexual Abuse*. 283.
39. *RCFR*, 16, 2, 695.
40. *RCFR*, 16, 2, 689.
41. *RCFR*, 16, 2, 702.
42. Delgado and Stefancic, *Critical Race Theory*.

Clerical Errors

The damning conclusions listed in this chapter come from experts, both lay canonists and bishops.[43] It is a terrible irony that these efforts to conceal crimes have done worse damage to the Church's reputation and brought a much larger financial cost, than if the church had faced them honestly. The Irish *Murphy Report* reached similar conclusions. Some have described the church's legal system for dealing with abusers as a fiasco. Professor Nicholas Cafardi considers the system to have fallen apart. Kieran Tapsell remarked that the wheels have really fallen of a justice system when it requires the consent of criminals themselves to strike them off the professional list and deprive them of the income they receive from the institution they have betrayed.[44] Guilty priests would naturally prefer not to be disqualified, for it means losing their church income. The situation is as absurd, Tapsell says, as asking a lawyer who has stolen huge amounts of his clients' money to give his consent before being struck off the roll.

Again, it needs to be emphasized, that a basic reason underlying these enormous institutional failures is the claim that priests are "ontologically different". This clerical error has led other members of the church to see clergy as belonging to a higher caste and defer to the privileges they claim. The human consequences of the erroneous assumption can hardly be exaggerated. It has been further asked whether the ultimate source of the injustices can be found in Canon 1404, which declares that the pope is accountable to no one. Beyond the creation of clerics into a special caste, this declaration radically separates the human head of the church from other Christians and from the rest of the world.

The inadequacies of Canon Law do not excuse from serious guilt the bishops who followed it without question or objection. They were intelligent men, each with a conscience, and each able to discern whether severe, lifetime damage to children was less important than the "good name" of an individual cleric or of the institution. The same guilt is borne by the men who drafted and amended the church's defective laws. Once again, it is the central aim of this book to point out that Catholic, clerical leaders, trusted by generations of loyal Catholics to lead them towards God, have betrayed the principles of the gospel upon which the institution was founded.

---

43. Doyle, Beal, and Bishops Robinson, Gumbleton, Weakland, Smity, Malone, Pell and Hart.

44. Tapsell, *Potiphar's Wife*, Location 2202.

7

The Amoral Institution

The triumph of evil requires a lot of good people doing a bit of it, in a morally disengaged way, with indifference to the human suffering they have collectively caused.

—ALBERT BANDURA

POSSIBLE CAUSES HAVE BEEN suggested, in the preceding chapters, for the high level of child sexual abuse by Catholic clerics and religious. One of these is the institutional "shape" that the church has developed over centuries For the sake of victims, past and present, it is urgent that we identify and admit the truth about this, so this chapter will look more closely at institutions and how they can affect the behavior of the people who are their members. *Institution* can mean several things:

1. *an organization or society made up of people who share a particular goal;*
2. *a well-established and structured pattern of behavior and relationships that has become part of a culture*

Examples of the first kind of institution are universities, trade unions, parliaments and armies. The second kind is not a physical entity of people or buildings, but an established custom such as marriage; funeral rites; Independence Day or ANZAC Day; a country's legal system; and not least,

Clerical Errors

caste. In this chapter we will look at the church as a vast organization of people—an institution of the first kind—within which there has developed an institution of the second kind: a clerical caste.

The earliest human groupings were probably family clusters, formed naturally from blood relationships, in which individuals learned the obvious advantages of working together and being loyal to each other. While some have imagined that humans tend naturally towards conflict, like the marooned boys in William's Golding's *Lord of the Flies*, others take a much more optimistic view.[1] They point out that early humans, knowing the pleasures of companionship, affection and love, would readily help each other to achieve their material needs for food, shelter and security. Our ancient ancestors would probably have reinforced their findings about the advantages of collaboration from observing the ant hill, beehive, and hunting pack.

Institutions of the first kind mentioned above seem inevitably to develop a sense of identity and power, behaving in some ways as individuals do. The law sometimes grants them the status of being an artificial "person". Throughout history, political, religious and commercial institutions have formed alliances; stronger groups have overcome weaker ones, seizing their territories or enslaving their peoples. Such was the origin of city states, kingdoms, empires and the trading companies that exploited the "New World". From the earliest times too, large numbers of people have united in religious worship and collaborated, perhaps with some degree of coercion, to build megalithic tombs, pyramids and temples that still impress us.

Institutions tend to form among the followers of inspiring individuals who attract followers but may not necessarily have intended to found and lead an institution. It can be argued that this was the case with the Buddha, Socrates, Jesus, St Francis of Assisi and Gandhi. In times of social upheaval, to meet some need in contemporary society, charismatic leaders like Saints Basil and Benedict, Catherine McAuley, Edmund Rice, and Mary McKillop have deliberately led bands of women or men to educate poor children or nurse the sick. Other kinds of leaders, clearly driven more by self-interest, have founded empires: Napoleon, Lenin, Hitler, Mao Tse Tung and many others.

Institutions of every kind tend to symbolize their power by a heraldic emblem, motto, logo or mission statement. Some establish a rule of life or have their members wear a uniform. Institutions may glorify

1. E.g., Bregman, *Human kind*.

The Amoral Institution

themselves by creating their own myth or "back story," and the grand buildings that institutions erect declare their aim to inspire members, onlookers, or potential customers.

But while institutions can achieve much good, they can have seriously negative aspects. Philosopher Michel Foucauld in particular wrote extensively in criticism of modern institutions that have evolved to educate, punish and heal people: the school, the prison, the clinic. Adolf Hitler and other unscrupulous leaders have turned whole nations into powerful institutions by rewarding with material prosperity people who had known poverty and failure; and by attracting the wealthier with the promise of increased wealth, prestige and power.

Institutions can attract members by what is perhaps an even more potent motive: our desire to be included. C. S. Lewis considered this to be one of our strongest cravings, and warned of its possible negative consequences: "Of all the passions, the passion for the Inner Ring most of all makes a [person] who is not yet . . . bad . . . do very bad things."[2] Being included as a member allows us to feel secure, but whenever we entrust an institution with some of our freedom, we put at risk our adult status and responsibilities. It is not uncommon for members of an institution to allow it to become their essential support system, a kind of exoskeleton, to the point where they see life mainly in terms of their membership and are constantly checking whether they are keeping the institution's rules, conforming to superiors' wishes and earning the rewards due to them. This "shell" may appear to give security, but it can seriously restrict personal growth, cripple individuality and creativity and seriously distort the member's moral choices. Associates can find themselves performing mainly in order to please the leaders who largely control their lives. This loss of freedom would be bad enough if it affected only their own maturity: it becomes worse when it leads the institutional member to make ruthless or inflexible decisions that seriously harm other people. The institution can seriously damage its members if they feel compelled to stay within it when they know it is destructive or evil: when they stay because if they dared to criticize the institution they would be shamed, punished or expelled and left with no other livelihood for their family. Alternatively, members of institutions may be tempted to misuse their institutions' resources and power to enrich themselves or to exploit victims, and then exploit the power of the institution to conceal their wrongdoing. This has happened in every kind of

---

2. C.S. Lewis, *The Inner Ring*.

institution from political parties to police forces; from banks to churches. Public inquiries have often been called to eradicate such corruption but are usually only partly successful.

The leadership positions of institutions attract personalities who are "driven"; who may be highly skilled at manipulating others but may lack feeling for people. It has been found that persons who have these qualities to an extreme extent—who are in fact psychopaths—reach the "top of the tree" at a greater rate than ordinary individuals. Their superficial charm and cunning often enable them to flourish in top positions, at least until the destruction they cause leads to their undoing.[3]

One of the most serious disadvantages of large institutions is that they are impersonal. There is a wide gap between the people who draw up plans and those who carry out orders. This can lessen or even eradicate compassion in the workings of the institution. When higher officials are remote from the people whom their actions affect—when they do not see the faces or hear the voices of those whom their decisions impact—this distance and anonymity can deaden their sensitivity. Lower functionaries may see the effects of the harmful decisions, but since they did not make the decisions, they can claim: "We are only following orders." The effects of this gap can be illustrated by abundant examples.

The book *Ordinary Men* tells the story of a Nazi Reserve Battalion of middle-aged family men who from 1942–43 repeatedly obeyed orders to kill in cold blood thousands of Polish Jews.[4] In another war, hundreds of US and Australian military personnel obeyed orders to spray twenty million gallons of the herbicide Agent Orange over the Vietnam landscape and people. The poison is still causing birth defects in the fourth generation.

The gap can operate in peacetime too. In 2016, office workers in the Australian social service Centrelink sent to thousands of pensioners and beneficiaries computer-generated invoices claiming that the clients owed the Department grossly inflated amounts. Receiving these invoices—"robo-debts"—caused enormous trauma to many fragile people and even drove some to suicide. The debacle resulted in a huge class action against the government.

In the church context, some bishops admitted to the Royal Commission that this same gap, which sociologists call diffusion or displacement of responsibility, must also have existed between the offices of Vatican

---

3. Martha Stout, quoted in Ronson, *Psychopath Test,* 113.
4. Browning, C., *Ordinary Men.*

The Amoral Institution

congregations and children sexually abused by clergy. In each of these typical cases, executive decisions were made in a boardroom or office far from the people whose lives they partly destroyed. The choices were made by people who did not see the devastated landscape and populace; or meet the pensioners traumatized by crippling false debts they could not hope to repay. And executive decisions were made by high-ranking clerics who may never have met a sexually abused child or listened to its grieving parents.

All these examples appear to illustrate Albert Bandura's theory of *Selective Moral Disengagement*, by which persons may act according to strong moral-based reasoning but fail to base their conduct on a true understanding of human—including deviant—behavior. More than rational thinking is needed. When making their decisions, the officials in institutions—including bishops and Roman bureaucrats—have judged situations according to their own inadequate understanding but lacked contact with the emotional realities of human suffering. Christian leaders sanitized the horrific effects by using euphemistic labels, and even redefined as "protecting the church" their own harmful conduct in concealing crimes. The institutional behavior summarized here was bluntly summarized in the report of the Victorian Inquiry, called *Betrayal of Trust*. It showed that prior to the 1990s, senior leaders of the Church had *contributed* to abuse by not disclosing it or responding to it; by trivializing the problem and by ensuring that the Victorian community remained uninformed about it. Those leaders had failed to hold perpetrators accountable, with the tragic result that more children continued to be abused when this could have been avoided. The Report added that the Catholic church as an organization had many features that created high risks that its personnel would perpetrate criminal child abuse. These included its complex hierarchy; a structure which gave great power to bishops and priests; and some flawed beliefs that led to poor processes for reporting or responding to abuse. The *Report* also criticized the Church's self-perception as an institution. Its image of itself as a "perfect society" makes self-criticism very difficult and causes it to treat harshly those who dissent from its institutional behavior, or who advocate for its victims.[5]

Experiments have been conducted which attempted to show how the authority wielded by persons in institutions can affect those people's behavior. At Yale in 1961 Stanley Milgram had official-seeming "supervisors" ordering volunteer "teachers" to administer punishments to volunteer

---

5. *VPI*, xxxi; Cahill and Wilkinson, *Child Sexual Abuse*, 111, 113.

Clerical Errors

"learners" each time they made errors in the tasks they were given.[6] The punishments were electric shocks that increased to a level that the "teachers" believed to be severe. The shocks were merely simulated, but some "teachers" would keep administering them even when they could hear the "learners" crying out in pretended agony. Milgram concluded that his volunteers were doing this solely in obedience to the authority of the grey-coated supervisors.

In 1972 Philip Zimbardo's Stanford Prison Experiment attempted to demonstrate how people might behave when given almost unlimited authority over others. In a make-believe prison, he found that young male volunteers who were arbitrarily assigned to be "guards" soon began to maltreat volunteers arbitrarily assigned to be "prisoners". The "guards" were soon submitting the "prisoners" to dehumanizing indignities. Zimbardo concluded that his experiment demonstrated that when people are given authority and a uniform, and are directed by a forceful leader, they will treat people under their control in ways that their moral sense would not otherwise permit.[7]

Milgram's and Zimbardo's experiments have been criticized as seriously defective in various ways. The critics point out that, besides the fact that some dubious record-keeping was found in both situations, the volunteers were all aware that they were in an experimental, quasi-theatrical setting. This alone would allow them to react differently than in real-life situations. In addition, the complex human motives that operate in such experiments can be variously interpreted. For instance, Milgram's critics point out that his volunteers did in fact resist, more than he admitted, in subtle and indirect ways. The critics also challenge his conclusion that there is a strong capacity for evil lying dormant in everyone, which can be easily awakened in "authoritarian" circumstances.[8]

Those criticisms are no doubt valid, but some decades later, in 2003, events in Iraq made the artificial experiments seem tragically prophetic. Soon after the United States and their allies had invaded Iraq, ordinary soldiers guarding Iraqi prisoners in Abu Ghraib and other military jails were

6. https://en.wikipedia.org/wiki/Milgram_experiment.
7. Zimbardo, *Lucifer Effect* 354.
8. Perry, *Behind the Shock Machine*; Bregman, *Human kind*.
  Also https://news.wisc.edu/infamous-study-of-humanitys-dark-side-may-actually-show-how-to-keep-it-at-bay/.

The Amoral Institution

found to be demeaning and torturing prisoners to extreme levels, in ways that cannot be called human.

The official investigation of the Abu Ghraib atrocities, as well as an independent psychological analysis, found that the monstrous abuses resulted not from extraordinarily evil individuals, but from *ordinary* guards responding in the institutional setting.[9] The guards learned from what others were doing; they collectively obeyed authority; they were encouraged to act-out their emotional prejudices against the "enemy" that were prevalent in the army. Deeper investigation has revealed that it was military commanders at the highest level who had given permission and encouragement to treat prisoners in *whatever ways* the guards might think useful to make them give up information.[10] In other words, the inhuman behavior was strongly assisted by the institution to which the soldiers had sworn allegiance.

Lest we are inclined to dismiss Abu Ghraib as an anomaly, the same combination of institutional factors has produced similar crimes in every war: physical power; a sense of being morally unaccountable; psychological distance from their victims and anonymity in the perpetrators. Some atrocities are well-documented, like the massacre in 1968 of some 500 men, women and children by US troops at My Lai in Vietnam, but again, deeper investigation shows that there were many similar massacres of non-combatants during that prolonged invasion.

Despite their original high ideals, institutions can lose their first enthusiasm. Monasteries and religious orders were founded in poverty and simplicity, with exalted ideals of following Christ, but when they grew to have hundreds of members, they faced entirely new challenges. The need for large-scale material supplies and complex management inevitably changed the original vision. The Christian church itself began as a fast-growing network of small communities of enthusiastic people, but by the fourth century it had taken on a considerable institutional structure. Liberated and helped by Constantine and later emperors, it acquired new wealth and property. Its large basilicas and complex politics were vastly different from the small communities of mostly poor people among whom it began. Chapters 8 and 9 will look more closely at the evolution of its priesthood and Eucharist.

It is when institutions begin to lose their original fervor that they make self-serving decisions which, although small, can accumulate and

---

9. Zimbardo, *Lucifer Effect*, 354.
10. Greenberg and Dratel, *Torture Papers*.

lead to larger errors, changing the organization in crucial ways. Small errors can accumulate like snowflakes piling up on a branch, until they eventually bring the institution to a point where it betrays its principles, catastrophically. In the case of the church, cumulative clerical errors have come to betray seriously the gospel on which it was founded. When this happens, reform becomes essential. Through two millennia, the church has profoundly influenced humanity by bringing to millions of people the incalculable benefit of discovering the transcendent Good News of the gospel. But inseparably entangled with these benefits have been serious errors and abuse of power, stemming largely from the institutional structures that its members have added to the church.

Previous chapters have already amply shown how structures within the church-institution have come into conflict with the gospel. Do we need to be reminded of some notorious historical examples? That the papacy officially condoned the violent treatment and enslavement of Indigenous races; that *Inquisitions* attempted to maintain conformity of belief by inhuman punishments; that even under recent popes, church bureaucrats—particularly the secretive CDF—have denied natural justice to authors, theologians, and bishops by the threat, or the sentence, of excommunication? Theologians Leonardo Boff, Tissa Balasuriya and Paul Collins; Bishop William Morris of Toowoomba, and many others, are witness to these abuses of power.[11]

Clerical legislators have made laws that favored and protected clerical reputations, inevitably at the expense of victims. Senior clerics, to their credit, are now admitting what this failure can lead to. When the report on Cardinal McCarrick was published, Cardinal Cupich of Chicago admitted that it laid bare four decades of institutional decision-making which had led to lamentable failures.[12]

Cardinal Clancy, as President of the Australian Bishops' Conference, wrote to Pope John Paul II conveying the Conference's unanimous request that two statutes in canon law be urgently reviewed. Clancy did not even receive a reply.[13] Likewise, Auxiliary Bishop Pat Power of Canberra-Goulburn sent letters to three popes in succession, recommending improvements to regulations. None of his letters was even acknowledged. They were probably never delivered, but deflected by the bureaucrats who surround the pope as they encircle every monarchical leader. The situation within

11. Collins, *Modern Inquisition;* Morris, *Benedict, Me and Cardinals Three.*
12. *NCR* November 16, 2020.
13. *RCFR,* 16, 2, 326.

The Amoral Institution

the church-institution was summed up by an experienced lawyer who had served in a wide range of roles in the US legal system, including that of State Supreme Court judge. He remarked that he had never encountered an organization as duplicitous and manipulative as the Catholic Church.

There is sufficient evidence to show that the whole enormous disaster of clerical child abuse and its concealment is closely linked to the presumption that the church-institution is "holy" and so must be free of the problems that afflict other institutions. To expect or demand that the church is exempt from being judged in the same way as other institutions is the nadir of clericalism. Crime is crime, whoever commits it.

Far from being unchanging or "eternal", the papacy has evolved to resemble the absolute monarchs of former times or modern totalitarian dictatorships. As a hierarchical pyramid the church often breaches the principal of subsidiarity, a basic principle of Catholic teaching on social justice. The bureaucrats in Vatican Congregations (Departments) often ignore bishops' ancient rights as leaders of local churches by bullying them, for instance, by presuming to set the agenda for bishops' synods. In 1997 the Vatican congregations that oversee bishops and evangelization forbade diocesan synods to discuss such pastorally important matters as the ordination of married men or of women, birth control within marriage, and homosexuality. They also advised the bishops that it would be "imprudent" to discuss any matters concerning the life and ministry of priests.[14]

Caste

Caste is an example of the second kind of institution that this chapter is examining: *a well-established and structured pattern of behavior and relationships that has become part of a culture*. As such caste is an artificial and fixed ranking of persons according to their imagined value and standing in a society.[15] To understand clericalism, we need to understand caste, for clericalism shares most of caste's characteristics.

Each person is unique, each different from all others. We may rank them by their different *acquired* skills and by their achievements; but it is against natural justice, and simply untrue, to claim that any person or class is *essentially* superior to another. However, it is precisely on this false claim that any caste system is established. The assertion of superiority has been

14. Cahill and Wilkinson, *Child Sexual Abuse*, 32.
15. Wilkerson, *Caste*, Location 1302.

Clerical Errors

variously based on historical conquest, superior wealth and power or even the authority of Scriptures. Caste is found not only among Hindus, but to varying degrees exists in most societies. Caste is more fixed than social class and creates stronger boundaries. It is a kind of script that earlier generations have written for the current generation, allotting character-roles for each group.

A person might change their religion or move to a different social class by being educated or acquiring wealth, but it is much more difficult to move out of the caste into which one is born. The result is that in many societies the *imaginary* divisions of caste generally produce a *real* division. People who have wealth, power, and security are separated from those who are poor, vulnerable, and de*nigra*ted [sic]. People in upper castes, who may be otherwise good and kind, have their own reasons for not questioning the institution of caste, or doing anything towards changing it. Curiously, those in a lower caste can be content to uphold the caste system, for at least it provides them with a secure place in the hierarchy.[16] It has been reasonably argued that racism, one of the commonest examples of caste, is not just a manifestation of personal bigotry or animus but is systemic: embedded in institutions, culture, values and laws. Critical race theory is exposing the truth that even the legal advances that help people of color, tend even more to serve the interests of the dominant white society.[17]

The institution of caste can lead people to treat others in ways that are totally amoral. Caste has been shown to affect African Americans in the USA and First Nations in Australia as much as it affects Dalits in India, and formerly impacted on Jews in Nazi Germany.[18] Its assumptions become unquestioned, like the common laws of physics, not even needing to be spoken. In 1919 it was the madness of caste that led white people on a public Chicago beach to stone and drown the black youth Eugene Williams, because he inadvertently waded past an imaginary line dividing the "white" beach from the "black".

It was also caste that in Australia enabled Europeans to take the lands of the First Nations people while officially declaring that no one was occupying those lands. Although most white Australians do not appear to think in terms of caste, it was deep assumptions about Indigenous inferiority which enabled Europeans to massacre and dispossess tens of thousands of First

16. Wilkerson, *Caste*, Location 1325.
17. Delgado and Stefancic, *Critical Race Theory*.
18. Wilkerson, *Caste*, Location 585.

Nations people; and to remove eight generations of "half-caste" children from their parents. In the twenty-first century, assumptions of caste still allow Australia to jail Indigenous persons at an enormously higher rate than Whites and tolerate them dying in jail at a rate much higher than White prisoners. Submerged feelings of caste can emerge with ferocity, on slight provocation. This was seen in 2013, when champion Aboriginal footballer Adam Goodes dared to challenge a young spectator who had called him an ape. Although the matter between them was soon settled amicably, at all future matches, large sections of the crowd continued relentlessly to "boo" every move Goodes made until he felt forced to abandon his outstanding football career.

A caste system has no more basis in science or logic than does a system that classifies people by "race". In 1922 the US Supreme Court denied citizenship to a Japanese man because, the court said, the legal term "white" does not mean skin color but depends on "Caucasian" ancestry. When analyzed however, *Caucasian*, like *Aryan* is a totally artificial category, now abandoned by scientists. Again, as late as 1983 a Louisiana law defined all persons as "Black" who had as little as 1/32 of "Negro blood".[19] Despite being irrational and arbitrary, caste and race lead to a kind of collective madness that feeds on lies and half-truths and draws real boundaries between groups which keep them in their "proper place".

Clericalism as Caste

Is clericalism, which pervades the Catholic Church, a form of caste? The question is important, because especially in situations involving crime and the law, the concept can deeply affect the physical and mental health of the persons against whom it is used. Our detour into the effects of caste was necessary in order to understand the powerful persistence of clericalism and the results it can produce. The central evil of caste is that it *divides* people, whereas the Good News of Jesus, which the church professes to teach, is that all people are *united* by being radically equal as children of God, are actually "one body".[20] Hence the existence of caste among Christ's followers is particularly evil. But early in the history of the church, when clerics assumed unique control over the Eucharist, the church's central means of attaining unity, the foundations of a clerical caste were laid. The evolution

---

19. Wilkerson, *Caste*, Location 582, 1555.
20. The expression is common in the New Testament: e.g., Rom 12:5.

Clerical Errors

of this caste eventually produced a kind of apartheid in the church. Like other caste systems, clericalism has produced attitudes, even a culture, which idealize and favor the more powerful group. In crucial ways clerics came to be seen as different from and superior to "ordinary" members of the church.

That clericalism does this can be seen by comparing some of its foundational "pillars" with those which support other forms of caste.[21]

1. Caste is said to originate in the Divine will and the laws of nature. Canon 107 of the 1917 *Code* declared that "it is of divine institution that there are in the church clerics, distinct from laity". Like all Catholics, I was taught from childhood that the clerical hierarchy was founded by Jesus, when he ordained men as clerics to lead the Eucharist. Chapter 8 will show that in fact Jesus did *not* do this, and that the theory that clerics are ontologically different from other people arose from medieval interpretations of the sacraments. The 1917 *Code* also declared that only clerics have the power of "orders" and of "jurisdiction",[22] and that all the faithful owe reverence to clerics, "according to [clerics'] different levels". The faithful were also warned that to harm a cleric seriously is to commit the sin of sacrilege.[23] This canon contains a terrible irony, when we consider the countless children whose innocent lives have been sacrilegiously damaged by clerics' sexual crimes, but who have been silenced in favor of the clerics who abused them.

2. and 3. These pillars do not apply to clerics, for they deal with how caste is inherited, and with prohibitions of marrying outside one's caste.

4. Contact with "inferior" castes is considered to pollute "higher" castes. Blacks were banned from using public facilities in northern and southern states of USA and in South Africa. Christians from ancient times received the bread of the Eucharist as they received any food, in their hands. The clerical caste later banned anyone but clerics from touching the consecrated bread or even the "sacred vessels". For centuries, until the 1970s, lay people were obliged to receive the consecrated bread by having it placed on their tongue, as infants are fed. They were not even permitted to wash the cloths used to wipe the

---

21. Wilkerson, *Caste*, Location 1696.
22. *Codex*, Canon 196. Schillebeeckx, *Church with a Human Face*, 205
23. *Codex*, Canon 119.

The Amoral Institution

chalice at Mass,[24] and women were forbidden to enter the sacred space of the "sanctuary", when Mass was being celebrated.

5. Caste dictates the occupations one can engage in. In the southern states of the US after the Civil War, "persons of color" were forbidden by law from being artisans, mechanics, shopkeepers etc., unless they paid an impossible $100 for an annual license. Blacks were therefore confined to farm work and domestic service and later found success through music and entertainment. Conversely, Canon Law forbade clerics from lessening their dignity by bearing arms, practicing medicine, joining political parties or frequenting theatres or taverns.

   Christine Schrenk assures us that "There is absolutely no question that women served as deacons in both the eastern and western churches,"[25] and probably led the eucharistic ceremony. But the church forgot the gospel's radicalism and quite soon succumbed to the caste system of patriarchal societies, as we see in the commands given to women in the post-Paul Letters to Timothy and Titus.

6. Lower castes are controlled by being dehumanized. Black slaves and Indian Dalits—"Untouchables"—were strictly forbidden to become literate. The Negro caste was ridiculed; used as targets in fair-ground games or mimicked by Whites in "black-face" concerts. Aborigines and slaves were given mocking nicknames; Jews were made to wear yellow stars, and as prisoners were tattooed with a number that replaced their name. On a similar principle, Indigenous people in colonial territories were not permitted to become priests. Nor could any man be ordained who had a disability such as epilepsy, or whose appearance might cause ridicule. Early and Medieval theologians, following Greek philosophers, judged women as inferior, so that still, today, they are forbidden by clerical law—not Scripture or theology—from being ordained.[26]

7. Caste is enforced by fear. Extreme violence has been used against those who dared to transgress caste boundaries. Slaves were often tortured to death for escaping. As late as the first decades of the twentieth century, every three or four days a black person was lynched in the USA, usually on false charges of liaising with white women.

---

24. *Codex*, Canon 1306.
25. *NCR*, July 22, 2021.
26. Wijngaards, *What They Don't Teach*.

Clerical Errors

Similarly, clerics have made liberal use of the doctrine of eternal torment in hell to encourage people to lead moral lives. In addition, during many centuries, clerics enforced conformity to their view of orthodoxy by Inquisitions that used torture and executed obstinate dissenters. Today, any cleric who challenges "orthodox doctrine", or tries to restore equality to the church by, for instance, adapting liturgy to people's needs, will soon be pressured by self-appointed guardians of clericalism. These have often been known to report priests or bishops, anonymously, to Roman authorities. Many "liberal" bishops and priests, such as Bishop William Morris in Toowoomba, have been reported in this way, and as a result dismissed from their position or "suspended" from working as clerics.[27]

8. Higher castes claim to be inherently superior. Blacks and Dalits were compelled by law to address their "superiors" by the titles "Mister", or "Sir"; and to give way to them in the street. In the clerical caste titles abound: Reverend, (literally, "to be revered"); Most Reverend; Monsignor, (literally "My Lord"); Your Grace; Your Eminence. Clerics of "higher" rank expected "lower" clerics and laity to kiss their ring on coming into their presence. From the eleventh century until the twentieth, the bishop's house was called his "palace".

A deference to caste has often led otherwise good clerics to disregard the suffering of abuse victims. Whenever a bishop moved a pedophile priest, he was implicitly deciding that the children who were the criminal's victims were less important and of less value than the reputation of the cleric, and the clerical caste as a whole. It was not uncommon for church authorities to be hostile towards families who sought justice against criminal priests, and senior clerics often felt justified in lying to complainants. The tragic lists in chapter 2 show the results of this imbalance of power between castes.

The Trinity as Model

We can recognize the evils that institutions commit, and we may strive to eradicate the clerical errors that caste has led to, but what exemplar or standard can we use to reform this institution? It may seem surprising that the most obscure mystery of Christian faith, the mystery of God as a Trinity, offers the best model for community. Early Christian thinkers discerned

27. Collins, *Modern Inquisition*.

The Amoral Institution

from the New Testament that God is not a solitary monarch or despot, but a mystery of three distinct "Persons", mutually indwelling and interpenetrating. The Persons are three, but more profoundly one. Early theologians used a quaint metaphor to describe them as engaged in *perichoresis*, an eternal dance of equal, loving exchange.

Christians are familiar with the idea that the gospels urge us as *individuals* to imitate God by being compassionate,[28] but it is less noticed that Jesus also urged us as *communities* to become like the Trinity. The gospel of John has Jesus saying to the community: "love one another *as* I have loved you",[29] but he had previously said: "*as* the Father has loved me, *so* I have loved you."[30] In whatever community we find ourselves, we are challenged to strive towards the absolute equality of selfless love that is shared between Father and Son: the Infinite Love which in fact *is* the Holy Spirit.

There is no supremacy or hierarchy within the Trinity: it is a community of totally equal Persons. It is the model for Christians living and working together, giving and receiving without subordination or opposition; as friends who mutually care for each another. In sad contrast, our church's pyramid structure has become distorted into a monarchy, a pyramid constructed of lesser pyramids: of dioceses and parishes ruled by officials of decreasing rank, all of them male. One of the worst effects of this structure is that it continues to distort the way we think about God. The main concept of God given to the world by two millennia of Christianity is the concept of *Almighty* God. This model suggests a supremely powerful male dictator, like the Roman emperor or similar absolute monarchs who ruled their pyramid-society by fear. Can we imagine what the church would be like if it had preserved in its structures the *equality* that Jesus taught, and had evolved into a network of communities based on love?

When institutions, including the church, do evil, to what extent are the individual members responsible? The question is complex. Each of us is a member of many large, overlapping institutions: we belong to a nation which may engage in unjust war; we daily consume the products of multinational corporations, thus augmenting the profits of institutions that are often guilty of exploiting, even enslaving, the workers who supply their products. When we buy our cheap clothing, mobile phones and other equipment we contribute constantly to this abuse. These corporations also cause

28. Luke 6:36.
29. John 15:12.
30. John 15:9.

Clerical Errors

enormous destruction to the environment and augment the global warming that will burden the lives of future generations. While we benefit from the comforts and convenience that these purchases bring us, can we be excused from their grave negative consequences that we do not care to see?

We have seen how persons in authority can put pressure on their subordinates to do wrong; and, how distance and anonymity may let both groups feel less responsible when the victims being hurt are not known as individual persons. What of us who are church members? To what extent are we responsible for the errors of the clerical institution and those who lead it? One of the consequences of those distorted structures and personal errors was the higher-than-average percentage of little ones who have been abused. If we accept a clericalized church, to what extent do we bear responsibility? If more church members had been alert to clericalism, would not the crimes have been sooner noticed and reported?

Isn't there mutual influence here? Institutions form us, and at the same time we contribute to forming them by accepting their flaws. Our choices contribute to the quality and behavior of the institutions we belong to, including the church. Members build up a sound institution by their wisdom and love, but by semi-deliberate ignorance, by their errors and malice, members can make an institution sick. A sick institution can exert strong pressure on its members which further distorts their actions. In all this, however, each member always retains an inner core of freedom. In World Wars I and II, governments exerted immense pressure on their citizens to take up arms, but a few conscientious objectors bravely resisted. Some found the courage even to face execution rather than surrender their personal integrity.[31]

People who face dilemmas in any setting deserve our compassion. The poem *Eighth Air Force*, by Randall Jarrell, shows how complex the situation can be for persons within an institution. Jarrell was one of the millions of young people drawn to fight in World War II, largely ignorant of what lay ahead. Many soon found themselves commanded, under threat of severe military discipline, to do what they would never otherwise have done: to kill innocent people. Can we condemn them as guilty?

Those combatants who did not die young were often haunted for the rest of their lives by the evil they had committed or witnessed. Jarrell was part of a US bomber crew, and in the poem reflects on his flights over "enemy" cities, killing and maiming countless unknown people. After the war

---

31. Baxter, *We Will Not Cease*; Jaegerstetter, *A Hidden Life*.

The Amoral Institution

he returned to writing poetry, but post-traumatic stress led to depression and an early death, possibly by suicide.

His poem shows bomber crews resting in their quarters between "missions". Some relax with a game of pitch or play with their mascot puppy. One sergeant, still drunk at breakfast-time, whistles as he shaves. Another lies on his bunk, near-hysterical from the stress of facing death almost every night. The young airmen are hardly aware of the human devastation they are committing on each raid, but Jarrell frankly calls them "murderers" and includes himself in the accusation. But he wrestles with the ambiguity of their situation, and then excuses them, but has to admit he is lying when he does so. He concludes by comparing himself to Pontius Pilate:

> Men wash their hands, in blood, as best they can:
> I find no fault in this just man.

But can we Catholics claim to be wholly innocent of our church's guilt? As a whole community, are we doing as much as possible to prevent and to heal the guilt? It has taken us a long time to see through the errors of clerical power: can we see, at last, that we need to change radically the pyramid structure of the institutional church? The church's hierarchical structure and the aberration of a clerical caste were constructed by human beings. Therefore they can be transformed by the efforts of its own members. After chapters 8 and 9 examine the clerical errors made during the evolution of the priesthood and Eucharist, the final chapter will propose practical steps towards correcting those errors: towards transforming and renewing the church.

8

Temple and Priesthood Restored

THE GOSPEL OF MARK reports that at the moment Jesus died, "the veil of the temple was torn in two, from top to bottom".[1] Whether or not this actually happened, Mark was telling the Christian community for which he was writing that the temple was no longer the center of their belief and worship. During his lifetime Jesus had respected the temple, which was central to his Jewish heritage. As child and adult, he went there for the great feasts,[2] but he was about to fulfil and transcend both the temple and the Jewish Law: ". . . something greater than the temple is here."[3] John's gospel presents him saying that true worshippers will no longer use *any* temple but will worship God "in spirit and truth."[4]

At the climax of his public life Jesus symbolically "cleansed" the temple by driving out the people who were buying and selling there, thereby challenging the authorities who permitted such abuse. John's gospel, written after the temple had been destroyed by Roman armies, also recalls Jesus saying: "Destroy this temple, and in three days I will raise it up," referring to his resurrection.[5] A few decades later, the Letter to the Hebrews would describe in metaphor how Christians, who had intimate

1. Mark 15:38.
2. Luke 2:41.
3. Matt 12:6.
4. John 4:23.
5. John 2:19–21.

Temple and Priesthood Restored

contact with God because Christ's Spirit was in them, could now enter the true sanctuary "not of this created order". The "door" of this sanctuary was the risen Christ himself.[6]

But for some time after Jesus' resurrection the first Christians continued to pray each day in the temple: "Peter and John used to go up to the Temple for the afternoon prayer".[7] But Luke adds a new thing: they met regularly in their houses "for the breaking of bread".

The temple where those Jewish Christians prayed was centuries old, but much older temples had preceded it. Millennia before Jerusalem existed, humans had wondered about a Transcendent Reality, a realm beyond their senses. What could explain the incomprehensible violence and majesty of storms and volcanoes? What lay behind the enigma of birth and death? Trying to connect with that mysterious realm, they built shrines and temples. The earliest that we know is in modern Turkey, at Gobekli Tepe, which dates from around 10,000 BCE, and many later temples can be found in Egypt, China, Persia, India, and the Americas. The Hebrew people's tradition describes them coming gradually to believe in a sole, supreme God, for whom they built a temple under Solomon, around 1000 BCE.

Humanity has attempted to describe the transcendent Mystery with words that separate it from ordinary life. Typical is the ancient Greek *hagios;* literally "separate from earth"; or the Roman word *templum,* derived from the Indo-European root "to cut". It describes a place "cut off" from everyday activities and dedicated to the gods. The Hebrew people, whose word for holy—*qadosh*—is also derived from "separate", hung a veil in their Jerusalem temple to separate the outside world from the Holy of Holies where the One whose name they would not utter was thought to dwell among them.

The Hebraic tradition, as expressed in the mythical language of Genesis, was gradually learning that the unseen Creator was friendly. God is described as walking and conversing with the first human couple. Even after they had rebelled against the divine commands, God still kindly provided them with clothes.[8] The prophets described God's friendship in even more intimate terms, and the summit of Judeo-Christian revelation saw the Wisdom of God

---

6. Heb 9:12, 10:20.
7. Acts 3:1, 2:46.
8. Gen 3:21.

Clerical Errors

joined to humanity in Jesus of Nazareth. He is called *Immanuel*—God with us—for "The Word became flesh and lived among us".[9]

The heart of the Christian gospel—which means Good News—is that God is our friend, with whom we can achieve intimate union. Jesus taught that for those who base their lives on love ". . . my Father will love them, and we will come to them and make our home with them".[10] Saint Paul told his disciples that "You [the community] are God's temple."[11] He went so far as to say that this intimate link could become shared identity: "Now you are the body of Christ and individually members of it".[12] The uncreated Sacred is no longer separate from "profane" creatures, and this intimacy is the foundation of Christian prayer and worship. Mark's symbol of the torn temple-veil stated powerfully that we no longer need temples. However, within a few centuries of Jesus' resurrection, Christians were once again building temples which resembled the Jerusalem Holy of Holies. It can be shown that this about-turn was one of the major "clerical errors" that are the subject of this book.

Ritual is an integral part of human life. We create formal ceremonies to mark the events of birth, marriage and death and many occasions in between. We use small rituals when we greet each other or eat and drink together, and we devise more solemn rituals by which we try to worship the Transcendent. In themselves, rituals are functionally useless for material life, but they deepen our humanity in real ways. Even the simplest symbols and rites can lift us beyond the physical plane, but like any human activity, they can also seduce and enslave us.

When the emperor Constantine's *Edict of Milan* freed the church from persecution in 313 CE, Christian communities were able to gather safely for public prayer. They were given, or soon built, public halls called basilicas, similar to the pagan temples that were abundant in every city. Since these Christian buildings needed a staff of officials to maintain and protect them and conduct the worship within them, the development of the church as an institution took a great leap forward.

It is curious that about a century later there began to appear in these Christian churches a structure known as the *templon*, which separated the ministers who led the Eucharist from the people attending the ceremony.

9. John 1:14.
10. John 14:23.
11. 1 Cor 3:17.
12. 1 Cor 12:27.

Temple and Priesthood Restored

The oldest surviving example of a *templon* (ca 463 CE) is in the basilica of St John the Baptist at Stoudios in Constantinople. It is a low wall separating the main nave of the church from the sanctuary, or "holy area", which could be entered via three doors in the *templon*. What could have moved the custodians of Christian churches to build this structure? Was it merely the practical purpose of keeping the crowd back from the leaders' activities? If this was the original reason, the simple physical structure soon took on ritual and spiritual significance. It developed into a higher wall called the *iconastasis* which is still found in many Eastern churches. In the West, it later took the form of the *rood screen*, on which hung a large cross. In each case, the structure eventually re-created an area like the Jewish temple's Holy of Holies, into which no "lay persons", and certainly no women, could enter. The rood screen played less part in the liturgy than the *iconastasis*. It was gradually reduced to low "altar rails" with a central gate, and was removed in the liturgical reforms following the Second Vatican Council.

Those who installed the first *templons* in their churches might have been remembering the veil which cut off the holy of holies in the Jerusalem temple. Although that temple had been destroyed in 70 CE, the stories in the Old and New Testaments kept it constantly before the minds of Christians. The *templon*-builders may also have had in mind the *proskenion* wall behind the stage of every Greek and Roman theatre. This screen had three doors through which the actors came and went and was itself derived from the grand facades of pagan temples. Like those temples, the *proskenion* was adorned with statues, and the *ikonastasis* in churches also came to be covered with icons of Christ and the saints. The first *templons* did not obscure the congregation's view of the eucharistic table, but as time passed, the *iconastasis* grew higher and completely concealed it.

But the *templon* also concealed a fundamental error. Although probably built first for practical reasons, and later intended to add beauty and mystery to people's worship of the Holy One, the *templon* caused Christians to lose sight of Christ's revolutionary teaching that God lives within each person. Our attention is easily turned aside from this profound and fundamental belief to the less personally demanding, and more external, celebration of the "holy mysteries" in a "holy place" Although the shift of attention may not have been deliberate, the return of a "temple" with two distinct areas also undermined the radical Christian teaching that all people are fundamentally equal.

Clerical Errors

The *iconastasis* and rood screen became spaces where beautiful art was displayed. Temples of all kinds can move us to a deep sense of awe and of prayer, but this considerable benefit cannot justify the distortion to which church architecture eventually contributed. As will be seen in chapter 9, the simple community meal that Jesus exhorted his followers to celebrate became a mysterious rite conducted behind a wall, largely unseen by those who had been invited to "do this in memory of me".

How could it be that within a few centuries of Jesus resurrection, both "temple" and "priests" were re-established in the Christian church?[13] Among the complex reasons for this evolution, two dubious developments stand out:

1. The error of likening the Eucharist to First Testament sacrifices.

2. Errors in the development of leadership in the Christian community.

Errors about the Eucharist as Sacrifice

At Jesus' death, the ripped dividing-curtain showed that the temple was now superfluous and the Jewish priesthood redundant. Those priests had functioned as mediators between God and the people: they explained what God wanted, and offered sacrifices for the populace. The primary meaning of sacrifice—*sacrum facere*—is "to make holy". A sacrifice was something offered to improve one's relationship—to bring about at-one-ment—with God.[14] The first Christians were mostly Jews who had been raised in the ancient culture centered on the temple. Not surprisingly they saw everything by its fading glow, and naturally used analogies and metaphors drawn from its cult to explain the wonderful new situation in which they found themselves. They realized that Jesus' resurrection and the gift of his Spirit gave them a new and profound union with God: made them holy. Is it surprising that they called Jesus the Lamb of God, who had been sacrificed?[15] But they were inventing a metaphor: Jesus was not a sheep!

The Jewish people had cherished the covenant which God had established with their ancestor Abraham. At the Last Supper Jesus expressed in

13. Armour *Call*, 38.

14. 'a true sacrifice is every work which is done that we may be united with God in holy fellowship ...' St Augustine, quoted in Aquinas, *Super Sent.*, lib. 3 d. 9 q. 1 a. 1 qc. 2 arg. 1.

15. John 2:29, Acts 8:32, 1 Cor 5:7, 1 Pet 1:19, Rev 5:6.

Temple and Priesthood Restored

words and a simple ritual that he was establishing a *New* Covenant which made that divine bond even stronger. The intense love that drove Jesus to give his whole life for humanity, defying our worst injustices and lies, showed him to be priest *par excellence*. The author of the Letter to the Hebrews repeated this in many ways: that Christ is the ultimate high priest whose own life and death was a gift that surpassed and replaced all temple sacrifices.[16] But it not suggested in Hebrews, a late New Testament writing, nor anywhere else in the New Testament, that Jesus ordained anyone as a priest to offer sacrifice.[17] Jesus' reported invitation at his last meal, to "do this in memory of me", did not institute any person as a priest (*hiereus*). His words as reported in the gospels were eventually used in most eucharistic Prayers, but not in all of them. It is also significant that the presider at the Christian Eucharist does not pronounce those words as if he is presuming to stand in Jesus' place: he speaks them as *quoting* Jesus.

Christians began to realize that by obeying Christ's central command to love, they were imitating his life and uniting themselves to him. Since they depicted Christ's life metaphorically as *resembling* a sacrifice of the old kind, they used the same metaphor to describe their own efforts to live as he did.

New Testament writers often describe ordinary Christians as a "holy priesthood who offer *spiritual sacrifices* acceptable to God" and urge them to "present your bodies as a *living sacrifice*",[18] but in no place is this metaphorical Christian "priesthood" linked with the role of leading the Eucharist.[19] And although the New Testament writers speak of many diverse gifts that the Spirit gives to Christians, they never mention a special gift or power to "consecrate" or lead the Eucharist.[20] Nor was any follower of Christ described as priest in that context.[21] The first-century *Didache* used the word sacrifice in the same analogical sense, and when discussing the Eucharist, that document did not use the term priest for the person who presided. Only later would that metaphorical title come into use.[22] When the earliest Christians worshipped God, "no animals were harmed", and no priests were needed!

16. Heb 2:17, 3:1, 4:14, 5:5–6, 9, 6:20, 7:11, 17, 20–21, 26, 8:1, 3, 9:11, 10:21.
17. Brown, Priest and Bishop, 16.
18. 1 Pet 2:5, 9; Rom 12:1, 15:16; Heb 13:15; Phil 2:17.
19. Brown, Priest and Bishop, 16.
20. Schillebeeckx, *Church with a Human Face*, 119.
21. Congar, *Priest and Layman*, 74–78.
22. Brown, *Priest and Bishop*, 16.

Errors in the Development of Christian Community Leadership

The restoration of the temple and priesthood is linked with the misuse of authority. Although the first Christian communities were joyful and charismatic, they faced the same problems as any community. If they were to survive to share Christ's Good News with the outside world, they needed leaders with authority to keep order among their diverse members and to correct any behavior that endangered the community. More fundamentally, they needed to preserve the nature of the group by defining what they believed and where they were going.

All leaders, whether of small communities or large institutions, must resist the temptation to misuse their power or the material resources in their care: the inclination to serve themselves rather than those they are appointed to serve. History is littered with leaders who have abused their wealth and power, and the Christian church, including the modern Vatican, has not been exempt. The First Testament contains stories warning about this danger. The people of Israel were warned *not* to ask for a king,[23] advice that has since been amply justified by the countless leaders who have degenerated into tyrants.

In the New Testament, leadership is always spoken of as *diakonia*, service to the community. Jesus turned upside down the concept of greatness by pointing to a child as the ideal.[24] He rebuked his disciples for their incipient clericalism,[25] and himself washed his followers' feet, a task normally done by slaves.[26] The *Third Letter of John* criticized a certain Diotrephes "who likes to put himself first", going against the explicit advice Jesus had given to his followers.[27] Clearly, in Christian communities, there was to be no hierarchic relationship of masters and subjects, but when the New Testament frankly admits lapses within Jesus' own team, we can know that this very human error has been occurring in the church from its earliest days.

Who were the leaders in the new Christian communities? Jesus chose twelve men, whom he called apostles,[28] whose main function seems to have

---

23. Judg 9:8–15; 1 Sam 8:11–18.
24. Mark 9:35–37; Matt 18:1–6; Luke 9:46–48.
25. Mark 9:38–40; Luke 9:49–50.
26. John 13:3–6.
27. 3 John: 9.
28. Matt 10:2–4; Mark 3:14–19; Luke 6:13–16.

Temple and Priesthood Restored

been to symbolize the twelve tribes of ancient Israel in the new spiritual Reign of God. The twelve served as witnesses to Jesus' Resurrection and took a leading part in crucial decisions of the early Jerusalem community.[29] They are never mentioned as leading specific communities, and were not replaced after their deaths, but fade from the written story. Jesus singled out Peter as leader,[30] but also gave to the community of disciples the authority to bind and loose.[31]

Leadership did not develop uniformly everywhere: there was variety in the way the churches were led. Paul advised Timothy to appoint elders[32], and the *Didache* advised each community to "Select for yourselves *episkopoi* and deacons..."[33] The word *episkopos*, from which the English term bishop would later be derived, meant an overseer or supervisor. In some communities the leader was called by the earlier term presbyter (*presbuteros*), a term from Judaism, meaning an elder. In most of the New Testament and the *Didache* both terms are used as equivalent,[34] but St Paul used only the term *episkopos*.[35] Presbyters are sometimes mentioned in the plural, possibly showing that some communities were led by a council of elders. By whichever name they were called, these leaders were not seen as superior to the itinerant, charismatic prophets, and the idea of bishop as sole "monarchical" leader did not emerge until well after the New Testament era.

The Acts of the Apostles and the Letters to Timothy and Titus describe leaders of local churches being appointed by prayer and the "laying on of hands".[36] Paul and Barnabas were also selected in this way for their special mission to preach. The ritual action focused the gifts of the Spirit-filled community onto the chosen person, but the power being handed on was not to lead at Eucharist, but to guard and preach the tradition.[37] Neither the *Didache* nor any book of the New Testament suggests that one of the Twelve or anyone else ordained any person to lead the Eucharist. This is a significant absence and would seem to indicate that there was no such

---

29. Acts 15:6, 22–23.
30. Matt 16:17–18; Luke 22:32; John 21:15.
31. Matt 18:18; John 20:23.
32. Titus 1:5.
33. Didache 15: 1, 2.
34. Schillebeeckx, *Church with a Human Face*, 127.
35. Schillebeeckx, *Church with a Human Face*, 126.
36. Acts 14:23; 1 Tim 1:11, 4:6, 6:20; 2 Tim 1:13, 2:2.
37. Schillebeeckx, *Church with a Human Face*, 101.

specific role. Later theologians, such as Thomas Aquinas, looking backward from what had been long-established by his time, presumed that the role of the New Testament presbyter was identical to that of the medieval priest, and that John 20:22 described Jesus as ordaining the apostles,[38] but such theology was based on limited and too-literal understanding of the Scriptures, before deeper scriptural studies brought further knowledge.

As the early charismatic Christian communities developed into more organized assemblies, by the end of the New Testament period the roles of presbyter and *episkopos* had begun to dominate over the charismatic gifts, and the prophets were fading from the scene.[39] The writings of Clement, the *Letter of Barnabas* (70–132 CE) and *The Shepherd of Hermas* (towards 200 CE) show that in the Western church, including Rome, the naming and function of Christian ministers was still in flux, at least until the end of the second century.[40] Within those early centuries too, the role of leader of the eucharistic ceremony was becoming more firmly established. This simple task, which the *Didache* had described as open to various persons—householder, community leader or charismatic prophet—had gradually became institutionalized as the exclusive right of men specifically designated. A tendency can also be seen, to formalize and standardize the Eucharist, and to centralize the way authority was exercised in churches. In the writings of Ignatius of Antioch there is a clear tendency to create hierarchy.

Ignatius was martyred during Trajan's rule (98–117 CE), but some claim that the *Letters* bearing his name may date from as late as 140 CE.[41] These letters, addressed to a cluster of cities in western Asia Minor, were concerned to promote unity between each community and its "monarchical" *episkopos* and group of presbyters. We cannot conclude that what Ignatius was describing, or trying to promote, was the universal practice. Christian communities developed differently, and monarchical bishops were not common throughout the church until the end of the third century. In contrast to Ignatius, a letter by Polycarp (ca 110–30 CE) to the Greek city of Philippi does not mention an *episkopos,* but only presbyters and deacons, who seem to have governed that church as they did many others.[42] Ignatius

38. Supplement. Q.35.4 *Sed Contra*.
39. Schillebeeckx, *Church with a Human Face*, 103.
40. Osborne, *Priesthood: a History*, 95.
41. Richard Pervo; Timothy Barnes. https://en.wikipedia.org/wiki/Ignatius of Antioch.
42. Schillebeeckx, *Church with a Human Face;* 128. Armour, *Call,* 4.

Temple and Priesthood Restored

does not claim "apostolic succession", i.e. that *episkopoi* and presbyters had received authority from the Twelve their authority to govern the community or to preside at the Eucharist.[43] We can now see that by promoting the role of the "monarchical" *episkopos*, Ignatius was in fact opening the way to *division* in the community of believers. The hierarchy he was seeking to promote and justify contained the real risk of domination, because it gave special power to bishops and developed an attitude of powerlessness in "subjects". These developing attitudes were eventually to open the way to the disastrous results of clericalism. The role of *episkopos* was gradually swallowing up other roles. The "temple" and "priesthood" were returning. By promoting them the leaders were, no doubt unconsciously, beginning to betray the gospel.

Irenaeus (d. 200–203) was *episkopos* at Lyons. He implies that by his time every Christian community was led by an *episkopos* appointed by the apostles or their successors. This bold assertion does not prove a direct line of descent, for other sources describe the history differently: the *Didache*, for instance, had said that the *prophets* were the successors of the apostles.

Tertullian (c 160–c 220 CE) consistently referred to church leaders as forming an "ordo", the term used for several classes within Roman society. There was the *ordo* of the senate, into which one was born; the *ordo* of the *equites* (knights) to which one might be raised by the emperor. Those who belonged to an *ordo* were seen as superior to the lower classes or *plebs*. As an *ordo*, clerics had taken a big step towards claiming to be above the laity. Thus by imitating the civil structure, these leaders had moved away from the gospel, quite forgetting St Paul's warning: "Do not be conformed to this world".[44]

The oldest known ordination rituals for *episkopos*, presbyter and deacon are found in the *Didascalia Apostolorum (The Apostolic Tradition)*, which claims to be by Hippolytus (c.170–235 CE). In fact, the *Didascalia* may have been written as late as 380 CE, by which time these three officials were becoming solidly established as hierarchical liturgical ministers. The document described the bishop as "like a high priest".[45]

Again, Hippolytus' claim to link the *episkopoi* of Rome's established hierarchy to the twelve apostles must be treated with caution. Such pious assertions are comparable to the custom of attributing one's writings to a

---

43. Schillebeeckx, *Church with a Human Face*, 70.
44. Rom 12:2.
45. Schillebeeckx, *Church with a Human Face*, 144–45.

Clerical Errors

famous author in order to get them accepted. Like writers before him, Hippolytus noted that the *episcopos* and presbyters were chosen by the community, and it seems that the role of the *episkopos* as leader at Eucharist grew out of his prior role as community leader. The *episcopos* described by Hippolytus was not expected to be celibate, but husband of one wife, as New Testament texts had also demanded.[46] This expression often appears on secular tombstones of the period, and so may not have been intended to prohibit a widowed bishop from re-marrying, but to encourage every bishop to be a truly committed husband.

The ordination rituals for all three levels of clergy focus on the bishop's laying hands on the candidates, accompanied by prayer to the Father to give them power. The candidates were not anointed, although this would later become an essential rite. It is surprising that in some cases the entire ceremony of ordination was dispensed with. When the would-be presbyter had survived persecution and so earned the title of "Confessor", his sufferings sufficiently qualified him, so he did not need to be "ordained". This exemption presents a serious problem for those who would later maintain that ordination causes an "ontological change" in the presbyter.[47]

Origen (ca.184–ca. 253 CE) had a highly symbolic way of interpreting the Scriptures. He regularly described presbyters by the Greek word *hiereus*, (Latin *Sacerdos*), the same word used for Hebrew and pagan priests. Using similar analogies, Origen compared the Eucharist to the sacrifices of the First Testament. This usage became common after Origen, bringing with it the danger that people would understand it in a literal sense and assume that the Eucharist is *literally* a sacrifice offered on an altar, when in fact the word "sacrifice" in this context refers to Christ's life and death in total self-giving love.

By Origen's time, clergy had clearly become a special, privileged group. From his angry accusations we learn that they were often mercenary and corrupt, indulging in "... the most sordid ... intrigue and demagogy ... as soon as there is a chance of snatching an office, especially the highest and most lucrative office, that of bishop. Clergy brag about their seniority, and try to ensure that their children or relatives will succeed them ... These 'tyrants' will not take advice even from equals, much less from a lay man or a pagan".

---

46. 1 Tim 3:2; Titus 1:6.
47. Schillebeeckx, *Church with a Human Face*, 93, 152.

Temple and Priesthood Restored

To summarize: until the end of the second century, Christian communities recognized many different spiritual gifts in their members, but presiding at the Eucharist was not specifically identified. Nor did these gifts constitute distinct hierarchical "ranks". Communities elected one or more of their members as their leaders—presbyter or *episcopos*. This natural democracy was being eroded by around 200 CE. A three-fold *ordo* of *episkopos*, presbyter and deacon was evolving, distinct from "laity", and the *episkopos* was often appointed by his predecessor, with the community merely being asked to acknowledge the choice.[48]

Leadership at the Eucharist was becoming restricted solely to *episkopos* and presbyter, whose power and prestige was thereby increased. They were coming to be called "priests"—*hiereus, sacerdos*—and seen as mediators, "holding the place of God in relation to people".[49] Their place in society became equivalent to that of the Pagan cultic priests. The clerical caste was becoming established.

The roles of presbyter and *episkopos*, once interchangeable, were diverging.[50] To enhance the office of *episkopos*, a questionable theory was being promoted that they were successors of the twelve apostles. Although the church had preserved the teaching of Jesus, to which the Twelve had borne witness, the radical truth was being forgotten that *all* Christians, with Christ's Spirit within them, shared with Christ in offering their lives to God. To use the same metaphor, Christ and all Christians were "priests".[51]

When, in 313 CE, the decree of Constantine and Licinius allowed all religions to worship freely, the public worship performed by Christian clerics was seen as contributing to the welfare of the empire. As noted previously, they were given the same status as pagan priests: exemption from taxes and from prosecution in civil courts. "Higher" clerics began to adopt the insignia of noble Roman families. "Priests" and "temple" had returned.

The imperial favor might seem to promise a great liberation, but its impact on Christ's followers was ambiguous. Clerics became increasingly separated from ordinary believers and their role became more cult-like. The gospel was further compromised when Christians began to serve in the empire's armies, whereas for the first three centuries—as all writers of the period attest—Christians had obeyed Christ's radical call to love even their

---

48. Schillebeeckx, *Church with a Human Face*, 130.
49. Connolly, *Didascalia*, xxxviii, quoted in Osborne, *Priesthood: a History*, 130.
50. Schillebeeckx, *Church with a Human Face*, 136–37.
51. 1 Pet 2:5, 9; Rom 12:1, 15:16.

enemies and refused to kill.[52] Once taken, the step to bear arms and use violence had to be justified, and attempts were made to find theological arguments vindicating warfare, such as Augustine's theory of the "Just War".

Another effect of Constantine's edict was that Christians, especially bishops, could become wealthy. The bishop could direct the community's wealth to help widows, orphans and victims of famine. These civil and administrative roles of the bishop became more important as the empire's civic structures declined. Some bishops controlled resources that fed many thousands of people. In the 4th and 5th centuries the patriarchs of Alexandria had a fleet of ships and controlled the grain trade. Bishops sometimes became judges in civil courts, a task that weighed heavily on St. Augustine in Hippo. These charitable and civic works could be reconciled with the gospel, but they brought their own temptations, as Jesus had warned.

During and after the barbarian invasions, bishops were drawn to fill the civil power vacuum and sometimes played significant roles in holding society together. The *Code of Justinian* (527–65 CE) had ratified the bishops' social role,[53] but a crucial line had been crossed and another clerical error committed when some bishops became directly involved with military defense. The transition would have seemed natural, for most bishops of the time came from landed noble families already deeply involved in politics and war. Nonetheless, it further betrayed the gospel.

Through the Middle Ages bishops were often directly involved in warfare. For example, Bishop Odo of Bayeux was a capable military man and rode in battle with his brother William the Conqueror. In 1096 Bishop Adhemar de Puy rode on the First Crusade against the Seljuk Turks. In northern England, Durham was traditionally controlled by a "Prince Bishop" who fought to protect the border against the Scots. In Umbria and the Papal States Cardinal Giuliano delle Rovere (1443–1513) led an army to restore papal rule. When delle Rovere became Pope Julius II, besides hiring Michelangelo to adorn the Vatican, he often personally commanded his army in the field.

In Hungary, archbishops and bishops fought and died in combat against the Tatars (1219–41) and against the Turks (1475–1526). Faced with physical threat, these bishops chose violence and killing to defend their community, having abandoned the position of early Christians who in obedience to Christ faced execution rather than bear arms. Although these bishops' intentions

---

52. Kalantzis, *Caesar and the Lamb*, 7.
53. *Codex Iustinianus*, (Ed. Kruger) I, 4, 26.

Temple and Priesthood Restored

were understandable, as warrior-priests they too were fundamentally betraying the gospel. The church had not only come to resemble the empire of Rome, but by a supreme irony, was replacing it as it died.[54]

Clerics became progressively more separate from the majority of church members. In the fifth-century, pope Celestine had forbidden bishops and other clergy to dress distinctively, warning that they "should be distinguished from the common people by our learning, not by our clothes; by our conduct, not by our dress."[55]

But older styles of clothing retained by the clerical *Ordo* eventually became distinctive clerical garb. Around the beginning of the sixth century the monks' tonsure—the shaven crown—was being copied by most clerics and was made compulsory by the Lateran Council of 1215. Centuries before that, however, the western church began to demand of all its clerics an even more distinct separation: celibacy. This will be discussed later.

In his treatise on the priesthood, John Chrysostom (d.407) eulogized the priest, who ought to be holier than the people on whose behalf he prays, just as rulers excel their subjects. Because he "constantly handles the . . . Lord . . . ought not [the priest's] soul . . . be purer and holier than anything in the world?" Chrysostom's view was shaped by an understanding of the Eucharist which, as we will see in the following chapter, had evolved to emphasize the presence of Christ in the consecrated bread and wine at the expense of recognizing Christ's presence in the people gathered for the Eucharist. He also compared the priest to the political ruler, on the assumption—which cannot be found in the gospel!—that rulers were more excellent than the people they governed. Chrysostom's exaggerated praise of the priest continues to run as a strong current through the church's thinking. By the nineteenth century it reached extraordinary proportions in statements like that by Saint John Vianney, Curé of Ars: "O, how great is the priest! . . . If he realized what he is, he would die . . . After God, the priest is everything!"

Clerical power and prestige increased as other tasks were reserved to the priest alone. By 1000 CE it was made essential to have a priest witness marriages. From 1100 CE, the anointing of the sick was reserved to priests. Ordination was declared to be one of the seven sacraments, and it was achieved after passing through six preliminary stages. The candidate became a cleric by receiving the tonsure. He then received in succession

---

54. Schillebeeckx, *Church with a Human Face*, 150–51.
55. Mansi, *Concilia*, IV, 465.

the "orders" of doorkeeper, reader, acolyte, sub-deacon, deacon and lastly priesthood. If consecrated as bishop, he was said to receive the "fullness of the priesthood".

In the theological schools that developed towards the end of the first millennium, the sacraments were much discussed, and debates arose about what actually happens when a priest is ordained. Back in the fourth century, Augustine had helped settle the Donatist dispute by teaching that baptism did not need to be repeated if a person repented after renouncing it. He compared the "character" conferred by baptism to the identifying mark that was tattooed or branded onto Roman soldiers. So the question was asked: since at baptism a Christian is "sealed" by the Holy Spirit, might not ordination also bring about another permanent change in the one who received it?

Peter Lombard (c.1096–1160 CE) defined "Orders" as "a certain sacred sign *(signaculum)* by which a spiritual power and office is given to one ordained". Some scholars took this *signaculum* to mean not just the symbolic ritual action by which the power was conferred, but—as in baptism—an inner, spiritual sign that remained with the ordained person, even beyond his death. The Third and Fourth Lateran Councils (1179 and 1215 CE) accepted this sacramental "character", as did some later theologians and eventually the 1917 *Code of Canon Law*. The change brought about at ordination has come to be described as ontological, meaning a change in the ordained person's being or nature. One twentieth-century writer described it as: "a mark impressed on the soul . . . inseparable from it and together with it constitutes one reality . . . the mark is "indelible" . . . nothing can erase it."[56]

This is rather more than was claimed by St. Thomas Aquinas, a reliable source of sacramental theology. He did not say that ordination causes a change in the *being* of the ordained person, but simply that it gives the person a capacity or power *(potentia)* to administer the other sacraments,[57] although he did speculate that this power would last beyond death.[58] Aquinas considered that our "powers" such as intellect, will and senses are clearly distinguished from our being itself. Comparing the sacrament of ordination with the eucharistic sacrament, Aquinas explained that the

---

56. Galot, *Theology*, 197.
57. *S. Th.* IIIa 63 2 c.
58. *S. Th.* IIIa 63 5.

Temple and Priesthood Restored

Eucharist does not confer a "character" on the recipient, because the Eucharist contains Christ... the "fullness of Christ's priesthood".[59]

This raises the question, that if the person to be ordained has already been incorporated into Christ by baptism, and receives the fullness of Christ's priesthood in the Eucharist, does that person's "nature" need to receive any more of Christ? Can ordination do any more than simply depute the person to preside at the eucharistic ceremony? A more reasonable interpretation would seem to be that ordination puts the ordained minister into a new and profound *relationship* with the community that they are to serve, rather than claim that the sacrament changes the minister's *nature*.[60] Seeing ordination in this way would restore our understanding of the Eucharist as the action of a Christ-filled community thanking God "through Christ, in the Spirit", rather than a specially empowered individual bringing Christ present by speaking the "words of consecration".

Contemporary theologians have seriously challenged the concept of "ontological change".[61] The truth of the matter is debatable, but there is no question that the assumption has had a profound effect on the way Catholics have viewed priesthood, and enormously reinforced clericalism.

Celibacy and Priesthood

In Matthew's gospel, Jesus spoke positively of the option of remaining unmarried "for the sake of the kingdom of heaven".[62] Paul echoed this advice in his letter to the community in Corinth.[63] Through the centuries, many Christians have continued to make this life-choice, but as already mentioned, despite efforts to prove otherwise,[64] there is no early tradition that celibacy was required of persons who preside at Eucharist. Many third century bishops were married, and before the fourth century there was no general practice, much less an obligation, for clerics to be celibate.

In the fourth century, church authorities began to demand that married presbyters refrain from sexual intercourse before celebrating the Eucharist. The reasons for this were linked with First Testament regulations

---

59. S. Th IIIa 63 6c.
60. Bishop Mark Coleridge, *RCFR*, 16, 2, 620.
61. E.g., E. Schillebeeckx, *Christian Community*.
62. Matt 19:12.
63. 1 Cor 7:34.
64. E.g., Cochini, *Apostolic Origins*.

concerning ritual purity. The idea that sex is in some way incompatible with The Holy is an ancient one. For instance, in the Book of Exodus, when the Israelites were being prepared to encounter God at Mt Sinai they were commanded to abstain from sexual intercourse.[65] Similarly, in the First Book of Samuel, the temple priest Ahimelech reluctantly gave David's hungry warriors the bread offered to God, "provided that the young men have kept themselves from women".[66]

Were leaders in the early church motivated by this same suspicion that sexual activity was ritually unclean, or even intrinsically impure? The error is a central tenet of Manichaeism and recurs throughout history in various forms of puritanism and prudishness. St Jerome revealed this prejudice when he wrote: *omnis coitus immundus*—"all intercourse is unclean"—and it can be widely seen in the writings of Augustine, a reformed Manichee.[67] Fully aware of the trouble that sexuality can cause, churchmen "justified" these opinions, and began to demand abstention from sexual activity by blaming Adam and Eve's disobedience, which had lessened our reason's control of our now-disordered emotions. But any disparaging of sex clashes with the fundamental truth contained in the same Genesis story that sexuality is intrinsically good because humans are an image of God.[68]

Presbyters in the western church were eventually asked to abstain from sexual activity not only before celebrating the Eucharist, but permanently. This was probably because they were celebrating the Eucharist more often, even daily. It is not surprising that the proposal was not universally accepted. At the Council of Nicaea (325 CE) it was proposed to compel all married clergy to separate permanently from their wives. The proposal was rejected, but soon afterwards, married bishops were commanded to live with their wives "as brother and sister".

The bias against sexuality seems to be another of the major errors that accompanied the growing power of the clergy. Whatever the clerical legislators' deeper motives, the reasons given in church documents for demanding clerical celibacy have usually been pre-Christian examples of ritual purity: explanations which stem from the clericalist mistake of seeing the presbyter as too closely equivalent to the priest of the First Testament.

---

65. Exod 19:15.
66. 1 Sam 21:3–6.
67. Schillebeeckx *Church with a Human Face*, 242–43.
68. Gen 1:26–27, 31.

Temple and Priesthood Restored

The fourth-century church fathers Ambrose and Jerome argued—questionably—that the First Letter to Timothy demanded that a married man who became a bishop must abstain from sexual relations. The emperor Justinian (530 CE) passed a law making null and void all marriages contracted by clerics in Holy Orders and declaring illegitimate the children of such marriages. The Council of Trullo (692 CE) ordered that a bishop's wife should retire to a convent or become a deaconess. Despite this, great numbers of the Latin clergy, even as late as the tenth century, were married. Most rural priests were either married or living with a woman partner and many urban clergy and bishops had wives and children. In Northern Italy the severe critic St Peter Damian lamented that a large number of the priests and even bishops openly took wives and begot children to whom they bequeathed church property. After the 1066 invasion, many of the higher Norman clergy who came to England had wives, and even a century later the Council of London (1129 CE) had not succeeded in solving this "problem".[69] The Western church continued to demand celibacy, not only by declaring at the First and Second Lateran Councils (1123 and 1139 CE) that clerical marriages were henceforth invalid, but by commanding clerics who were *legitimately* married to send away their wives.[70] Latin clergy who disobeyed would now be doing illegally what Greek clergy were encouraged to do by law: living with wives and raising families.

The problem of priests' sons inheriting church property was one reason for imposing celibacy, but not the whole story, for the church could and often did confiscate priest's property. Other motives were at work. Even into the mid-twentieth century, all Papal documents demanding clerical celibacy were still quoting the previously mentioned texts from Exodus, 1 Samuel, and Leviticus[71] which state that sexual contact renders a person ritually "unclean". It has to be asked: if the demand that presbyters maintain lifelong celibacy has been based on pre-Christian concepts and a distorted suspicion of sexuality—as found in the writings of Jerome and Augustine—is this demand yet another clerical error that betrays the gospel of Jesus?[72]

Does celibacy benefit the person who preaches the gospel and presides at the ritual of the Eucharist? *Any* self-giving for the purpose of better loving and serving others surely deepens a person's life and their sharing

---

69. Campion, Edmund, Priesthood in the Middle Ages, in Gleeson, *Priesthood*, 28.
70. Schillebeeckx, *Church with a Human Face*, 243 Note 33.
71. Lev 15:16, 22:4.
72. Schillebeeck, *Church with a Human Face*, 242.

in the "kingdom of God". In this way celibacy can be a strong witness to the reality of the Transcendent that is being taught and celebrated. This was the motive Jesus gave for celibacy. But *obligatory* clerical celibacy can distort a person if it is not whole-heartedly accepted and integrated. It was not uncommon, for instance, for some medieval offenders to try to justify their sodomy or abuse of the young by claiming that it was more "acceptable" than illegal involvement with a woman. Peter the Chanter, of Paris (d.1195 CE) and Robert of Courson (d.1219 CE) claimed that while vows of continence might have benefited the church in the past, in their own time these vows served only to foster sodomy, immorality and damnation, and should be abolished.[73]

The Western church's long struggle to impose celibacy on its diocesan clergy seems to have had more success after the Council of Trent, (1563 CE), but modern surveys indicate that the success is by no means complete. The Second Vatican Council (1962–65) acknowledged the situation of the early church and the continuous tradition of the Eastern churches and then reaffirmed that the nature of the presbyterate does *not* require celibacy. The Council also emphasized that celibacy is "for the sake of the kingdom . . ." and that it gives a "living sign of the world to come . . . in which the children of the resurrection neither marry nor take wives".[74]

Is celibacy a "higher state"? Until the Second Vatican Council it was generally assumed and taught that celibacy is a "higher state" than marriage. This is a long-held view, and has greatly contributed to clericalism, Even the Vatican Council's Decree *On Priests* might appear to be maintaining that the priest is superior. That document stated that presbyters, by celibacy, adhere to Christ "more easily with an undivided heart".[75] These comparatives, and a number of others, might seem to suggest that non celibates don't "adhere to Christ" as well as celibate priests, and that therefore there are two classes of Christians. That would be fundamental clericalism. But the Council had earlier stated definitively that *everyone* is called to holiness: clerics, bishops, and those to whom they give pastoral care. All Christians, receiving the Holy Spirit when they are baptized, are capable of loving God with their *whole* mind and heart. All share in God's nature and are truly made holy. "All . . . of whatever rank or status", are called to the fullness of

---

73. Elliott, *Corrupter of Boys*, 232.
74. *PO* 16, quoting Matt 19:22. Abbott, *Documents*, 565.
75. *PO* 16. Abbott, *Documents*, 566.

Temple and Priesthood Restored

the Christian life and to the perfection of charity.⁷⁶ This plain statement quietly corrects centuries of error promoted by and about clerics.

The Council reinforced the point by emphasizing that baptism makes the whole church priestly, pastoral and prophetic. The laity are not merely "non-clergy", but are no less Christ's disciples *(christifideles)* than persons ordained to preside at the table of the Eucharist. This teaching, based solidly on Scripture, shows that to allow the formation of a clerical *caste* distinct from the majority of Jesus' followers has been a primal error. Having examined the errors of restoring temple and priesthood, the following chapter will look at similar errors in the evolution of the Eucharist.

76. LG 40. Abbott, *Documents*, 67.

9

How Clerics Have Changed the Eucharist

THE PREVIOUS CHAPTER DESCRIBED how Jesus' resurrection had made both the temple and its priests redundant for Christians, because the Spirit of the risen Christ now provided a radically more intimate way in which people could connect with the Transcendent. The first Christians rejoiced in the Good News that Jesus had taught: that God loved them and had commissioned them to build up the Reign of God, based on love. They exulted in the promise of eternal life. The central means by which those Christians maintained their link with the Risen One was the simple meal which Jesus had instructed them to share in his name. Celebrated regularly on the Lord's Day, that meal's primary function was to thank God, so it became known as the Eucharist, from the Greek word for thanking: *eucharistein*.

It is hardly surprising that they chose to express their joy and gratitude by a party or feast of love (*agape*). Those who had known Jesus before his death recalled how he often used meals as an occasion for teaching people about the Reign of God. Luke's gospel alone records Jesus taking part in meals in the houses of several Pharisees and of the converted tax-collectors Matthew and Zacchaeus. He also dined in the home of his friends Martha, Mary and Lazarus. The story was told how—perhaps on several occasions—he fed a large crowd in a remote place. Luke also recalls that on the night after Jesus' resurrection, in the village of Emmaus, he was recognized by Clopas and his wife or companion as the stranger who had met them

How Clerics Have Changed the Eucharist

on the road, and broke bread at their evening meal.[1] The Gospel of John recalled Jesus at a wedding feast in Cana; and after his resurrection, cooking breakfast for his friends by the lakeshore.[2]

Because Jesus did not keep the customary fasts he was criticized as "a glutton and a drunkard"[3] but his followers remembered with delighted hope that he described the future Kingdom of God as a great feast, where people from east and west will come together to rejoice.[4] They also remembered that when Jesus was sharing a meal with friends, or providing food for a crowd, he would first thank or bless God—the words mean the same—then break the bread and share it around. All four gospels record him doing this at the last meal that he shared with his followers, but on that occasion he made the remarkable statement that he was establishing a new covenant between humanity and God, and asked his friends to "do this in memory of me".

Built on these memories, the first Christians' regular thanksgiving meal was a joyful and precious experience. It was a simple meal, yet extraordinary in several ways. The people who gathered for it knew that the Spirit of the risen Christ was present within each of them, and among their assembly. They saw their action of sharing the loaf and the cup as a powerful symbol of this love which united them, just as the wheat-grains and grapes from which it was made had become united as bread and wine.[5] The extraordinary meal set aside all social barriers and conventions: poor people and rich; women and men; slaves and free; gentiles and Jews all shared the same table. Their fellowship transcended the Mosaic Law that would call some of them "unclean" and others "pure". During the meal they broke and shared the one loaf, and all drank from the same cup, explicitly obeying Jesus' words at his last meal with them.[6]

Christ was for them not just a memory. Since his gruesome death, they had all encountered him in some kind of transforming experience. Some had "seen" the risen Christ on Easter day or soon after. They had all received his Holy Spirit: some on the morning of Pentecost; others when

---

1. Luke 4:39, 5:2, 7:36, 10:38, 11:37, 14:1, 19:5, 9:13, 22:15–20, 24:13–35, 5:33, 7:34, 13:29.
2. John 2:1, 21:9.
3. Matt 11:19.
4. Matt 8:11, 22:1–14, 25:1–13; Mark 2:19.
5. Didache, 9:3.
6. O'Loughlin, *Eucharist: Origins*, Location 2748.

they were baptized, or even before their baptism, as happened to a group of Samaritans and to the centurion Cornelius.[7]

Only the most determined sceptics deny that people are capable of experiencing a transcendent dimension of reality in a "mystical" experience. When people have such an experience, they often say that it was "indescribable", but then struggle to describe it in familiar words and images. Saul of Tarsus had such an experience on the road to Damascus; through the centuries many other people have had similar mystical experiences. Today, when great numbers of people are revived after being "clinically dead" for a short time, with no activity in their brain or heart, many report a similar mystical experience in which they had a profound encounter with the Transcendent. These encounters have come to be known as the Near-Death Experience, and their transcendence is proved by the fact that during some of them, the person learns of facts that they could not have known otherwise. Many—even atheists—communicate with a "Being of Light", whom according to their culture they may call the Buddha, Krishna or Christ. The experience always has a radical impact on the person's future life.[8] The post-resurrection meetings with Jesus which his followers reported were similarly "impossible to describe", but nonetheless were retold as the metaphorical post-resurrection stories found in the gospels and in 1 Corinthians. Jesus' followers would surely have recounted these stories whenever they met for their thanksgiving meal.

The focus of the eucharistic meal was thanking the Father in Jesus' name. The prayers used resembled the Jewish grace, the *birkat hamazon*, for most of the first Christians were Jews. They thanked God for the created world; for the food and drink which brought them joy, and for the promise of eternal life. They also prayed for those in need and were conscious of being united with Christians in other places celebrating the same kind of meal. The action of sharing the one cup was as unique and surprising in first-century culture as it is in our own day. People did not normally share the same cup then, just as we do not share the same coffee mug or wineglass today, but in this meal they did it deliberately as Jesus had instructed. It was a striking way of declaring that they were united, despite all physical and social differences. It was a visible statement that they were one in Christ.

It is vain to search for the "original" exemplar of the Eucharist. The four last supper accounts give only conflicting fragments, preserving only

---

7. Acts 2:1–4, 8:15, 10:44.
8. Moody, *Life after Life*; Alexander, *Proof of Heaven*.

the key actions of Jesus. They do not describe a ceremony or rite, but simply recall the precious fact that Jesus *took* bread, *thanked* God, and *broke* it, and that he mysteriously referred to it as "my body" before inviting them to share it. Likewise, he referred to the wine-cup as "my blood, of the covenant", comparing his own blood, which would be shed the following day, to the blood of the animal sacrifices which had ratified the previous covenant.

It is safe to assume that in the first decades of the Christian church, each community would have celebrated the meal with slight differences each time they ate it. Just as the gospels preserve a variety of memories of Jesus, so his living presence in the eucharistic gathering was celebrated in a variety of ritual actions. It is instructive to see how some of the early Christian writers described the Eucharist. Justin Martyr, (100–165 CE) mentioned the same basic elements that can be recognized in twenty-first-century Sunday celebrations of the Eucharist, but with significant differences.[9] In the *Didache*'s brief description of the Eucharist, we see the community which gathered on the Lord's Day not so much attending an event, as people today "attend Mass", but rather as *doing* something together: actively thanking and worshipping God.[10] Nor does the *Didache* give a standard format for the meal as if there were only one way to arrange it. As in Justin's account, a form of prayer is *suggested*, with the comment that if the one leading is a prophet, he is free to use a different formula from the words given.

Apart from mentioning that a prophet may sometimes lead the Eucharist—and some prophets were women—neither the *Didache* nor Justin says anything explicitly about who was to preside.[11] The issue of who led at Eucharist does not seem to have been important enough to point out in those writers or anywhere in the New Testament. The *Didache*'s instructions about the meal seem arranged so as to be easily memorized. This might indicate that *most* members of the community, even women who were not prophets,[12] were able to lead the eucharistic meal when called upon, just as today we invite various people to "say grace" before an important meal.[13] It is also noteworthy that the *Didache* refers to women's ministry *(leitougia)* in

---

9. *First Apologia*, chapter 65–67.
10. O'Loughlin, *Didache*, 81.
11. O'Loughlin, *Didache*, 108.
12. *Didache*, 10.7.
13. O'Loughlin, *Didache*, 23.

connection with the Eucharist on the Lord's Day.[14] As noted in the previous chapter, the silence of the New Testament may be sufficient to show that there was at first no specific ministry of presiding.[15] We might expect that the Twelve always presided when they were present at Eucharist, but there is no evidence for this. The presbyters or overseers (*episkopoi*) appointed to lead first-century Christian communities may have also led the community's thanksgiving meal, but it is just as likely to have been the head of the house where the meal was eaten. Paul often mentions by name the men or women householders who hosted the communities he had founded: Lydia in Philippi; Crispus, Stephanas, Onesiphorus and many others.[16]

Can we know that women led the Eucharist? Jesus had treated women with revolutionary respect and courtesy and included women among his disciples and travelling companions. He drastically broke convention by talking with the foreign Samaritan woman and by accepting, in public, a woman's loving caress.[17] We know from Paul that the first communities followed Jesus' radical position when he wrote: "... there is no longer male and female; for all of you are one in Christ Jesus".[18] But Jesus' followers soon found themselves in conflict with the constraints of Graeco-Roman patriarchal culture. Nowhere do we hear of a woman chosen to lead a community as presbyter or *episkopos,* and later epistles, possibly written by Paul's disciples, limited the extent of women's participation at Christian assemblies, even warning them of unacceptable hairstyles.[19] By the end of the second century, such attitudes certainly would have restricted leadership at Eucharist to males only.

Is the Eucharist a sacrifice? The previous chapter discussed the metaphorical use of the word sacrifice to describe Christ's death, the lives of Christians, and later, the Eucharist. Like many generations of Catholics, I was often taught that the "sacrifice of the Mass" somehow repeats Jesus' sacrifice on Calvary, but I never understood how that worked. As a seminarian I read that the Council of Trent condemned those who deny that "in the Mass a true and proper sacrifice is offered to God".[20] But—as with

14. *Didache*,14.1, 15.1.
15. Armour *Call,* 40.
16. Acts 16:15, 18:8; 1 Cor 1:15; Rom 16, 2; Tim 1:16.
17. John 4: 5; Luke 7:36–39.
18. Gal 3:28.
19. 1 Tim 2: 11–12.
20. Trent, Canon 1. Dz 948.

the Scriptures—the language of church Councils needs to be interpreted in the cultural context in which they were written. Trent was opposing the Protestant rejection of the Catholic overemphasis on sacrifice.

After being ordained, I found myself using the word "sacrifice" about twenty times throughout the only Eucharistic Prayer then permitted. Was it right to emphasize the Mass as a sacrifice? Not—as has often been done—if this led people to imagine that the Eucharist, like First Testament sacrifices, is offered as a gift to persuade or "appease" God. People often request Masses to be offered, seemingly with the intention of persuading God to grant some favor or benefit. But the Good News of God's infinite love assures us that it is blasphemous to imagine that we need to persuade or bargain with God, as if we were dealing with an offended or angry tyrant. Jesus assures us that God attends to our needs far more lovingly than any human parent.[21]

A more sinister error about sacrifice is to suggest that God was "pleased" by Jesus' suffering and death; or is pleased by anyone's pain; even by the pain it costs us to love and serve each other. It is indeed a human tendency, but an evil one, to feel a sense of satisfaction when we "pay back" someone who has hurt us; or when we find a "scapegoat" to blame and punish for a disaster. This human feeling of satisfaction is neither permanent, nor does it satisfy us at the deepest level, as many studies have shown.[22] When Eucharistic Prayer I asks that God will be "pleased" to accept "a holy sacrifice, a spotless victim" this needs careful explanation. If the sacrifice of Jesus "pleases God", this cannot mean Jesus' murder, or the pain he suffered. It can mean only his *life* of total love. When Jesus endured the worst that human evil could do to him, God was intimately present *in* Jesus. So, when in their eucharistic meal Christians make an "offering" of themselves to God, their action is indeed a sacrifice, a making-holy, not to appease God, but to unite themselves with the living Christ—with God—in thanks, praise and love.

The ancient *Didache* warns the community to resolve all disagreements among its members before "offering your *sacrifice*" to God. The community was told to "confess your sins that your *sacrifice* may be a pure one".[23] The *Didache* was not saying that the consecrated bread was the sacrifice. Only later did the bread come to be called the "host" (Latin *hostia*, victim). As the New Testament authors had done, the *Didache* was

21. Matt 7:11; Luke 11:13.
22. Muller, Death Penalty; Radelet, Retributive Impact.
23. *Didache* 14, recalling Matt 5:23.

describing how Christians offered their own *lives*, including the Eucharistic meal, in union with Jesus' total self-giving. Such love was and is more truly called a sacrifice than were the slaughtered animals of the Old Law.

Four Changes to the Eucharist?

In the generations after Jesus the eucharistic meal gradually took on a standardized form, but always continued to evolve. It underwent significant changes in the fourth century, when the church became assimilated into the empire and the members of the clerical *ordo*, now described as priests, were growing in power. The liturgical historian Thomas O'Loughlin has summarized four basic changes or "displacements".[24]

Change 1

At some time in the second century the agape meal became separated from the eucharistic rite. The meal continued to be shared in the evening, but the Eucharist was celebrated the following morning. Then the meal disappeared, leaving the Eucharist isolated. Why did this happen? Perhaps people found it too difficult to bridge the wide cultural gaps that sharing the meal challenged them to bridge. Perhaps, as Paul once complained, the wealthy didn't share their food and drink with the poor or were over-indulging.[25] Whatever the reasons, the decision to abolish the meal because of abuses was like discarding the proverbial baby with its bathwater. Its loss severely weakened the Eucharist's benefit to the community, for in every culture people know that eating together is the most effective way to unite people. Deep hostilities can be resolved when people sit down to share food, and any parish community knows how sharing even tea or coffee and biscuits can draw locals and strangers together after the service. When the *agape* was discarded, it was easy to lose sight of the Eucharist's function to unite people into community. Without the shared meal, the Eucharist was no longer the community's common action, the but was on the way to becoming each person's private attempt to draw closer to the Divine by eating a marvelous *object*.

---

24. O'Loughlin, *Eucharist: Origins*. 191.
25. 1 Cor 11:17–34.

Change 2

The focus of the Eucharist gradually shifted from being the action of re-membering, *(anamnesis)* praising and thanking the *Father*, to become more an event at which *Christ* became present when the bread and wine were consecrated. From the beginning, communities had known that Christ's Spirit was continuously within them as individuals and among them as a community: "Where two or three are gathered in my name, I am there among them".[26] This second change led to adoring *Christ* rather than the *Father* and enhanced the role of clerics who "brought Christ into the community". Clerics were coming to be seen as special persons who could *re-enact* what Christ had done at the Last Supper, where formerly the whole community had joyfully joined together to *remember* it.

As has been mentioned, the New Testament does not describe anyone as having power to "consecrate" and transform bread and wine to make Christ present in those elements. On the contrary, important witnesses from the first centuries told how it was *the people* that were transformed in the Eucharist. For Ignatius of Antioch and for Augustine, it is not the presider but the faithful *recipients* who make Christ present by increasingly *becoming* the Body of Christ. In his hundreds of sermons, Augustine often speaks of the sacrament being valid not because of the *leader's* words or actions, but because the *recipients* are increasingly one with God and with each other. It is we who are taken into Christ's body, rather than he into ours. For Augustine the Eucharist transforms the *community* into a single thing, uniting its members under the symbol of bread made from many grains, and of wine from many grapes.[27] While Augustine does say "That bread, made holy by the word of God, which you see on the altar, is the body of Christ."[28] he knows that the risen Christ is an indefinable, unbounded mystery, including the entire church, and more.

In medieval times Christ's "real presence" in the consecrated elements came to be heavily emphasized. St Thomas Aquinas focused on this, but could still maintain that the *purpose* of the Eucharist, the *res sacramenti* or the reality which the sacrament both symbolizes and achieves, was the *unity*

---

26. Matt 18:20; 1 Cor 3:16–17.

27. *Interpreting John's Gospel* 27.6; *Sermon* 227 PL 38.1100, quoted in Wills, *Papal Sin* 142.

28. Sermon 227.1.

Clerical Errors

of the people within the Body of Christ.[29] Since the shared meal had been abolished and the "real presence" of Christ in the elements had become the main focus, there was a real danger that the people "attending Mass" could forget the deepest purpose of Christ's presence in the Eucharist was not just to make each person holy, but to help each community to be more united, and eventually to bring *all* people into one community, the "Reign of God".

Change 3

At first the *community* was the agent that praised and thanked God in the Eucharist, but later the *presider* came to monopolize this role. He began to be called the "celebrant", as if he alone celebrated and thanked God; and special power began to be attributed to him. This shift of focus was accompanied by the development of elaborate vestments which added grandeur to the person of the "celebrant". For centuries Catholics have considered vestments as essential for Mass, but in fact they were a relatively late innovation. In the fifth century, St Augustine presided at the eucharistic wearing everyday clothes.[30]

Change 4

This change removed the Eucharist from the midst of everyday life and made it into a sacred ritual in a "sanctuary", performed by a "priest" who came to be seen as necessary mediator between ordinary people and God. The development caused people to forget that in the tremendous fact of the Incarnation, when "the Word was made flesh and lived among us", the distinction was dissolved between sacred and profane. Holiness became accessible to all people, enabling them to become themselves temples of God. Reversing this seismic shift in human awakening, clerics were transforming the table around which Christians met to give thanks, into an altar of sacrifice raised several steps above them and presided over by clerics.

This evolution of the Eucharist was gradual, but the four changes were basic and substantial. By the Middle Ages they had radically transformed the Eucharist into a ritual totally controlled by "consecrated" specialists.[31]

29. E.g. S *Th*, IIIa, 73, 3, c; IIIa 73, 4, c.
30. Van der Meer, *Augustine*, 317.
31. Schillebeeckx *Church with a Human Face*, 146, 192, Note 80.

How Clerics Have Changed the Eucharist

The presider stood with his back to the community and was often barely visible through a roodscreen. He conducted what had become a kind of magic ritual, muttered in Latin, a language that most people no longer understood. Congregations would not regain a speaking part until the "dialogue Mass" was permitted [sic] in the 1950s. Presiders would not again face the community whom they were leading in prayer, until the reforms that followed the Second Vatican Council.

With the community reduced to more-or-less passive spectators, the priest was said to *immolate the sacrifice*, *consecrate* the bread and wine, or *confect* the Eucharist. The community no longer shared one loaf or a single cup, for the loaf had been replaced by separate fragile wafers. Clerics had long since forbidden lay persons from obeying Christ's command to drink from the one cup: it was considered sufficient for them to receive Christ in the consecrated wafer. Even that was no longer their daily bread, for most people felt unworthy to "receive Holy Communion" except on rare occasions, and then only after fasting from the previous midnight.

At Mass, most people merely watched the cleric "bring Jesus present" and then show him to the waiting people. The Fourth Lateran Council ordered the presider to pronounce the "words of consecration" loudly and clearly in the otherwise muted Eucharistic Prayer, and to lift up the "host" and chalice so that the people behind his back could view them. A bell was rung to advise when the moment was approaching.

People were *commanded* to attend. The Synod of Elvira (ca 305 CE) had imposed penalties for missing three Sundays,[32] and the Fourth Lateran Council in 1215 CE repeated the demand that people receive Communion at least once a year. The 1917 *Code* confirmed this universal obligation. It became common for people to ask the priest to "offer Mass" for some special intention. The priest's actions and prayers at the Eucharist were presumed to be more efficacious than their own in obtaining such outcomes as healing for a sick person, success in an enterprise or the freeing of souls from purgatory.

As early as the fourth century "private" Masses were being celebrated at the shrines erected to venerate the relics of martyrs. These Masses provided an income for a priest, and they continued to multiply, particularly in monasteries, in the sixth century and beyond. Few of the earliest monks were ordained, but in time this changed, and monks from Ireland and England brought into mainland Europe the custom of multiplying Masses.

---

32. *Code,* Canon 21, Mansi, *Concilia.* II, 9.

Their monastic churches had many altars where "private" Masses were offered for the dead or in devotion to the Blessed Virgin and to saints. Just before the Second Vatican Council a new seminary was built in Melbourne, whose chapel had nineteen side altars for the daily "private" Masses of newly-ordained priests.

In the days when severe public penances were given for certain sins, the custom arose of evading them by paying *weregeld* to have Masses said as a substitute. This transaction was further complicated when spiritual rewards or "indulgences" were allocated to specific Masses, altars and churches. The profits from offering such special Masses became a significant temptation for priests, and partly for this reason the Synod of Seligenstadt (1023 CE) directed them to limit their Masses to three per day.

The early Christians were keenly aware that the Spirit of the risen Christ was present in them as individuals and as a community,[33] especially when they gathered to bless and thank God through, with, and in Christ. One cannot be a Catholic Christian without believing that Christ is really present in the Eucharist, but since Christ is infinite, can this presence ever be de-*fined*? The truth is so awesome that it seems unnecessary and even absurd to argue *how* Christ is present; or try to decide at *what moment* of the Eucharistic Prayer he "arrives". This has not stopped people from putting forward numerous theories attempting to explain the mystery, or from defending their opinions by going into schism or fighting savage wars.

The Gospel of Matthew—written after Jesus' resurrection—recalled Jesus' promise: "where two or three are gathered in my name, I am there among them". That text echoed the Jewish awareness of the *shekinah*, God's glorious presence protecting the community, and it may have been suggesting that Christ's presence fulfilled and replaced the *shekinah*.[34] But St Paul pointed out to the Christians of Corinth that Christ might *not* be present when they tried to celebrate the Eucharist without first reconciling the factions within their community; or when they failed to share generously the food and drink of the *agape* meal. "When you come together, it is not really to eat the Lord's Supper".[35] His rebuke warned them that since they were lacking in genuine love, Christ was *not* present and so, in modern parlance, they did not have a "valid Eucharist".

---

33. Acts 8:17, 11:15; 1 Cor 3:16; Gal 3:5; Eph 1:17, 3:16.
34. Congar, *Temple* 133.
35. 1 Cor 11:20.

How Clerics Have Changed the Eucharist

This reprimand by Paul appears to conflict with the later belief in the efficacy of the words of an ordained minister: the belief that his words and actions—the *opus operatum*—are inevitably effective in bringing Christ present, regardless of the priest's personal moral state. This conclusion may have spared communities from concern about the "validity" of the sacrament when there were doubts about the priest, but it veers dangerously towards seeing the Eucharist as magic.

An absurd conclusion that has followed from excessive focus on the cleric's power to "bring Christ present" can be seen in Canon Law's strict prohibition that priests must not attempt to consecrate bread or wine by repeating Jesus' words from the Last Supper *outside* of Mass.[36] Presumably it would "bring Christ present" when he was not wanted.

From the earliest times, Christians began to reserve some of the consecrated bread to take to the sick. Around the time of Gregory of Nyssa (330-395 CE) more emphasis began to be placed on the presence of Christ in that consecrated bread, and this continued to increase in the following centuries. From the medieval period, devotions such as the forty hours vigil before the Sacrament sometimes overshadowed the eucharistic meal itself. The "reserved sacrament" began to be worshipped in a special ceremony: "Benediction of the Blessed Sacrament". An unfortunate result of this shift of focus was to minimize and even lose sight of how Christ is also really present, albeit differently, in the proclaimed Word of God and—as Augustine had emphasized—in the community of people joined in Christ.[37] The Second Vatican Council began to restore this awareness.[38]

It may seem incredible that clerics, even over a span of many centuries, could so drastically change the central act of Christian prayer and worship. But it becomes more understandable if we compare the process to the way languages have changed over the same two millennia. First-century Latin evolved into mediaeval Latin, then eventually into twenty-first-century Italian, French, Romanian, English and various other languages. The process has been gradual and almost imperceptible, but the resulting differences are vast.

Try as they might, academies cannot control the evolution of languages, which mutate because of the small daily choices that ordinary people make as they speak. The Eucharist, like language, is never static and there

---

36. *Code*, Canon 927.
37. *Civ. Dei*, X, 6. Quoted in Congar, *Priest and Layman*, 78.
38. SC 7. Abbott, *Documents*, 141.

Clerical Errors

is no permanent "ideal form". From earliest times, various rites evolved in different places: Coptic, Syriac, Armenian, Byzantine, Malabar, Roman, Visigothic, Sarum etc. But in most of them, what Jesus asked us to do has been distorted in the four ways mentioned above: errors made by clerics who gradually took full control in the church-institution, causing serious loss to the community at large.

It would be rash to suggest that the distortions described above were done with deliberate intent. There is no need to claim conspiracies. The evolution has come about by small incremental adjustments, many of them unfortunate human errors, motivated often enough by good intentions. All too often though, the changes happened when clerics—who claimed the authority to instigate change—succumbed to the temptation to increase their own power and prestige. Some of the changes, such as the early abolition of the *agape* meal, may have been partly intended to prevent irreverence, but it was a change that already altered the meaning of the Eucharist, for the New Testament texts use the names *agape* and *Eucharist* for the same event.

Today, wherever there are not enough priests to serve great numbers of people, the expedient of the "communion service" is often used. Because no ordained presider is available, consecrated bread is retrieved from an earlier Mass, perhaps in a distant place. After readings and prayers it is distributed to the congregation. But this "solution" does a grave injustice to about half of the world's Catholics. It has to be asked why any community of baptized Christians is deemed incapable of thanking God, in Jesus' words, at their own sacred meal. Jesus' is reported as telling us to "do this" in his memory. Can it be right that restrictive *human* laws prevent communities from obeying this *divine* command? Why cannot each community choose a suitable person to lead them regularly in the simple action of breaking bread and sharing the cup as they thank and praise the Father in Jesus' name?

Clerical control has changed eucharistic practice in many other ways. As already mentioned, lay persons were forbidden to receive the consecrated bread on their hand but waited for the cleric to place it in their mouth. Only recently has the ancient practice been restored. Although the consecrated bread and wine, the "eucharistic species" were not originally the central point of the gathering, the desire to protect them has further destroyed the Eucharist's main symbolic meaning.

Around the ninth century, clerics in the West made the choice to use unleavened bread on the assumption that the Last Supper was a Passover meal. The changeover also minimized crumbs, which were thought to be

How Clerics Have Changed the Eucharist

somehow irreverent. The decision not only deepened the rift between the Eastern and Western church; it also led to using bread pre-cut into separate wafers, thereby abolishing the main symbolism of breaking and sharing *one* loaf. In the twentieth century, clerical choices and industrial mass-production have further "improved" these morsels by sealing their edges so that they are totally crumb-free. These wafers, unfortunately, often resemble plastic, and bear little similarity to real food.

In the case of the cup, many elaborate ways have been devised to *avoid* sharing it. Eastern rites chose to use straws or spoons. Others dip the wafers into the cup. Some Christian churches use a separate little cup for each person. Most drastic of all, the Roman rite, from as early as the ninth century, chose to deny the cup to the laity altogether. This latter change is an example of how an institution will defend its position more strongly to prove one's opponents are wrong. In the sixteenth century, some of the main Protestant objections against Rome were the changes that clerics had made to the Eucharist. In particular, they wanted the cup restored to lay people. This caused Roman clerics to defend their defective practices even more strongly. They found "theological reasons" to continue withholding the cup from non-clerics. Sweeping aside the deep natural symbolism, they pointed out that Christ was totally present in the least portion of consecrated bread. Similarly, when Protestants questioned the Catholic theory of transubstantiation, Catholics more strongly emphasized that theory, drawing attention away from the other ways in which Christ is really present in the world.

Today clerical control still restricts people from sharing fully in the Eucharist. In 1980 Catholics were forbidden to say aloud with the presider the words that best express how the Eucharist is a community praising the Father through, with and in Christ. They were told that the Eucharistic Prayer is reserved to the priest, by virtue of his ordination, and that it is an "abuse" for "the faithful" to say parts of it.[39] Again, the ancient practice of the "kiss of peace" was restored after Vatican II, to express the communal nature of the Mass. Many presiders are still reluctant, or refuse outright, to allow the congregation to express and deepen their unity through this simple gesture.

In 2011 clerical control was exercised, without proper consultation, when a Vatican committee imposed a new translation of the Mass text on churches around the world. In a shameful abuse of power, a Vatican group discarded the work of an appointed committee of experts and imposed on

---

39. *Inaestimabile Donum* (1980).

the church their own translation which has since been widely scorned. The presumptuous clerics based their work on a novel principle, that God must be addressed in "sacral vernacular".[40] To demand that we address God in special language is to return to the gross error of imagining that God is remote from us. It undermines faith in the Incarnation itself, the uniquely Christian understanding that in Christ, God is intimately *united* with humanity and addresses us as friends.[41] It comes suspiciously close to Docetism, the error that believes Christ's body was not truly human but merely a phantasm or made of some celestial substance.[42] When clerical power is abused, it can lead to absurdity, perhaps even heresy.

The new translation also reasserted the division between the priest and laity by restoring such usage as: ". . . *my* sacrifice and *yours*" where the post-Vatican missal (1969) had seen that "*our* sacrifice' better expressed the reality. Such changes, enforced by a few powerful clerics, further obscured the truth that the Eucharist is a prayer of the whole community acting together.

Who may partake of the Eucharist? The sacrament prefigures the unity of all humanity in the Kingdom of God. The Infinite Love of God is working to bring about this kingdom, which excludes no one. It may be sometimes necessary for a community to exclude from their Eucharist members whose lives are in blatant conflict with the ideals of the community—as Saint Paul did in the Corinthian church.[43] But such measures are temporary, and are intended to bring the offenders to repentance. The situation is quite different with Christians of other denominations who value the Eucharist but may differ from Catholics in their theological understanding of its mystery. When they gather to do what Jesus invited us to do, believing that Christ is present in the action of their community, how can we deny that he is with them? When they visit our eucharistic gatherings, and vice versa, why may we not share the Eucharist with them? In recent times, the Vatican has allowed this, but only on quite limited occasions. Why be parsimonious in this fundamental matter, which affects the unity of Christians, and the example we show the world? When we give thanks for God's universal love, but refuse to share our loaf and cup with Christian neighbors who pray to the Father through the same Christ, don't we commit a contradiction,

---

40. Congregation for Divine Worship, *Liturgiam Authenticam*, 2001.
41. John 15: 13–15.
42. O'Loughlin, *Eucharist: Origins*, 196.
43. 1 Cor 5:11–12.

not to say blasphemy? When Catholics exclude other Christians because their Eucharist is not "valid", aren't we uncomfortably similar to the disciple John, whom Jesus rebuked when he tried to stop someone from healing people in Jesus' name, "because he does not follow with us"?[44] Was John exhibiting one of the first examples of clericalism?

Perhaps Catholics could be more generous in sharing Eucharist with other Christians if they examined more closely the distortions that it has suffered since the beginning. At its lowest ebb, the joyful thanksgiving meal had evolved into an elaborate ritual where "ordinary" Christians merely looked on while a cleric performed a secret ceremony and then showed them the bread that had been "transformed into Christ" by the cleric's words. Presiders and congregations alike had ceased to notice how absurd it was to come to a celebratory meal where most of the guests did not eat or drink.

44. Luke 9:49.

10

Reshaping the Pyramid

> *When we study history, we realize that there is very, very little about the church that cannot change.*
>
> —RICHARD MCBRIEN

> *The church and theology have the task to begin anew at the beginning, every hour.*
>
> —KARL BARTH

IT IS NOT OUTRAGEOUS to suggest that the church, like every human institution, needs to be reformed. Jesus warned his followers that they would be "pruned" to make them more able to bear fruit,[1] a warning that surely applies to the whole church as well as to its individual members. This book began by considering the gross clerical error of child abuse, and the institutional church's further errors of concealing the crimes and depriving their victims of justice. The institutional structure of the church was then identified as contributing significantly to the problem. Other clerical errors have been noted, by which church laws were distorted and the church's basic structure altered by the restoration of "temple" and "priesthood". Lastly, we have shown how clerics distorted the Eucharist from its original form. Each

---

1. John 15: 1–2; Mark 8:35; Matt 16:24–28; Luke 9:23–27.

Reshaping the Pyramid

of these errors has to some extent betrayed the gospel. What was founded as a community based on love has been distorted into an pyramid-shaped institution, built on power. It remains for us to ask how this church-institution might be changed, so that clericalism is eradicated.

The accumulated clerical errors still contribute substantially to the crisis in which the church finds itself, particularly the drastic drop in church attendance. Young people are "voting with their feet" against a cleric-dominated institution which fails to attract, or even repels them. It is not an exaggeration to compare the church's illness to an addiction which may not yet have destroyed a person, but which, unless cured, will continue to drain them of life. The church's destructive errors need to be transformed radically, in the original sense of that word, by returning to its roots.

Can there be hope? This book answers with a confident "yes". On the broadest scale, Christian values have contributed substantially to shaping the cultures and laws of world civilization. Through respect for persons and the advancement of their human rights; through international law and the constant search to improve the administration of justice, the "yeast" of the Good News continues to work in in people's hearts and minds. Without the gospel, handed on by the Christian church, the turbulent history of the last two millennia would surely have been much worse.

Today there are countless Christians, ordinary good people who live and work in relative obscurity to raise families and build up society. Most of these have long since ceased attending cleric-led Masses, but they hold on to their belief in the eternal, transcendent God. While clerics may accuse them of having "lapsed" from their Catholic or other traditions, in fact they have walked away largely because they have seen through the errors of clericalism. Perhaps they have not "left the church", but rather taken it with them, but have not yet found new ways to share their search within a community.

It will not be enough for the clerical church merely to change a few details. It needs to be deeply *transformed*. The difference is critical. A house, for instance, is changed when it is re-painted or extended: it has merely been given a new appearance. When something is *transformed* it becomes radically different, as a caterpillar is transformed into a butterfly. Anyone seeing its cocoon for the first time could never predict what would emerge, although its adult beauty is all contained in the creature's DNA. None of us can know what a transformed church might look like, but we recall that, at various points in its history, radical innovators like Saints Benedict, Francis, Dominic and

Catherine of Siena; Hildegarde of Bingen and Angela Merici, have created new prototypes, which have turned the church in radical new directions.

To transform or to reform—the terms are equivalent—means more than correcting the crimes of *individuals*: it is a question of *structures*. Many voices today are making practical suggestions towards transforming those aspects of the church by which clerics have deformed it. The ideas presented here are not claimed as original—most are already being acted upon—but we can hope that further discussion will encourage more people to explore them.

Two main areas where change is urgently needed are the use of authority and the celebration of the Eucharist. To transform these radically, we must consider the church's roots in the Scriptures and in the Tradition that has been authentically derived from them.

Transforming Authority

To look first at transforming the use of authority, we might call on St. Cyprian, bishop of Carthage, (ca 200–258 CE) who advised the church to "do nothing without the council of presbyters and the consensus of the people". Well before the second millennium however, clerics began to monopolize the exercise of authority. When leaders of an institution impose their will on the majority, they often act unjustly.

The Second Vatican Council, returning to the model St Cyprian had described, re-emphasized that true dialogue between church leaders and the laity was essential when decisions are being made about Christian communities.[2] Pope Francis has worked strongly to implement the principles of the Council and has emphasized the concept of *synodality*. This appropriately describes the way all the church's members need to negotiate if the church is to be transformed. *Synodality* describes a collaborative process of consultation which strives for more than the "democratic majority" and is more than collecting opinions or running surveys. *Synodality* involves dialogue and means seeking consensus. Dialogue is not mere intellectual debate, but includes feeling the emotions of all participants, and seeking genuine solidarity between all parties. Synodality is based on the truth that participants are truly sisters and brothers, whose diverse gifts and opinions need to be respected. *Synodality* does not eliminate the authority of bishop or pope, but affirms and strengthens it. However *synodality* demands that

2. *LG* 27. Abbott, *Documents*, 51.

Reshaping the Pyramid

these leaders consult sincerely and seek consensus. Building true community can only be based on genuine relationships, which often demand individual conversions. The gospel expects this, in asking that authority be truly a service to the people.

The collective belief and understanding of the whole Christian community is referred to as the *sensus fidelium*.[3] This collective belief is based on what Christians have derived from the Scriptures and what they hold about the major mysteries of their faith, such as the Incarnation; the Trinity; the role of Mary. The transforming of the church does not demand that these dogmas be questioned or reformed—although our understanding of them can always grow deeper. It is the instructions from lesser dimensions of the church's teaching authority—of its *magisterium*—which need to be based more solidly on listening to the followers of Christ. In making pronouncements, popes and bishops are inevitably influenced, favorably or unfavorably, by pressures from the world around them. Some papal statements which in the past were written without genuinely hearing the *sensus fidelium* were Pius IX's 1864 *Syllabus of Errors* and Pius X's 1906 encyclical. The former rejected the propositions that: "... Catholic countries [ought] to allow any public worship other than Catholic [78]; ... those in other religions might have a good hope of eternal salvation [17]; ... the pope can and ought to come to terms with progress, liberalism and modern civilization [80] ... that the church would benefit from losing the Papal States." [76]. The latter declared: "The church is essentially an unequal society". Such documents do not reflect what the whole Catholic population of that time was experiencing, understanding and believing. The same can be said of many lesser papal statements and decisions of Roman Congregations, some more recent examples of which will be discussed below.

The "voice of the faithful" is important because, while Jesus indicated Peter as a leader, he also gave authority to the community.[4] Christ, who encouraged fraternal correction,[5] shares his Holy Spirit with *all* his followers.[6] The Holy Spirit does not work only "from the top down".[7] The New Testament records how the community was consulted about important

---

3. *CCC*, 92–93; *LG* 12; St. Augustine, *De Praed. Sanct.* 14, 27: PL 44, 980.
4. To Peter: Matt 16:17–18; Luke 22:32; John 21:15. To the community: Matt 18:18.
5. Matt 18:15–17.
6. John 20:23. *LG* 4, 7, 9. Abbott, *Documents*, 16–26.
7. Brown, Priest and Bishop, 85.

Clerical Errors

decisions.[8] Clearly, just as it is a responsibility of the church at large to challenge individual wrong *actions* of priests or bishops, it is also a loyal act to question errors in the *statements* of bishops or popes. Canon Law recognizes this: "Christ's faithful ... have the right, indeed at times the duty ... to manifest ... their views on matters which concern the good of the church".[9] This is the *sensus fidelium* at work: the faith of all Christians playing their necessary part in keeping the church faithful to the gospel.

Discerning what the faithful believe means listening to the voices not only of a few celibate male clerics but of *all* Christians, most of whom are sexually active, and half of whom are women. The many different minorities also need to be heard, whether Indigenous, sexual or of other kinds. As one way to hear these voices, Vatican II recommended the creation of parish and diocesan pastoral councils, but it is scandalous that more than half a century later, many bishops and pastors have failed to establish these. This is a tragic deficiency, for there are now many "lay" Christians with extensive knowledge of Scripture, theology and empirical sciences who have much to contribute to their Christian communities. To be effective, however, councils need to be more than consultative. They must be able to make real decisions for the life of their communities, even to elect their pastors and bishops, as was done in the beginning. At present, the cleric has the right to veto anything that these councils might recommend. This severe imbalance of power in all Christian communities has a frustrating and crushing effect, not only on the laity whom it oppresses, but also on fair minded clergy who are trapped behind such a barricade.

Individual Catholics have the *right* to be heard, in every area of Christian community life. This includes shaping their local liturgy, educating children and seminarians, and dealing with the crimes of clergy. Witnesses at the Australian *Royal Commission* often remarked that if lay men and women had been more broadly consulted, perpetrators and victims/survivors of sexual abuse would have been dealt with sooner and more justly.

Christians have the *responsibility* to voice their disagreement where they see false steps being taken in the church. Besides the historical examples mentioned above, more recent blatant failures to consult the *sensus fidelium* have been *Humanae Vitae*, Pope Paul VI's encyclical on the regulation of births, and the continuing papal insistence on obligatory clerical celibacy. In issuing the 1968 encyclical, Paul VI did not accept the advice

8. Acts 6:2, 15:12.
9. *Code*, Canon 212 §3.

of his body of consultors, even after expanding it to include many bishops. When he eventually published his teaching, eleven episcopal conferences and the majority of Catholic laity did not accept some of its basic claims.

In the matter of obligatory clerical celibacy, Vatican II reiterated that celibacy it is *not* essentially linked to ordination; and at their 1971 synod more than half of the world's bishops saw the ordination of married men as a pastoral necessity. The 2019 Amazonia Synod voted even more strongly (128 to 41) in favor of married clergy for Latin America, but in 2022, celibacy for diocesan clergy is still compulsory.

It would be interesting to know what the *whole* church thinks of Canon Law's description of the church, written by clerical authorities: "*By divine institution* [emphasis added], among Christ's faithful there are in the Church sacred [sic] ministers, who in law are also called clerics—the others are called lay people".[10] It has for long been emphasized that clerics are the main channel by which we have access to God. How can this be squared with the New Testament, and with the statement from Vatican II, that *all* Christians have the gifts of the Holy Spirit; and *all* are called to minister to, and share their faith with each other and with those who do not yet believe?[11] Without proper consultation, how can we know what the majority of the church believes on such matters? Until now, assemblies at every level, even the church-wide Synods of Bishops, have notoriously been dominated and effectively gagged by clerical officials. The statement is often made in defense of the church's pyramid structure that "the church is not a democracy". This needs to be countered with "nor did Jesus establish an absolute monarchy".

Transforming the Eucharist

Authority is abused particularly in the way that clerics control the Eucharist, the primary means that Jesus gave his followers to encounter him in the heart of their community. It is an error to see the Eucharist merely as a sacrament by which the *individual* becomes holy. The church will be transformed only by re-building communities around the regular celebration of this beautiful way of giving thanks to God. It is scarcely surprising that people—especially the young—no longer find the Eucharist life-giving. Clerics have made it into a fixed performance by an ordained minister who

10. *Code*, Canon 207.
11. *LG* 31. Abbott, *Documents*, 57.

Clerical Errors

in today's large, combined parishes often does not even know most of those taking part. The ritual has become almost entirely detached from any sense of community and bears little resemblance to the thanksgiving meal that Jesus shared with his friends. Controlled as it is by clerical authorities, it no longer meets most people's needs.

If St Thomas Aquinas could state that the purpose of this sacrament—*res sacramenti*—is to signify and bring about the unity of the church-community, then the church must rediscover ways of celebrating Eucharist that tries realistically to unite contemporary people of all ages. This obviously means that Eucharist will be celebrated differently in various places. To resist such developments for legalistic reasons seems remarkably like worrying about gnats while ignoring camels.[12]

Jesus did not specify any particular way in which to "do this" in memory of him. The Eucharist does not have to be celebrated identically by every Christian community on the planet. Unity is not uniformity, and rigid uniformity is unhealthy, even lethal, for in nature and human life unity flourishes within diversity and amid constant change. When persons in authority demand uniformity, we need to ask whether they are seeking to augment their own power, or to help those whom they are meant to serve.

Even within current legal requirements, many simple choices can be made to improve the rich symbolism of what happens at Eucharist.[13]

The arrangement of the *place* of worship affects the community's action.

Whether the group is small or large, it is better to sit or stand in a semicircle, or around three sides of a rectangle rather than to face in one direction. When people "gather round" and can see each other, a stronger sense of community is automatically formed. In a church building which has fixed pews that extend back dozens of rows from the presider, people cannot see and communicate with each other, even if the clerical leader allows them to share the Sign of Peace.

The typical current Sunday Mass is anything but a gathering of equals, for the presider dominates the ceremony. The congregation's relationship with the *Word* is restricted, for only the presider shares, in the homily,

12. Matt 23:24.
13. See, e.g., Darragh, *When Christians Gather*.

whatever impact the readings have on *his* life and faith. Others have no opportunity to be heard.

The *bread* used for the Eucharist needs to be recognizable as everyday food, preferably baked by the celebrating community.

The ancient symbolism of breaking and sharing the *one loaf* is basic to the eucharistic action. Then, as we do when hosting a meal in our own households, the persons who distribute the Body and Blood of Christ ought to show *hospitality* to others by serving them before receiving it themselves.

The *one cup*, shared by all, is also an essential symbol.

The profound meaning of this unusual, indeed shocking, practice needs to be pondered and explained, and the custom restored. Where there may be a risk to health, as in a pandemic, the alternative which best retains the cup's symbolic meaning would seem to be that each communicant, having been given the consecrated bread, dips it into the chalice proffered by a second minister.

Not least, the *language* used in prayers obviously needs to be contemporary, vernacular, and inclusive.

The parish in its present form is not a community. Innumerable good clergy have labored, and still labor in parishes as pastors, preachers of the Word, and spiritual guides. But despite their heroic efforts to serve people, they usually fail to build Christian communities among most of the Catholics in their territory.

Many committed Christians admit that they find parish liturgies insipid and uninspiring but loyally refrain from criticizing the hard-working clergy, believing that clergy cannot make significant changes. Seeking to better nourish their spirit, such people often "shop around" for a more inspiring presider, preacher or ceremony. Not finding any sense of community, such people reasonably seek to satisfy their *individual* needs, as if the Eucharist were a consumer product.

One basic reason for this failure is that parishes originated in village society, in a church already clericalized. They are now too large. In most parishes neither the pastor nor the members can know more than the names of a few of its hundreds, if not thousands, of people. Some parishes make a special effort to welcome people arriving at Mass; and some work hard to form small groups within the parish, but these efforts seldom last very long. The groups rarely become a living group of Christian friends that provide long-term support for their members. It can be argued that this is principally because they cannot regularly share the Eucharist together.

It is not surprising that today the numbers are dwindling, of men willing to give their lives to be ordained to lead such parishes. In wealthier wealthy countries other "solutions" are being tried. One common tactic is to merge several parishes into one, but this "solution" is obviously based on the needs of the clerics, and not of the people. Merging parishes weakens and destroys whatever elements of community remained in the parishes that were merged; and the merger is often done without proper consultation. The church leaders usually fail to follow the path of *synodality*, but put the needs of the clerical minority above the needs of the majority: a clerical error of giant proportions.

Another common "solution" is to import clergy from poorer churches in the Philippines, South Asia and Africa. This too is seriously problematic, since it is unjust to the poorer countries, which need their clergy more than our wealthier churches do. Often this "solution" proves unjust also to the people whom the imported clergy come to serve. While differences of language can eventually be overcome, many of the imported clerics come from countries where the church still suffers from entrenched clericalism, having so far failed to implement the teachings of the Second Vatican Council. *Synodality* is not to be expected from such leaders, but where parish members reject patriarchy and clericalism, serious conflict is inevitable.

A radical way to heal the church is through small eucharistic communities. Every person responds to the warmth of friendship and good relationships. The statement in Psalm 133 is as profound as it is obvious: "How very good and pleasant it is, when kindred live in unity!" As we have seen, the Eucharist was originally the action of small communities that gathered in Jesus' name, rejoiced together, shared food and gave thanks to the Father. Could it be that rebuilding a network of such communities is the path most likely to transform and re-create the Christian church? Creating true communities would also be a step towards healing and uniting the whole of humanity, for such communities can effectively resist the worst elements in our contemporary world: consumerist greed, prejudice, violence and militarism.

Reshaping the Pyramid

In recent times, a variety of new Christian movements are rediscovering how the welcoming atmosphere of a community can powerfully transform people's lives.[14] These new organizations consist of committed face-to-face groups that either live together or meet regularly around a shared meal. In them, individuals and families become friends and grow together in maturity. They effectively demonstrate that small, committed groups are much more effective at forming community than is the traditional parish.

In addition to the organizations just listed, small eucharistic communities known as Basic Christian Communities have been successful for many decades. Mostly originating in poorer countries, they have faced criticism and opposition from Vatican clerical authorities—for they challenge clericalism—but they have provided an ideal human setting in which Christian life can flourish. The members readily help each other with their ordinary and extraordinary needs: childcare, sickness and bereavement, transport and finances. In meeting these mutual needs, the face-to-face community is much more likely than the larger parish to attract and engage people of all ages. In these smaller groups, members have equal status and can readily share, as friends, the exploration of all life's questions, and in doing so, grow together in faith.

Small eucharistic communities have all the ordinary human weaknesses and conflicting interests which tend to divide people, but they are better equipped than most human groups to overcome these. Because their constant focus is on Christ's call to love and forgive each other, they have a much better chance of facing the truth and preserving unity than any larger institution.

Celebrating Eucharist in small, enduring local groups is a truly radical idea: it returns to our Christian roots; to how the church began. Could such groups effectively renew and transform the church by becoming again its basic unit? The respected theologian Gabriel Moran was not alone in proposing that the entire church would benefit by becoming a worldwide network of such groups. He suggested that they have less than twelve adult members, but opinions differ about the ideal size.[15] To bring about this transformation there is no need to discard the present legal structure of the

---

14. E.g., *Bosé, Communione et Liberatione, Focolare,* Marriage Encounter, Neo Catechumenate, Teams of Our Lady, Catholic Worker. Outside the Catholic tradition: *Bruderhof.*

15. Moran, *What Happened to the Roman Catholic church?*

territorial parish, for such communities could thrive *within* it, while their members would relate to the parish in a radically different way. The small communities would normally celebrate Sunday Eucharist at a member's house or other suitable meeting-space. The community would be the focus of most of its members' activities: within it they would find their strongest friendships and mutual help. But their community would also be alert to the needs and activities of the wider neighborhood, and the very existence of the group, as a loving community, would constantly proclaim the Good News to those observing it. The community would be a true source of the four basic Christian activities: worship, fellowship, service and proclaiming the gospel. On special occasions like Easter, Christmas and patronal festivals, the small communities within a parish could gather for a more elaborate celebration. Through the development of such small communities, the parish could eventually become a strong "communion of communities."[16]

Basic Eucharistic Communities need to be small enough for all members to know each other as friends: the maximum size might be less than fifty adults, but the optimum will be found by experience. When a community grows to a size that becomes impractical, it will need to make the painful but courageous decision to divide. This is essential if communities are to thrive, and founding a new church in this way is a powerful way to spread the Good News of God's Reign. Founding a new group will challenge the community to live out the gospel's call to "lose one's life" in order to deepen and share that life.

It is convenient if members of a small community live in the same physical neighborhood, but exceptions will obviously occur. As far as possible the community will include people of all ages, sexes, marital status and local racial groups. The community will welcome all, especially persons with special needs, and reach out to invite people newly arrived in the neighborhood. Some communities will be strong enough to welcome people whom wider society often rejects, such as persons trying to find a place in society after leaving jail. Joining an existing community or helping to form a new one will be an effective way for any Christian to share in transforming the church and the world.

Who would preside at Eucharist in such communities? There is no need to surrender to the so-called "shortage of priests" and imagine that this plan cannot succeed because of the lack of ordained ministers. As we saw in

---

16. The *Movement for a Better World* teams work towards this goal in trying to renew parishes, but the *Plan* they set up often fails when subsequent pastors do not support it. (From personal experience).

Reshaping the Pyramid

chapter 9, in the earliest days of the church there were no Christian priests. The role gradually evolved, until the cleric became the only person considered competent to perform what is properly the action of the whole community. It was clerical law that established the specialized "priest" as sole "celebrant" of the Eucharist and established him as quasi "lord" of the territorial parish.

Today, each eucharistic community will need to choose a competent person to be its pastor and guide, and to preside at Eucharist. As was the custom among communities in the early church, the community would present its chosen leader to the local bishop to be ordained to lead that specific local church. The proposed leader would need suitable formation in Scripture, theology and liturgy, but on a simpler model than the current clerical priesthood. The wider church will always need specialist scholars in Scripture and theology, but to be a pastor who leads a small community, academic qualifications are no more intrinsically necessary than is celibacy. So the pastors or leaders of small communities could be married men, and there is no reason why they could not be women, for we have seen in chapter 8 that the reasons given to prohibit women from eucharistic leadership are not valid. Only when women take their rightful role in sharing leadership in the community and at the Eucharist will the church be able to claim that it is truly a community of equals.

The work of pastor and guide for a small community would not be a full-time task but might perhaps occupy two or three days each week. Leaders would not need a salary, being supported from their own employment or retirement funds, supplemented, if necessary, by a stipend from the community.

What if the local bishop is not willing to ordain this kind of leader for local communities? It is important that communities collaborate with the bishop, who is symbol of unity in the local church, but the church must proceed by true dialogue and *synodality* between its members. This demands genuine listening and mutual respect. Christians have a right to experiment with new forms, especially in the current situation where the old forms are in serious decline. If the local bishop or Bishops' Conference is reluctant to ordain the persons whom small groups elect to lead them, would they not be stifling the Christian life of those people? Faced with such opposition, local communities will need to discern, with prayer, how best to proceed.

They will need to recall the sad history of clerical errors made even by those who have compiled the church's laws. They will also need to recall that current laws about leadership of the Eucharist—about who can

Clerical Errors

be ordained priest—are in conflict with the gospel, for Jesus told us to "do this in memory of me", but human laws about who can be ordained to lead the Eucharist are, world-wide, preventing about half of Christ's followers from celebrating Eucharist. Such laws are clearly unjust. Can unjust laws command our obedience?

Christians need to ask, in view of the massive exodus from the church and the constant damage that clericalism is doing to people, what price are we paying to *pretend* that we have church unity? The basic decision facing each small community will be whether it is more important to obey Christ's *divine* command, or to allow flawed *human* laws to restrict the life of that Christian community. Ultimately, local communities will need to discern how best to proceed, as they try to follow Christ and to transform the church.

Like any crisis, the church's present grave predicament is an opportunity. If compels us to reflect deeply on the church's origins and purpose: to see the church honestly in the context of history, identifying aspects that need urgently to be re-formed: to be changed so that new growth can happen.

This book emphasizes what many other voices are saying: that even within the world-wide decline of religious institutions, the Catholic church is sick with its own diseases. It is failing largely because of basic errors still being made by clerics. The fundamental clerical error has been to claim to be a superior caste, and to misuse the power thus claimed. Clerical abuse of children, and the hiding of those crimes, have been the most obvious and abhorrent clerical errors, but another grave abuse of power has been to modify and control the Eucharist until most Christians are now deprived of this source of divine life.

The church can move towards transformation and healing only when its members act on the truth that all the baptized possess the Holy Spirit;[17] that all have a right to celebrate Eucharist in life-giving communities; and that the commands of the gospel are superior to human laws. Where there is conflict, the gospel must be obeyed, and the human laws reformed.

Our work as Christians will not be completed before the *Parousia*, the mysterious end times. Until then the church-institution will continue to evolve as it has evolved from its beginning, by the efforts of each member to bring about the Reign of God. We can have sure hope that Christian people in our time, alert to what that Spirit is saying to the churches,[18] will use the power of the Spirit in them to renew and transform the church.

---

17. *LG* 31. Abbott, *Documents*, 57.
18. Rev 2:7.

Bibliography

Abbott Walter M., SJ, ed. *The Documents of Vatican II*. London: Geoffrey Chapman, 1966
Alexander, Eben. *Proof of Heaven: A Neurosurgeon's Journey into the Afterlife*. Sydney: Pan Macmillan, 2012.
Allen, John L., Jr. *The Future Church, How Ten Trends Are Revolutionizing the Catholic Church*. New York: Image, 2009.
Ammicht-Quinn, Regina, Hille Haker, and Maureen Junker-Kenny, eds. The Structural Betrayal of Trust, *Concilium* 2004/3, SCM London, 2004.
Anderson, C.C. "When magisterium becomes imperium: Peter Damian on the accountability of bishops for scandal." *Theological Studies*, 65, 4, 2004.
Armour, Josephine E. *Call No One on Earth Your Father; Revisioning the Ordained Ministry in the Contemporary Catholic Church*. Eugene, OR: Wipf & Stock, 2019.
Baxter, Archibald. *We Will Not Cease, the Autobiography of a Conscientious Objector*. Whatamongo Bay, New Zealand: Tate Catley, 1980.
Beal, John P. "The 1962 instruction *Crimen sollicitationis*; Caught Red-handed or Handed a Red Herring?" *Studia Canonica* 41 (2007) 199–236.
Bianchi, Eugene C., and Rosemary Radford Reuther. *A Democratic Catholic Church: the Reconstruction of Roman Catholicism*. New York: Crossroad, 1993.
Boff, Leonardo. *Church: Charism and Power; Liberation Theology and the Institutional Church*. London: SCM, 1985.
Bonner, Gerald. *St Augustine of Hippo: Life and Controversies*. Norwich: Canterbury Press, 1986.
Bregman, Rutger. *Humankind, a Hopeful History*. London: Bloomsbury, 2020.
Brennan, Frank, SJ. *Observations On the Pell Proceedings*. Ballan: Connor Court, 2021.
Brown, Peter. *Augustine of Hippo: a Biography*. Oakland: University of California Press, 2000.
Brown, Raymond E., SS. *The Churches the Apostles Left Behind*. New York: Paulist, 1984.
———. *Priest and Bishop; Biblical reflections*. New York: Paulist, 1970.

Bibliography

Browning, Christopher. *Ordinary Men: Reserve Police Battalion 101 and the Final Solution in Poland*. New York: Harper, 2017.

Cafardi, N. P. *Before Dallas: the US Bishops' Response to Clergy Sexual Abuse of Children*. New York: Paulist Press, 2008.

———. "The Scandal of Secrecy: Canon Law and the Sexual Abuse Crisis". *Commonweal* July 21, 2010). http://commonweal magazine.org/scandal.secrecy.

Cahill, Desmond and Peter Wilkinson. *Child Sexual Abuse in the Catholic Church, an Interpretative Review of the Literature and Public Enquiry Reports*. Melbourne: Center for Global Research, 2017.

Carr, Anne E. *Transforming Grace: Christian Experience and Women's Experience*. San Francisco: Harper and Rowe, 1988.

Catechism of the Catholic Church: Rome: Libreria Editrice Vaticana, 2000.

The Catholic Bishops of Victoria and the Catholic Religious Orders, Congregations and Societies within Victoria. *Facing the Truth: Submission to the Victorian Parliamentary Inquiry by the Church in Victoria*. Melbourne: 2012.

The Centre International D'Etudes. *Ministerial and Common Priesthood in the Eucharistic Celebration: the Proceedings of the 1998 Fourth International Colloquium of Historical, Canonical and Theological Studies on the Roman Catholic Liturgy*. London: Saint Austin, 1999.

Chadwick, Henry. *The Early Church*. London: Penguin, 1967.

Cochini, Christian, SJ. *The Apostolic Origins of Priestly Celibacy*. Translated by Nelly Marans. San Francisco, Ignatius, 2002.

The Code of Canon Law in English Translation. London: Collins, 1983.

Collins, Paul. *The Modern Inquisition*. New York: Overlook, 2002.

Congar, Yves. *The Mystery of the Temple: the Manner of God's Presence to His Creature from Genesis to the Apocalypse*. London: Burns Oates, 1962.

———. *Priest and Layman*. Translated by P. J. Hepburne-Scott. London: Darton, Longman & Todd, 1967.

Congregation for Divine Worship. *Liturgiam Authenticam: on the Use of Vernacular Languages in the Publication of the Books of the Roman Liturgy*. Rome: 2001. https://www.vatican.va/roman_curia/congregations/ccdds/documents/rc_con_ccdds_doc_20010507_liturgiam-authenticam_en.html.

Connolly, R. H. *Didascalia Apostolorum*, Oxford: Clarendon, 1929.

Cornwell, J. *The Pope in Winter: the Dark Place of John Paul's Papacy*. UK: Penguin, 2005.

Cozzens, Donald. *Faith that dares to speak*. Mulgrave: John Garratt, 2004.

Crothers, John. *The Clergy Club*. Hindmarsh: ATF, 2018.

Cwiekowski, Frederick J. *The Beginnings of the Church*. New Jersey: Paulist, 1988.

Daly, Robert J., SJ. *Sacrifice Unveiled; the True Meaning of Christian Sacrifice*. Bloomsbury: T & T Clarke, 2009.

Darragh, Neil. *When Christians Gather Issues in the Celebration of the Eucharist*. New Jersey: Paulist, 1996.

Davey, Melissa. *The Case of George Pell: Reckoning with Child Sexual Abuse by Clergy*. Melbourne: Scribe, 2020.

Delgado, Richard and Jean Stefancic. *Critical Race Theory: An Introduction*. New York University Press: 2001.

Denzinger, Heinrich. *Enchiridion Symbolorum*, Barcinone: Herder, 1957.

Donovan, Vincent J. *Christianity Rediscovered: an Epistle from the Masai*. London: SCM, 1978.

Bibliography

Doyle, Thomas P., OP, et al. *Sex, priests, and Secret Codes: the Catholic Church's 2000-Year Paper Trail of Sexual Abuse*. London: Crux, 2006.
Dziwisz, S. *A Life with Karol: My Forty-Year Friendship with the Man who Became Pope*. New York: Doubleday, 2008.
Edgar, Brian, and Gordon Reece, eds. *Whose Homosexuality, Which Authority? Homosexual Practice, Marriage, Ordination and the Church*. Adelaide: ATF, 2006.
Ehrman, Bart D. *Misquoting Jesus: the Story Behind Who Changed the Bible and Why*. San Francisco: Harper, 2005.
Elliott, Dyan. *The Corrupter of Boys; Sodomy, Scandal and the Medieval Clergy*. Philadelphia: University of Pennsylvania Press, 2020.
Fiorenza, Elizabeth Schussler. *Discipleship of Equals*. London: SCM, 1993.
Fitzmeyer, Joseph. *The Gospel According to Luke:* Garden City, New York: Doubleday, 1985.
Foster, Chrissie, and Paul Kennedy. *Hell on the Way to Heaven: An Australian Mother's Love; the Power of the Catholic Church; A Fight for Justice over Child Sexual Abuse*. Sydney: Bantam, 2010.
Galot, Jean, SJ. *Theology of the Priesthood*. San Francisco: Ignatius, 1985.
Geraghty, Christopher. *Dancing with the Devil*. Melbourne: Spectrum, 2012.
Gillion, Chris, and Damianne Grace. *Reckoning: the Catholic Church and Child Sexual Abuse*. Adelaide: ATF and Eureka Street, 2014.
Gleeson, John, ed. *Priesthood, the Hard Questions*. Petersham, NSW: E.J Dwyer, 1993.
Goosen, Gideon. *Clericalism: Stories from the Pews; a Workbook for Parishes*. Bayswater: Coventry, 2020.
Graff, Ann. "Women in the Roman Catholic Ministry; New Vision, New Ethics". In *Clergy Ethics in a Changing Society. Mapping the Terrain*, edited by James P. Wind et al., 215-30. Louisville: Westminster/John Knox,1991.
―――. "Infallibility: Have we Heard the Final Word on Women's Ordination?" *US Catholic* 61 (1996) 6-13.
Greenberg, K. J., and J. L. Dratel, eds. *The Torture Papers: The Road to Abu Ghraib*, Cambridge University Press, 2005.
Harris, Maria. "A Discipleship of Equals: Implications for Ministry". In Francis A Eigo, ed. *A Discipleship of Equals: Towards a Christian Feminist Spirituality*. Villanova, PA: Villanova University Press, 1988.
Hart, David Bentley. *That All Shall Be Saved: Heaven, Hell, and Universal Salvation*. New Haven: Yale University Press, 2019.
Healy, John. *A Perfect Heart: My Story*. Dublin: Liberties Press, 2012.
Heasley, Berise. *Call No One Father: Countering Clericalism in the Catholic Tradition*. Melbourne: Coventry Press, 2019.
Hellholm, David, and Dieter Sanger, eds. *The Eucharist: Its Origins and Contexts: Sacred Meal, Communal Meal, Table Fellowship in Late Antiquity, Early Judaism, and Early Christianity*. Tubingen: Mohr Siebeck, 2017.
Holland, Joe. *The Cruel Eleventh-Century Imposition of Western Clerical Celibacy: A Monastic-Inspired Attack on Catholic Episcopal & Presbyteral Families*. Washington, DC: Pacem in Terris, 2017.
Janis, Irving. *Groupthink: Psychological Study of Policy Decisions and Fiascoes*, Boston: Houghton Mifflin, 1982.
Jarrell, Randall. The Complete Poems, New York: Farrar, Straus, Giroux, 1969

Bibliography

John Jay College of Criminal Justice. *The Nature and Scope of the Problem of Sexual Abuse of Minors by Catholic Priests and Deacons in the United States*; City University of New York. https://en.wikipedia.org/wiki/John_Jay_Report.

Johnson, Elizabeth A. "Trinity: To Let the Symbol Sing Again". *Theology Today* 54 (1997) 299–311.

Justin Martyr. *Apologia pro Christianis*. Jean-Paul Migne, ed. *Patrologia Graeca*, Paris, 1857.

Kaiser, Robert Blair. *Whistle: Fr Tom Doyle's Steadfast Witness for Victims of Clerical Sexual Abuse*. Thiensville, WI: *Caritas*, 2015.

Kalantzis, George. *Caesar and the Lamb; Early Christian Attitudes on War and Military Service*. Oregon: Cascade, 2012.

Keenan, Marie. *Child Sexual Abuse and the Catholic Church: Gender, Power and Organizational Culture*. Oxford: Oxford University Press, 2013.

Kelly, J. *The Oxford Dictionary of the Popes*, OUP, Oxford, 1986.

Kelly, Michael Bernard. *Seduced by Grace, Contemporary Spirituality, Gay experience and Christian faith*. Melbourne: Clouds of Magellan, 2007.

Krueger, P., ed. *Codex Iustinianus.*, Oxford: Oxford University Press, 1877.

Lacugna, Catherine Mowry. *God For Us; the Trinity and Christian Life*. San Francisco: Harper, 1991.

Lathrop, G. W. "Sacrifice?" *Worship* 64 (1990) 30–48.

Lehner, U. L. *Monastic Prisons and Torture chambers: Crime and Punishment in European Monasteries 1600–1800*. Eugene, OR: Cascade, 2013.

Lennan, Richard. "Deconstructing the Priesthood". *ACR* 82 (2010) 162–77.

Lewis, C. S. *The Inner Ring*, Memorial Lecture at Kings College, London, 1944.

MacCulloch, D. *Silence: A Christian history*. London: Penguin, 2014.

Malick, Terrence. dir. *A Hidden Life* (Motion picture, 2019).

Maly, Eugene H., ed. *The Priest and Sacred Scripture*. Washington, DC: United States Catholic Conference Publications Office, 1972.

Martel, Frederic *In the Closet of the Vatican: Power, Homosexuality, Hypocrisy*. Translated by Shaun Whiteside. London: Bloomsbury Continuum, 2019.

McCormack, Irene. "Do this in Memory of Me". *Compass Theology Review* 25 (1991) 33–35.

McGann, Mary E., RSCJ. *The Meal That Reconnects: Eucharistic Eating and the Global Food Crisis*. Collegeville, MN: Liturgical Press Academic, 2020.

McGillion, Chris, and John O'Carroll. *Our Fathers*. New South Wales: Charles Sturt University, 2003.

Michalski, Melvin. *The Relationship Between the Universal Priesthood of the Baptized and the Ministerial Priesthood of the Ordained in Vatican II and in Subsequent Theology*. Lewiston, NY: Mellen,1996.

Milligan, Louise. *Cardinal: the Rise and Fall of George Pell*. Melbourne: Melbourne University Press, 2017.

———. *Witness*. Sydney: Hachette Australia, 2020.

Mohler, James A., SJ. *The Origin and Evolution of the Priesthood; a Return to the Sources*. New York: Alba House, 1970.

Moody, Raymond. *Life after Life*. Bantam, 1975.

Moran, Gabriel. *What Happened to the Roman Catholic Church? What Now?: An Institutional and Personal Memoir*. Pennsauken, NJ: BookBaby, 2021.

Bibliography

Morris, William Martin. *Benedict, Me and the Cardinals Three; the Story of the Dismissal of Bishop Bill Morris by Pope Benedict XVI.* Hindmarsh: ATF, 2014.
Muller, R. "Death Penalty May Not Bring Peace to Victims' Families." *Psychology Today*, October 19, 2016.
O'Brien, John. *Women's Ordination in the Catholic Church: Historical and Theological Reasons.* Eugene, OR: Cascade, 2020.
O'Loughlin, Thomas. *The Didache: a Window on the Earliest Christians.* Grand Rapids: Baker Academic, 2010.
———. *The Eucharist: Origins and contemporary understandings.* London: Bloomsbury Academic, 2015.
O'Malley, J. "The Scandal: A Historian's Perspective". *America* 186 (2002) 14–17.
Osborne, Kenan B., OFM. *Priesthood: a History of the Ordained Ministry in the Roman Catholic Church.* New York: Paulist, 1988.
Parvis, Paul, OP. "History of Celibacy." CR, 1981, 322 and 354.
Pell, George. *George Cardinal Pell: Prison Journal.* San Francisco: Ignatius Press, 2021.
Perry, Gina. *Behind the Shock Machine: The Untold Story of the Notorious Milgram Psychology Experiments.* New York, Perseus, 2013.
Pius X, Pope. *Vehementer Nos.* Rome: Libreria Editrice Vaticana, 1906.
Pius XI, Pope. *Quadragesimo Anno, Encyclical on Reconstruction of the Social Order.* Rome: Libreria Editrice Vaticana, 1931.
Porteous, Julian. *The Life and Ministry of Priests at the Beginning of the New Millennium.* Ballan: Modotti, 2009.
Primavesi, Anne, and Jennifer Henderson. *Our God Has No Favorites; a Liberation Theology of the Eucharist.* Tunbridge Wells: Burns and Oates, 1989.
Radelet, M. "The Incremental Retributive Impact of a Death Sentence Over Life Without Parole." *University of Michigan Journal of Law Reform*, 49, 4. (2016).
Rahner, Karl. *The Shape of the Church to Come.* New York: Seabury, 1974.
Robinson, Bishop Geoffrey. *For Christ's Sake: End Sexual Abuse in the Catholic Church For Good.* Mulgrave: Garratt, 2013.
Ronson, Jon. *The Psychopath Test: A Journey Through the Madness Industry.* New York: Riverhead, 2011.
Ross, Susan. "God's Embodiment and Women". In *Freeing Theology: the Essentials of Theology in Feminist Perspective*, ed. Catherine Mowry Lacugna. San Francisco: Harper, 1993.
Schillebeeckx, Edward. The Christian Community and its Office Bearers, *Concilium* 133 (1980) 95–133.
———. *The Church with a Human Face: A New and Expanded Theology of Ministry.* London: SCM, 1985.
———. *Church: the Human Story of God.* London, SCM, 1990.
Schrenk, Christine. *Crispina and Her Sisters: Women and Authority in Early Christianity.* Minneapolis: Fortress, 2017.
Schussler-Fiorenza, Elizabeth. *Discipleship of Equals: a Critical Feminist Ekklesia-logy of Liberation.* Lawrenceville, GA: Crossroads, 1993.
Shupe, Anson. *Rogue Clerics: the Social Problem of Clergy Deviance.* New Brunswick, NJ: Transaction, 2008.
Stout, Martha. *The Sociopath Next Door: the Ruthless versus the Rest of Us.* London: John Murray, 2006.
The Swag, Australian National Council of Priests, Belmont, Victoria.

Bibliography

Tapsell, Kieran. *Potiphar's Wife: the Vatican's Secret and Child Sexual Abuse*. Adelaide: ATF 2014.
———. Submission to the Royal Commission into Institutional Responses to Child Sexual Abuse. 2015.
Tertullian. *Apologeticum*. Heinrich Hoppe, ed. *Corpus Scriptorum Ecclesiasticorum Latinorum*, Vienna and Leipzig 1939.
Torrell, Jean-Pierre. *A Priestly People: Baptismal Priesthood and Priestly Ministry*. New York: Paulist, 1989.
Van der Meer, F. *Augustine the Bishop*, London: Sheed and Ward, 1961.
Vanhoye, Albert, SJ. *Old Testament Priests and the New Priest*. Petersham, MA: St Bede's 1986.
Volf, Miroslav. *After Our Likeness; the Church the Image of the Trinity*. Grand Rapids MI: Eerdemans, 1998.
Werlen, Martin, OSB. *Embers in the Ashes*, New York: Paulist, 2012.
Wijngaards, John. *What They Don't Teach You in Catholic College; Women in the Priesthood and the Mind of Christ*. Lafayette, LA: *Acadian House*, 2020.
Wilkerson, Isabel. *Caste, the Lies that Divide Us*. UK: Allen Lane, 2020.
Wills, Gary. *Papal Sin: Structures of Deceit*. London: Darton, Longman, and Todd, 2000.
Wilson, George B. *Clericalism: the Death of Priesthood*. Collegeville, MN: Liturgical Press, 2008.
Winter, Michael. *What Ever Happened to Vatican II?* London: Sheed & Ward, 1985.
Wood, Susan. "Priestly Identity: Sacrament to the Ecclesial Community." *Worship* 69 (1995) 109–27.
Zimbardo, Philip. *The Lucifer Effect: Understanding How Good People Turn Evil*. New York: Random House, 2007.
Zizioulas, John D. *Being as Communion: Studies in Personhood and the Church*. London: Darton, Longman, and Todd, 1985.

Index

Abu Ghraib, 108, 109
abuse
   "models" to explain, 63
   by religious person, especially painful, 53, 54
   delay in reporting, 53, 58
   flawed definition of, in Canon Law, 93
   link to celibacy?, 67
   link to clericalism, 69, 72, 80
   link to power imbalance, 66
   psychological, 55
   rate of, by Catholic clergy, 57
   seen as normal, 53
   trivialised by church leaders, 67
   variation in rate of, 59
abuser
   deferent towards authority, 67
accountability, 114
Africa, sexual abuse in, 22
agape meal, 146, 152
Ahimelech, 136
Allison, James, 66
ambiguity, 38
Anderson, John, 48
Angus, Christopher, 55
Aotearoa New Zealand, 36, 42, 44, 63
apostles, 126, 129
Apuron, Archbishop Anthony, 43

Argentina, 27
art, 124
Asia, sexual abuse in, 28
Auchettl, Paul, 49
Australia, 35
   bishops confused, 84
   caste in, 112
   First Nations, 112
   institutional errors, 106
   Mass attendance, xi
   no statutes of limitations, 97
   number of clerics abusing, 36
   percentage of clerics abusing, xii, 36
   use of Agent Orange, 106
Austria, 29
authority, 108
   abusers exploit, 48
   as service, 159
   becomes centralized, 72, 128
   contributes to abuse, 81
   in institutions, 107–9
   not eliminated by synodality, 158
   shared by community, 159

Baker, Billy, 38
Balasuriya, Tissa, 110
Ballarat, 8, 36
Bandura, Albert, 107

Index

baptism
   change caused by, 70
   confers "character", 134
   confers the Holy Spirit, 142, 168
   makes person "priest, prophet, king", 139
baptized
   all are members of the church, 84
Barbarin, Cardinal, 31
Basic Christian Communities, 165
basilicas, 122
Belgium, 30
bella figura, 97
Benedictines, New Norcia, 36
Benediction of the Blessed Sacrament, 151
Best, Robert, 37, 41, 48, 63
Betrayal of Trust, 67, 107
Bevilacqua, Cardinal, 24
Bindoon, 55
bishops, 71
   "liberal", 116
   "like rabbits in the headlights", 84
   "should not report abuse", 95
   appointment process criticized, 99, 101
   assume civil powers, 132
   authority of local, 87
   become wealthy, 132
   children of, 137
   concealed abuse, 85
   condemned as incompetent, 98
   deny abuse, 80, 81
   distinctive dress, 133
   election of, 160
   England and Wales, 94
   exempt from civil trial, 90
   failed to protect, 85
   failed to report offenses, 90
   guilt of, 102
   ignorance of, 83
   laicized, 28
   married, 130, 135, 137
   military involvement, 132
   monarchical, 127, 128
   moved offenders, 84, 95
   ordained unsuitable candidates, 59
   power of, 66
   promise made by, 98
   relationship to priests, 94
   requests to Vatican ignored, 96
   resist inquiry, 58
   rights ignored, 111
   see through clericalism, 74
   selection of, 98
   short of priests, 20
   their synods manipulated, 161
   unable to dismiss offender, 96
   USA, 58, 97
   want married priests, 161
   wives of, 137
   wrong statements by, 160
Blenkiron, Peter, 13
Body of Christ, 122, 147
Boff, Leonardo, 110
Boston, 24
Boys Town, 54
Brady, Noel, 11
bread
   pre-cut, 153
   unleavened, 152
Brennan, Frank, 9, 13
Buddha, 104, 142
Byrne, Gerard, 53

Catardi, Nicholas, 93, 102
Cahill and Wilkinson, xii
Caldwell, John, 35
Canon Law
   and clerics "indelible character", 70
   change recommended, 101
   distorted by clericalism, 86
   fails to help victims, 95
   ineffectual against abuse, 93
caste, 104, 112
   no scientific basis, 113
Catholic Catechism, 70
Catholic church
   caste within, 113
   conspiracy against?, 60
   expansion post WWII, 59
   initatives to prevent child abuse, 60
   limits debate, 98
   major causes of abuse within, 80, 107
   massive failure to protect children, 45
   not essentially the institution, xv
   patriarchal nature, 81

Index

reasons for decline of, xi
secretive, 90
sickness of, 168
Catholic clergy
  and power, 66
  compared to other professions, 57
  majority successful, 68
  percentage homosexual, 65
  respected, 57
Catholics
  "traditionalist", xv
  leaving church, xi
  reluctant to report abuse, 23
  wanting women priests, 72
CDF, 35, 91, 96
  denied natural justice, 110
celibacy
  a higher state?, 138
  and ritual purity, 137
  as witness to the transcendent, 137
  does it lead to sexual abuse?, 67, 68
  imperfect practice of, 73
  many want it optional, 68
  not essential for priesthood, 115, 67, 138, 161
Central and South America
  sexual abuse in, 27
Cherubini, Stefano, 21
Chile, 27
Christ
  as priest, 125, 131
  as sacrifice, 125
  command to love, 125, 131
  in Eucharist, 135
  indefinable mystery, 147
  present in community, 133, 135, 154
  present in Eucharist, 133, 147, 150
  present in recipients, 147
  present in Word, 151
  present in world, 153
  real presence of, 147, 148
  risen, 141
  seen in Near Death Experience, 142
  women "cannot represent", 72
Christian
  prayer, 122
  values, 157
Christian Brothers, 23, 37, 41

Christians
  all are equal, 70
  all have Christ's Spirit, 131
  and military, 131
  as priests, 125, 131
  as temple, 122
  did not bear arms, 132
  Jewish, 121
  of other churches, 154
  two classes of?, 138
church
  and violence, xiv
  carries truth, xvi
  healing of, xvii
  is essentially people, xv
  needs to be transformed, 157
  not the only path, xv
  points to Transcendent, xiii
  pyramid structure of, 117
  sickness of, xvi
  two classes in?, xiv
Chute, Kostka, 41, 63
Clancy, Cardinal Edward, 110
Clement, 128
clergy
  as mediators between humanity and God, 131
clerical
  closet, 34
  concubinage, 20, 21
  marriage, 21
  monopoly, 72
clericalism
  and laity, 82
  condemned by Jesus, 75
  culture of, 17
  definition of, xiii, 69
  excesses of, 73
  in seminaries, 78
  in other institutions, xiii
  link with patriarchy, 72
  source of errors, xiii
clerics
  as mediators between humanity and God, 161
Coleridge, Archbishop Mark, 95
Collins, Paul, 110
Colombia, 28

Index

Commensoli, Peter Lewis, 40
community
   always capable of celebrating
      Eucharist, 152
   authority to bind and loose, 127
   destroyed by merging parishes, 164
   divided by abuse, 52
   needs to be inclusive of all, 166
   new forms of, 165
   proclaims the good news, 166
   sometimes needs to exclude, 154
   united by Eucharist, 147
compassion, xvi
   hindered by clericalism, 100
   lacking in institutions, 106
confession,
   "seal" of, 78, 136
   abuse within, 21, 78, 88, 89
conscience
   superior to external authority, 9
Constantine, 88, 109
correction, fraternal, 159
Council of
   Elvira, 19, 149
   Lateran, 133, 134, 137
   Toledo, 20
   Trent, 88, 138, 144
   Trullo, 137
Crimen Sollicitationis, 89–92, 94, 95, 97
Critical Race Theory, 101, 112
Croatia, 30
crusades, xiv
Čuček, Ivan, 30
Cunningham, Kit, 22, 63
cup, one shared by all, 142, 149, 163
Cupich, Cardinal, 110

Dalits, 112, 115, 116
Daly, Denis, 39
David (King), 136
Davis, Albert, 42
Day, John, 72, 84, 99
Deakin, Bishop Hilton, 84
Degollado, Marcial, 26, 34, 35, 62, 96
denial, 8, 80, 81, 90, 100
Didache, 125, 128, 129, 145
   and women's ministry, 143
   does not mention ordained, 127

Didascalia Apostolorum, 129
Docetism, 154
Dominicans, 32, 36, 42
Doveton, 11, 38
Dowlan, Edward, 14, 41, 49
Doyle, Thomas, 64, 78, 100
Duggan, Aidan, 40
Dziwisz, Monsignor, 34

Eastern rite churches, 68
Ellis defence, 40
Ellis, John, 14, 40
empires, xvi, 104
Encompass, 43, 64
ephebophilia, 65
episkopos, 127–31, 144
Eucharist
   action of the whole community, 167
   and community, 146
   and victim, 145
   as sacrifice, 124, 130
   cannot be defined, 150
   Christ present in, 142
   cup not received, 153
   denied to half of world's Catholics, 155
   excluding persons from, 155
   its purpose is unity, 148
   not valid, 150
   one cup, 149
   presider at, 125, 143
   received on hand / tongue, 114
   reservation of, 151
   transforms recipients, 147
euphemisms, 19, 24, 107
Europe, sexual abuse in, 29
Evans, Michael, 40

Facing the Truth, 100
Farrell, John Joseph, 82
Farrell, Stephen, 41, 52
Fichter, Stephen, 35
fire, eternal, xiv
First Nations, 23, 110
Fisher, Archbishop Anthony, 39, 84, 85
Fitzgerald, Gerald, 83
Fitzmaurice, Dominic, 42
Fletcher, James, 37
Fontino, 88, 92

Index

Fortune, Sean, 32
Foster (family), 12, 38
Fox, Julian, 42
Fox, Peter, 84
France, 30, 33
Freeman, Cardinal James, 39, 40
Fructuosus, 20, 21

Gaines, Bishop Edward, 44
Gandhi, Mohandas, 104
Gannon, Desmond, 38, 50
Garroni, Dom, 35
Gauthe, Gilbert, 24, 63
Geoghan, Fr, 24
Germany, xi, 31, 88, 112
Gilroy, Cardinal Thomas, 39
Glennon, Michael, 38
Grand Jury, 24, 25, 93
Gratian, 21
Groer, Cardinal Hans, 29, 30
Guam, 43, 75

Hart, Archbishop Denis, 82, 102
Heather, Bishop Bede, 83
hell, 48, 73, 116
Higgs, Victor, 42, 48
Hildegarde of Bingen, 158
Hippolytus, 129, 130
Hitler, 104, 105
Holiness accessible to all, 138, 148
homosexual-ity, 29, 60, 65, 66, 73, 98, 111, 138
Horan, Fr, 35
Hoyos, Cardinal Castrillon, 46, 94
Hullermann, Peter, 31
Humanae Vitae, 160

iconastasis, 123, 124, 193, 194
immigration, 59
Incarnation, 148, 154, 159
innocent persons convicted, 8
inquisition, 21
institution
    accepts abuse, 24
    achievements of, xvi
    attracts "driven" personalities, 106
    becomes person's main support, 105
    betrays its purpose, 32
    compassion lacking in, 106
    feared by laity, 22
    pattern of abuse in, 26
    trust destroyed, 47
    two meanings of, 103
    use of symbols, 104
institutional paralysis, 38
Inzoli, Mauro, 33
Ireland, 32, 40, 63, 100, 149
Italy, 33, 88, 137
Ivanov, Fr, 30
Ivereigh, Austin, 11, 14
Ivo of Chartres, 21

Jalandhar, 29
Japan, 29
Jarrell, Randall, 118, 119
Jesuits, 26
    Australia, 42
    Chicago, 26
    Oregon, 26
Jesus, 104
    and celibacy, 135, 138
    and Eucharist, 140, 141, 143, 149, 161, 162, 164, 168
    and New Covenant, 125
    and power, 126
    and sacrifice, 144–46
    and Temple, 120
    and women, 144
    as lamb of God, 124
    chose Peter as Leader, 127
    command to celebrate Eucharist, 152
    defended victims, xv
    gave authority to community, 159
    God with us, 122
    hierarchy founded by?, 114
    his resurrection made temple redundant, 140
    invites communities to imitate Trinity, 117
    post-resurrection appearances, 142
    present in community, 150
    rebuked clericalism, 155
    sharing meals, 140
    teaching about God, 145

Index

John Jay Report, 58
Justinian, 132, 137

Karadima, Fernando, 27
Kavanagh, Bishop John, 44
Keating, Patrick, 35
Keenan, Marie, 77
Kenya, 22
Kidd, Peter, Judge, 3, 15, 16
kiss of peace, 153
Kiss, Vincent, 62
Klep, Frank, 42
Knox, Cardinal James, 38
Kostelnick, Fr, 25
Kramer, Peter, 31
Krishna, 142
Krol, Cardinal, 24

Lacchin, Mario, 22
laicization, "administrative", 95
laity
    and Eucharist, 114
    and *humanae vitae*, 160
    and Vatican II, 139
    clerical *ordo* superior to, 129
    clerics favoured over, 92
    collude with clericalism, 67
    consultation of, 158
    failure to consult them, 160
    hierarchy distinct from, 131
    not receiving cup, 153
    want change to obligatory celibacy, 68
Law, Cardinal Bernard, 24
Leahy, Michael, 87
Legionaries of Christ, 34, 35, 75
Lenin, 104
Letter of Barnabas, 128
Licinius, 131
Linane, Clare, 13
Little, Archbishop Francis, 37, 38, 92, 98
Losirkale, Sabina, 22
Louisiana, 24
Lubičić, Drago, 30
Lyon, 31

Mackey, Bishop, 44
magisterium, 159

Maitland-Newcastle, 37, 75
Malone, Bishop Michael, 75
Manichaeism, 67, 136
Mannix, Archbishop Daniel, 38
Mao Tse Tung, 104
Marist Brothers, 36, 41
Martel, Frederic, 34, 73
Mass
    "intentions", 145, 149
    "private", 149, 150
McAlinden, Denis, 37
McAlinden, Kevin, 63
McAuley, Catherine, 104
McCarrick, Cardinal Theodore, 25, 26, 62, 64, 110
McCarthy, Fr, 25
McGuire, Donald, 26, 27
McGuire Patrick, 96
Melbourne, 37
Melbourne Response, 12, 14, 39, 54, 82
memory
    in victims of abuse, 4, 7, 40, 80
Mercer, Vincent, 32
Milgram, Stanley, 107, 108
Missionaries of Charity, 27
Moran, Gabriel, 165
Moreno, Archbishop, 94
Morris, Bishop William, 110, 116
Mortara, Edgardo, 88
Mortlake, 36
Movement for a Better World, 166
Mulakkal, Bishop Franco, 29
Mulkearns, Bishop Ronald, 11, 36, 37, 92, 98, 99
Müller, Cardinal Gerhard, 31
Mulvale, Gerard, 12
Murphy Report, 32, 100, 102
Murray, Bishop, 40
Murray, Magnus, 44, 63

Nagle, Philip, 52
Napoleon, 88, 104
Narcissism, 63, 64, 65, 74
Near-Death Experience, 142
Nestor, John, 96
Netherlands, 33
New Covenant, 125, 141

Index

New Zealand, See Aotearoa New Zealand
Newbridge College, 32
North America, Sexual abuse in, 23

O'Collins, Bishop James, 36
O'Donnell, Kevin, 11, 38, 39, 54, 63
Oakleigh, 11, 38
obedience, 58, 62, 75, 76, 82, 86, 108, 132, 168
    to Christ or human laws, 168
oblates, monastic, 19
Oceania, sexual abuse in, 35
ontological change, xiv, 70, 130, 134,134, 135
opus operatum, 151
ordination
    called "Holy Orders", 70
    causes "ontological change", 69, 70
    causes new relationship, 135
    dispensed with for "confessors", 130
    in Aquinas, 134
    not known in early church, 70
    of married men, 111, 161
    oldest known ritual, 129
Oregon, 26
Origen, 67, 130

Papal States, 88, 132, 159
paradigm shifts, xv
parish
    "pyramid structure" of, 117
    and small Eucharistic communities, 166
    as institution, 55
    being made "child-safe", 82
    good initiatives in, 164
    increase of, post WWII, 59
    ineffective when combined, 162, 164
    not effective as community, 163
pastoral councils, 160
Pecan, Bishop, 94
pedophile
    "fixated", 63
    appearance of, 13
    bishops failed to understand, 83
    protected by Canon Law, 93
    treatment of, 33, 43, 83, 99, 101

Pell, Cardinal George, xii, 1, 102
    accusations against, 10
    acquitted by High Court, 1
    and Foster family, 12
    and K.O'Donnell, 11
    and K.Toomey, 12
    and Melbourne Response, 12, 39
    charges against, 3
    conspiracy against?, 10
    denies crisis or systemic abuse, 80, 82
    knowing about abuse, 11
    not declared innocent, 1
    Prison Journal, 6
    Sworn statement to Royal Commission, 11
    Vatican connections, 2
perichoresis, 117
permissive '60s, 60
Philadelphia, 24, 25, 75, 93, 98
Phillipines, 29
Pickering, Ronald, 38
Piper, Eileen, 12
Pironio, Cardinal, 34
Poblete, Renato, 27
Poland, 32
Polding, Bishop John Bede, 35
pope, accountable to no one, 102
Pope Alexander II, 20
Pope Benedict XVI, 31, 39, 81, 96, 100
Pope Francis, xvi, 2, 14, 27, 33, 74, 92, 101
Pope Gregory VII, 20
Pope John Paul II, 20, 24, 30, 33, 34, 35, 92, 94, 95, 98, 110
Pope Julius II, 21, 132
Pope Julius III, 21
Pope Leo IX, 20
Pope Leo XIII, 89
Pope Paul VI, 83, 95, 160
Pope Pius IX, 159
Pope Pius V, 88
Pope Pius X, 79, 81, 159
power, abuse of, 110
Power, Bishop Pat, 110
presbyter, 127–31, 136–38, 144, 158
    married, 135
Preynat, Bernard, 31

Index

priest
  and narcissism, 63, 64
  and psychological stress, 68
  as God's representative, 48
  as holy, 74
  homosexual, 65
  increased numbers post WWII, 58
  lay people as, 70
  not in New Testament or early church, 125, 167
  numbers declined, 60
  power of, 50
  treatment of, 77, 83
  women as, 98
priesthood, its restoration a clerical error, 236
prophets, 191, 200, 201, 202, 219
proskenion, 193
purity, ritual, 209, 210

Rankin, David, 78
Rapson, David, 77
Ratzinger, Cardinal, 62, 163, 164
Ratzinger, Georg, 57
Regensburg, 57
reporting of abuse
  mandatory, 161, 168
  opposed by Vatican, 161
  late or never, 22
res sacramenti, 225, 243
responsibility, displacement of, 176
Rice, Edmund, 174
Ridsdale, Gerald, 29, 64, 65, 105
rituals, 13
Robinson, Bishop Geoffrey, 119, 123, 147, 151
Rodriguez, Cardinal, 161
rood screen, 193, 227
Rosminians, 44
Rubeo, Victor, 69
Ryan Report, 58
Ryan, David, 67
Ryan, Vincent Gerard, 37

"sacral vernacular," 154
sacramental character, 70, 134
sacred and profane, distinction dissolved, 148

sacrifice, 62
  as love, 130
  Christian, 145
  Christ's death as, 222
  Eucharist as, 144
  in *Didache*, 125, 145
  in temple, 195
  Mass as, 125
  meaning: "to make holy", 124
saint, See St.
Salesians, 42
Salvano, John, 12
Schrenk, Christine, 115
Scriptures, used to support caste, 112
Searson, Peter, 11, 38, 84
secrecy, link with privilege, 90
secrecy pontifical, 91, 94
Secreta Continere, 91, 94
seminaries
  clericalism in, 78
  gay culture in, 65
  hindered emotional development, 76
  inadequate screening, 68
sensus fidelium, 159, 160
sexuality
  Christian teaching on, 67
  suspicion of, 136, 137
shadow-side, xvi
Shea, Thomas, 54
shekinah, 150
Shepherd of Hermas, 128
Shiel, Bishop, 35
Shirres, Michael, 42
Simonds, Archbishop Justin, 38
sin
  structural, xiv
Sipe, 58, 64
Sisters of Mercy, 36
Sisters of St Joseph of the Sacred Heart, 36
Sleeman, Graeme, 52
Smyth, Brendan, 32, 63
Socrates, 104
Sodano, Cardinal, 34, 96
Somalo, Cardinal, 34
South Africa, 23, 114
St Alipius, 41, 48, 49, 52
St Ambrose, 137

Index

St Angela Merici, 158
St Augustine, 67, 132, 134, 136, 137, 147, 148
　on Eucharist, 151
St Basil, 19, 104
St Benedict, 19, 157
St Catherine of Siena, 158
St Cyprian, 158
St Dominic, 157
St Francis of Assisi, 104, 157
St Gregory of Nyssa., 151
St Ignatius of Antioch, 128, 129, 147
St Ignatius College Riverview, 42
St Irenaeus, 129
St Isidore, 20
St Jerome, 136, 137
St John Chrysostom, 133
St John of God (Brothers), 36
St John Vianney, 133
St Joseph Calasanz, 21
St Justin Martyr, 19, 143
St Mary MacKillop, 35, 104
St Patrick's College Ballarat, 14, 20, 41, 49, 51
St Peter Damian, 20, 137
Stanford, Peter, 63
statute of limitations, 25, 29, 59, 97, 110
Storero, Papal Nuncio, 94
subsidiarity, principle of, 86, 87, 111
suicide by abuse victims, 26, 39, 40, 41, 49
Sydney, 39
synodality, 158, 164, 167

Tanzania, 22
Tatchell, Paul, 14, 51
Tell No One, (film), 33
Tellicherry, 28
temple
　and authority, 126
　and Christians, 121
　and Jesus, 120
　before Judaism, 121
　its restoration a clerical error, 122, 156
　made redundant, 140
　persons as, 148
　source of power, xiii
　superfluous, 124
　veil, 120–23

templon, 122, 123
Teresa, Mother, 27
tonsure, 133
Toomey, Kevin, 12
Towards Healing, 39, 40, 82, 94
Towards Understanding, 36, 81
translation of Mass text, 153, 154
transubstantiation, 153
treatment programs, 43, 83, 99, 101
Trinity, as model for church, 116
Trujillo, Cardinal Alfonso Lopez, 28

uniformity is not unity, 162
unity, pretended, 168

Vangheluwe, Bishop Roger, 30
Vatican, 60
　abuse of power and wealth, 126
　control of bishops, 111
　refused mandatory reporting, 94
Vatican II, 34, 59, 60, 70, 87, 138, 149, 158
Vehementer Nos, 79
vestments
　and sexual abuse, 7
　not essential for Mass, 148
victim(s)
　and Eucharist, 145
　Canon Law failed to help, 110
　damaged spiritually of, 49
　delay or fail to report abuse, 6, 43, 58, 97
　failed by church, 55
　health affected by abuse, 47
　likely to offend?, 62
　need for compassion, 46
　not seen as part of church, 84
　paid billions in compensation, 45
　punished, 19
　silenced by fear, shame, power, 8, 53
　wrongly accept blame, 48
Victorian Parliamentary Inquiry, 43, 49, 67, 81

Walsh, Tony, 94
Washington, 25
weregeld, 150
Western Australia, 40, 41, 55

Index

Wilson, Bishop, 96
Wollongong, 40
women
    "unsuited to represent Christ", 72
    served as deacons, 115
    forbidden to enter sanctuary, 115, 123
    religious, offending by, 36
    were not presbyters?, 144

Woods, Stephen, 48
words of consecration, 135, 149

Xavier College, 42

Zimbardo, Philip, 108

www.ingramcontent.com/pod-product-compliance
Lightning Source LLC
Chambersburg PA
CBHW051925160426
43198CB00012B/2050